For Will

INTRODUCTION

Like a diamond, there are so many facets to one man's life. I have found myself in a time where all I can think is to write about my ride, my journey, or at least some part of it, the stories that might help someone else. It's always good to learn from another man's mistakes. And I have made quite a few mistakes. Maybe someone out there can learn from mine and not make the same ones.

This whole adventure called life that we go on is one long lesson. The ups downs and sideways are what defines us, and shapes us into who we become. Maybe not exactly who we want to be, but this comes with time and practice.

I never held back. I did whatever I wanted to do, when I wanted to do it. Chased my dreams no matter how far away or crazy. And lucky for me they were better than I even imagined when I got there. Most of the time anyway.

Life is what we choose to make it. How we roll with the punches is how well we will be able to take the beating life can bring. And life can really be a beating.

A book is something that takes people where they have never been. No one knows what I've been through, or the things I have seen other people go through, or the things I imagine people go through.

You learn from making mistakes. Smart people learn from watching other people make mistakes and not making the same ones. I have made so many mistakes because I was never afraid to try anything. And if some other human being can learn from my mistakes, maybe find the strength to keep on keeping on, or to find a better way, then putting myself out there, writing all the dirt and the glory, the ups and downs, taking my two fingers and typing out my journey is worth it. Even if it only helps just one person.

PROLOGUE

Miami....late 70's

"Gotta find someone to ride on the boat for one night, pick up some weed, for ten thousand dollars." Gary said.
"Look no further." I said. "I'm your man."
"Steve will never let you go, you know that." Gary was Steve's older brother. Gary was my best friend. We all grew up together, surfing, training Karate, smoking weed.
"Why not?"
"Cause he loves you. Anything can happen out there on the ocean. You could easily get killed or drown. Someone could try to rob you for the weed, there's Pirates out there. Or you could get busted and locked up for a century."
"My dad is the best attorney in town, if I get in trouble, he will get me out of it. I'm going." I grew up watching my Dad get everyone out of trouble. It was the hey day of drug trafficking in Miami and business was good.
It took me about an hour to convince Gary to take me over to Steve's house, then it took us both about three hours to convince Steve to let me go. Steve was always the big brother I looked up to. I had no idea how much Steve loved me till he was dropping me off three days later to go out on the open ocean in a boat and bring back five thousand pounds of weed. I got in the back of the truck with another kid who was about 16 years old also, named Harold and two older guys, Frank and Doug. I introduced myself. Steve walked up to the Driver's window and looked Frank in the eye.
"If anything happens to him don't come back here." Frank didn't like this. Steve was a second degree black belt and no joke.
"Fuck that Steve. He can stay here. Anything can happen out there, you know that."
"He's going. I'm just telling you to watch out for him, that's it."
Frank nods ok and we pull out of the driveway. As soon as we get off the street Frank turns around and looks at me.
"You don't stick your head up, you hear me?"

"Quit tripping, I'm not. I'll be fine." I had no doubt at all that I would be fine. In fact better than fine, I'm sixteen years old and I'm about to make ten thousand dollars. The excitement was overwhelming. I couldn't see past that.

We got to the dock and started loading the boat. These guys had done this a lot, so they knew enough to bring a lot of food, in case we get stranded out there or something.

The boat was amazing. A 40' foot Cigarette with four Evinrude engines and Loran radar painted gray to make it hard to see. It was state of the art for that time. Not even the Coast Guard had boats this good yet, not until they started confiscating them from the smugglers.

I was loading the groceries on to the boat and there were other crews with other speedboats loading up their boats up and down the docks. Everyone was happy, it was about six p.m. and the sun was going down. A really friendly Cuban guy came down the dock and stopped to talk to Frank. They talked for a minute, Frank shook his head no and the guy walked away. Frank watched him walk away then walked over to me.

"See that guy?" I looked over to the guy who was alone loading his boat. It wasn't as good as ours, no radar, not the best motors.

"Yeah I see him. Kinda shitty boat." I said. Frank treated me good, everyone did, it was a big operation, I was the youngest guy there which is kind of a special place to be.

"He just offered us a job. He needs help picking up a boatload of Coke. We could make almost a million dollars tonight. Three times what we will make on the weed. I turned it down. You know why?" I thought about it and shook my head no.

"Because that one boat load of coke is going to touch ten thousand lives. At least one thousand of them will go down the drain. That's nothing we want on our heads. Weed is the healing of the nation don't you forget that."

We looked back at the Cuban guy who was now pulling out of the dock.

"Wow, no radar, no crew. He 's just gonna pull up to the intersection and say, 'well I hope the cop aint there now,' and then floor it." Frank said in amazement.

"We don't worry about shit like that. We got three boats each with two men in them each, going up and down the coast from Miami to Ft. Lauderdale watching the Coast guard Boat and Helicopter." Doug said to me as he walked past with a load of groceries.

Frank picked up the handset of the CB radio and handed it to me. "You know how to use this?"

"Yeah, I had one I was a kid."

"Good, you are the radio man. It's on channel 19 now cause its Seven PM, that's military time. You count the hours until twentyfour. Starting now, then you turn it backwards every hour. The guys in the houses and on the boats are all listening. You got it?"

"Yeah, I got it." Frank smiled and went to the console and started the boat. Harold and Doug finished loading the food and got on the boat. I undid the lines and jumped on the boat and we backed out of the stall and headed out to the inter coastal towards Haulover cut, which is the beach I grew up surfing at, and the place where boats go out to sea. It was an eerie cool feeling as we pulled out of the cut with the sun going down to the blackness of the ocean.

We rode for about an hour till we got to a buoy, where two more boats were waiting. All the captains knew each other. These guys didn't have a care in the world. I sat in the back smoking joint after joint, not because I was nervous, but more cause I loved to smoke and was excited as a ten year old kid on Saturday morning. All I could think about was the money I was going to make. There was no worry about impending danger at all, getting killed or arrested, none of that, only excitement.

After a while we untied the boats and headed out to the blackness of the sea. In about twenty minutes we came up on a Columbian freighter. All three boats tied up and we loaded bails as fast and as quietly as we could. They all fit inside the hull and we took off towards Miami.

We got to the beach I grew up surfing at and I picked up the Handset and clicked it twice before I spoke into it.
"This is Spike, I'm two mile from the exit, hows it look? Over."
They used to call me Spike back in the day, and for no good reason, kind of like the big dog in that cartoon.
"All clear, come on and bring it." Frank looked at me and I gave him a thumb's up.
"All clear." Frank said, as he pushed the accelerator down and we pulled into the cut at about fifty. As we passed the two little fishing boats I saw Gary stand up and hold his arm up. He was smiling ear to ear. It was quiet about 3:30 am. One boat pulled in front of us and another boat pulled in behind us and guided us to the house.
We pulled in the channel and slowed the boat down to be quiet and not cause a wake. We were in a super rich neighborhood with all the houses on the water, with boats in their docks. We docked the boat behind one house and went inside. There were five guys inside all dressed in black. I knew two of them from the beach. Everyone was high fiving and hugging me. Everyone was making money now. We waited a little bit to make sure none of the neighbors called the cops, then we went out there and in a single file line and unloaded the boat. The house had plastic on all the carpets, which now was loaded to the ceiling with 50 pound bails of weed. Frank looked at me.
"You and Harold are going to take the boat back to the dock and clean it out, there is a dust buster on board. Throw the dust buster away when you are done. I will be there in about an hour."
Me and Harold took off and went out the back door. It was still pretty dark out. We took the boat to the dock and cleaned up all the weed that had fallen from the bails. We waited about an hour after that for Frank to show up. He walked down the dock got on the boat and looked all around the boat like an inspection.
"Good job. Where's the dust buster?"
"Threw it overboard." I said.
 Frank handed us each a brown paper bag we looked in them immediately. Inside the bag were stacks of twenties.

"There's seven grand each. I will get you the other three in a couple of days. We go again next week." Frank got out of the boat and walked away. Me and Harold looked at each other, then looked in the bags again.
"What you gonna do?" Harold asked me.
"Buy anything I want." I said with a smile.
I left the boat and got in my truck with the bag of cash next to me. At the first red light I opened it to look in again. It was more money than I had ever seen before. I was so excited and happy to have it. I had no idea the misery it was going to bring me.

1

"Tie them on tighter or they will never stay." Pauly said"I know what I'm doing." I was attaching playing cards to my frame with clothes pins so they made noise, when they hit the spokes of my bicycle wheel. Thats what we thought a motorcycle would sound like.
When you are ten years old the only thing you want is to grow up, get a motorcycle and ride around. At least that's what me and my friends wanted. We all dreamed about having motorcycles. Pauly, Johnny, Louie, Herman, Danny, Alex and me. That was my crew when I was a kid. My Pals, and they meant everything to me. Your PAL is the epitome of friendship, of Brotherhood. You would never let your Pal down. These guys were my first Pals.
Alex always had his big ass pit bull, Mako with him. Mako was huge and looked menacing but was a real sweetheart. Vince had a real big Pit Bull named Sebastian, who could swim to the bottom of the pool and pick up a quarter. Both these pit bulls were huge and really loving, which is cool. Bunch of kids with these big pits to protect them. Kind of Like Our Gang.
We all lived within a few blocks of each other, went to school together and basically did everything together. We started out by putting clothespins on our bikes, and riding around together. It was about 1972. Love-ins, gangs and drugs were

just starting to come to the forefront of society, at least for us. We rode around in a group everywhere we went. We built forts in vacant lots, which were our clubhouses. We went from there to stealing the old folks three wheeled bicycles, and from there to stealing mopeds, switching the parts in somebody's garage, then riding around in a pack.

"It's ready, let's go." I made the final adjustments on my cards and got on my bike.

"You guys equipped?" Pauly asked us. We all dug into our pockets and pulled out rocks and held them out. We were too young to get a knife so we carried rocks. In case we ran into other crews from around the neighborhood.

We took off and rode around the neighborhood causing mischief, knocking over garbage cans, ringing doorbells and running away, we did what ten year old kids do, raise hell.

We took off down the block riding our bicycles as fast as we could. The faster we went the louder the playing cards made in our spokes. We sounded like a swarm of bees coming down the road. I'm sure we looked like terror, seven kids riding as fast as we can with this big dog running behind us.

We rode across this golf course that was across the tracks and got chased out by the groundskeeper. We rode up to the mall and went flying through the parking structure till we were tired. We stopped at the highway over pass and Pauly and Johnny pulled out cigarettes and lit them up. Pauly held out the pack.

"Anybody want one? Don't be scared, twenty to a pack, enough for all of us."

"No way, my dad would beat the tar out of me." I said. Herman and Danny took one each and lit them up. We kicked back under the over pass while they smoked. Alex and me went right to adjusting the cards on our spokes.

" You ready?" Pauly said as he stomped his butt out. "Race you home." We all jumped on our bikes and took off. We rode fast as hell through the parking lot making people jump out of our way. We pulled up to the fence of the golf course and stopped.

"You think he's around?" Pauly asked us all.

"Only one way to find out." I said as I took off. I wanted to win. I always wanted to win. Second place didn't interest me at all. We went flying through the golf course and within twenty feet the grounds keeper came after us in his golf cart. He was in the main golf cart, which was bigger than the rest, and slower. He almost caught us but we ditched through a big hole in the fence and he is not allowed off the grounds. We all stopped and turned to look at him. He got out of his cart at the fence and was mad dogging us.

"ONE DAY I'M GONNA CATCH YOU KIDS AND WHIP YOUR ASS." He screamed at us. We gave him the finger and took off. This was the home stretch and we were all neck and neck riding as fast as we could. We turned the corner by the school and in the middle of the street was Lester, Bruce and Tommy Walker. We all slowed down to a stop. Three brothers, that lived at the end of the block. They were a couple grades ahead of us and spent most of their time shoplifting, smoking cigarettes and destroying whatever forts we built.

"Well, well, well, look who it is." Lester said. "Pauly and his crew. What you up to Pauly? Where you guys going in such a rush?" Lester said as he walked over and grabbed Pauly's handlebars so he couldn't go anywhere. Bruce grabbed mine and Tommy grabbed Alex's. Mako started growling.

"Better control that dog. If he bites me my mom will make sure he goes to the pound." Lester said.

"Better let go then. Who knows what he might do. He has a mind of his own."

"And what if we don't let go? You guys gotta pay a toll." We all looked at each other.

"We got your toll right here." We reached in our pockets and pulled out our rocks and threw them at them. They all let go and blocked the incoming assault. Once our rocks had been thrown we were unarmed.

"GET 'EM!" Lester screamed and it became a battle royal. It was the three of them against the seven of us. They were bigger and older so the odds were fair. We took a pretty good ass whipping and gave one too. Some parents came out and broke it up. We all got on our bikes and rode away as fast as we could. That battle with the Walkers raged on for years.

I put my bike in the garage and walked into the house.
"Go wash up for supper. Your father will be home any minute." As I passed her she grabbed me and took a better look.
"What happened?" She said as she looked at me up and down, I was a mess.
"Nothing." I went in and washed up.

2

"You are not from me." My dad said to me. We were sitting in the living room of the house we lived in. My parents had a restaurant when I was a kid. My dad's parents had restaurants when he was a kid and he went into that business. The restaurant business is a tough one. My dad would leave in the dark and come home in the dark. After ten years he decided he wanted to do something else so he went back to school then to Law school and became a criminal attorney. Miami was becoming the biggest hub for the drug trade at that time so there was always work for my dad. He was a great litigator. My mom was the art teacher when I grew up, and both my parents were all about being smart, using your head.
"What do you mean I am not from you?" I asked him.
"Your mother and I can not have babies. We adopted you."
"What does that mean?" I was about nine or ten years old. I think it was very cool of him to explain this to me at the first point of my life that he felt I could understand this concept.
"It means we got you and your sister from mothers that was not ready to have a babies."
"So she gave me away?"
"Yes, but not because she didn't love you. She gave you away because she loved you so much she felt that we could give you a better life than she could. I am sure it was a very hard thing to do." I thought about this for a moment. "You don't exactly look like your Mother and I, and you are going to hear this from other people as you grow up, I just wanted you to

hear it from me first. Do you understand?" I nodded my head yes.
" Are you ever going to give me away?" My dad smiled a smile of relief. I am certain this conversation was harder for him than me.
"Never."
"Can I go outside and play now?"
"Of course."
I remember walking outside thinking about how special I was. I am sure other people would get this news and feel inferior. I just didn't, on the contrary I felt nothing but special. It wasn't until many years later I found out my ethnicity and about my natural parents through non-identifying information from a Florida adoption agency. My entire life people would ask me what is my background and the only answer I gave was, that I don't know, I am adopted. And I was very OK with that.
I never felt anything but special about this fact. I didn't find anything about who I am according to my birth parents many years later, in my thirties. I realized long ago that who I am, is who I decide to be. Not what the paperwork says.

3

"Go on try it." I took the joint from my friend and took a big hit. I remember coughing my lungs out and everyone laughing. I was on the corner of my block with my sister and two neighbor kids that I hung out with when I was ten years old. That was the first time I smoked weed, or did any drug for that matter. After I was done coughing my lungs out I took another hit. This time it was a little smoother and I started to feel it. Panama Red. Sinsemilla wasn't invented yet. Cocaine hadn't hit the scene yet. This was about ten years before Scarface. Miami was desolate. The stores on Lincoln road were mostly empty. There were ten kids on the beach and I knew them all. Red sidewalks, I remember skate boarding on red sidewalks to the fishing pier to buy dime bags or nickels of weed then skating all the way to Haulover ramp to smoke it with my pals.

Miami was an amazing place to grow up as a kid. My dad would go to the racetrack on first street and drop me off to go surfing. It was a time of discovery for a lot of people. It was an enterprising time. A lot of people who could keep their head on straight got really rich in those first years. Miami was the hub. Wherever drugs were going in this country, they came through Miami first. Florida people always ran the show. It's in their blood. I can't tell you how many times growing up my friends would call me and tell me that bails were washing up on the beaches up and down the coast. We would be crawling through the sea oats pushing bails back to the car. Then we would get it home and have to lay it put and dry. We would make a coca cola water mixture and spray it out to get the taste of the ocean off it. We called it Seaweed.

After that first joint I bought an ounce of weed, five fingers, Panama Red for $25 dollars. I rolled up 50 joints and sold them at school a dollar a piece. I was sold out the first day. I was hooked. Damn sure beat working at the cement factory near my house which was my previous job.

 Pretty quickly I was buying Quarter pounds and selling ounces to my friends. I always had a good business mind. I had no problem doubling my money, which was the standard rate of profit I felt. I had even less of a problem spending what I made. I did that for a few years with no problems. I had a little bit saved up, a few thousand dollars is a lot when you are fourteen years old. I started living the life I dreamed about.

 I started going on surf trips a lot, me and a few of my friends would skip school and drive up the coast and surf all day then come home and skate an abandoned skateboard park near my house until the cops came and kicked us out. Later on we started taking real surf trips, we would fly to Puerto Rico or Costa Rica and surf for a week or two. I knew enough to put a bunch of weed on the street to sell, so that I had money waiting when I came back. I always had a dealer mentality. Everyone in Miami did. It's just how we grew up.

"So do you understand?"
I thought about it for a moment. It was a lot to take in when you are fourteen.
"I think so. Can you explain that auto pilot thing to me again?"
I was sitting in the park by my house with my friend Monty and his Dad, Michael, and his Uncle Tony smoking joints. These two were traditional hippies in the purest form. This was about 1976 I was a little more in tune, a little more into learning about the trip I was on called life than my buddy Monty, which didn't seem to matter to his dad, probably because he knew Monty had heard it before and he lived with him so he was going to hear it again and again. So they really focused on me.
Michael continued with the patience of a man that is trying to really teach a kid something very important.
"Basically you can control every single aspect of your life with your mind. Whatever you want you just have to see it in your mind's eye and it will be yours."
"My minds eye?" I asked.
"Yes. I am going to teach you a word. Manifest. Do you know what that means?
"No."
"It means to see what you want in your head first." Monty answered. He was so proud he knew something.
"Yes." Michael continued. "It means what ever you want, no matter how crazy it is, or far away is yours. You only have to see it first. And with practice you will get better and better at it. Your brain is the most powerful tool you have. Just like when you do pushups to build the muscle in your arm called your bicep, you can also do push ups for the muscle in your head called your brain. You can develop your bicep in a year, but your brain takes a lifetime. And it won't start until you have this awareness conversation. Until that time a person is on autopilot. Most people never get out of auto pilot, but in

the same respect they don't know what they are missing out on because they have never realized their brains potential."

Michael passed me the joint and I took a hit. Monty was goofing around a few feet away, which didn't seem to bother Michael or his brother. I was focused on learning this and he saw it.

"To take it one step further, whatever you put in your temple, or in your mind, is what you will get out. That is why we don't eat death."

"Eat death? I don't understand."

"Eating dead things will keep you from reaching a higher state of being. Meat. Soda, Alcohol, Cheese and dairy products are all dead things that will slow down your growth. Eating live food will enhance your awareness. Everything is connected. We are all connected, every living thing on this planet. You need to realize this. Killing a bug is the same as killing any living creature walking the earth. Just because something is smaller than you doesn't mean you can step on it. These are all living beings that have as much a right to exist as you do. The same as food, what you put into your temple is what you will get out. This is part of your training."

I thought about this for a moment as a large beetle crawled across the picnic table we were sitting at. I put my finger in front of it and it crawled on my hand. I walked a few feet away and set it free on a tree branch then sat back down.

"Well done." Michael said to me. "Now lets go one step further. Are you still with me?" I nodded yes.

"Your brain is the most powerful tool we have as human beings. We are no different than any other beings. They all communicate with eachother, we just do it through vocal chords. We have a third region in our brain, which lets us do this. But you can believe all creatures communicate with each other. That being said what you want to do is gain complete control of your brain. This is deep what I am about to tell you, so I want you to really pay attention." I sat up straight and listened like it was the most valuable information I ever heard. Years later I realized it was.

"The first chance you have to control your brain is to control your dreams. And the first chance you have to control your dreams is the waking hours of the morning. When you start to wake up, and you know you are still in a dream, go back to sleep, realizing you are in a dream and control your surroundings in that dream. This like anything else takes practice to accomplish the first time, and more practice to get better at it. Still with me?"

"Yes. My brain controls everything, and the sooner I realize this and start practicing, the better I will be at it."

"Exactly. And once you get comfortable with that, you will be able to control your dreams ay any time of the night. Once you get this it will never go away and you will be on the way to controlling ever aspect of your surroundings and the thoughts of other people."

"Other people?" I asked.

"Yes. A stronger mind will always be able to control a weaker or less developed mind. That is what I mean by autopilot. Most people never have this awareness conversation. When you speak to a lesser developed mind you will always know it. You will be able to project the answer you want to hear by thinking it first and sending it to their mind. I know it all sounds amazing and impossible but it's true."

"It doesn't sound impossible to me. In fact it all makes sense." I said. Michael smiled and handed me another joint.

"Do you know what Karma means?" Michael asked me, I nodded no.

"Karma is cause and effect. Just like everything is connected to you and you are connected to everything, whatever you do will come back to you. It's like the laws of the universe. If you are a good person and you are good to other living beings then good things will happen to you in return. In the same respect, if you are a bad person and you are bad to other living beings, no matter who or what they are, then bad things will come back to you. Understand?"

"If I'm bad then bad will happen to me, and if I'm good then good will happen to me." Michael smiled like he had achieved something special.

"Exactly. I think you're getting it."

"I've got it." I said with a smile. Michael looked at his brother with a reassuring smile then looked back at me.

"You really are smart as a whip aren't you? Try to understand this. You must always live in the now. The same way you just explained it to me. If you say you are going to be the best, it will never reach you because you are manifesting, or projecting it to the future. You have to say I AM the best. That way you project it to the now, to the present. That was my mistake saying you are getting it. You got it." Michael smiled.
"Now that you have had this conversation you are different than most people you are going to meet. Your job is to help them reach the same plane as you."
I nodded yes. I walked out of that park feeling different. Like I had been educated. I changed my diet and my train of thought from that day on and started manifesting every single thing I ever wanted in my mind's eye first.
I got on my bicycle and rode home. The whole way I thought and felt like a different person. Like I had been given a gift that no one could ever take away because it was inside me. I couldn't wait to go to sleep and start practicing what I had learned.
I got home that night and told my Mom about my new awakening and my new diet and she laughed and put hamburgers on the table for me to eat.
" I don't want to eat those any more." I said. My mom looked at me like I was crazy.
"What are you talking about, you love hamburgers."
"Not any more."
" We'll see how you feel about them tomorrow."
Three days later my mom was looking at me with great concern in her eyes.
"Just tell me what to buy and I will buy it. You have to eat."
Poor woman, she is trying to grow a tree. I handed her a list of things I would eat, basically a vegetarian diet. She got me what I wanted and started herself on learning about this whole plan. I think it helped both of us because the train of thought started to change after that. My parents were divorced, and my sister had moved out so it was just me and her. We have a very special bond, which I think opened her mind to a new train of thought. I never ate meat again, or soda or alcohol. It took me awhile to control my dreams, over

a year. But when I finally did everything else started to fall into line. Whatever I thought up happened. In fact it got so strong in me I had to be very careful to not to imagine bad things because they happened just as easily as the good thoughts. Basically the better I treated myself and my world, and my fellow man, the more powerful I got. I started to get addicted to it. I started to get comfortable with it. It became second nature to me. I began manifesting everything single thing I wanted. Looking back I can easily say whatever I wanted and manifested I got. It just took me awhile to only manifest the good. This was a big lesson to learn, and took some time.

5

I stood there watching the hippie next door sit on his porch for what seemed like forever. He sat upright and motionless with his eyes closed. I slammed the garbage can lid and he didn't open his eyes. I rang the bell on my bicycle over and over but he didn't open them. "HEY." I yelled but he didn't open them. I had seen him out there before, and I always wondered what he was doing. I was about twelve. When they first moved next door I thought they were weird. We had hippies on the right and Surfers on the left.
There were love-ins at the park near my house, and thousands of hippies would show up for these.
"Wake up." I yelled again. He didn't move a muscle. I stood there a while longer waiting, finally he opened his eyes. I walked over to him.
"What are you doing?" I asked. He smiled at me the way you would smile at a little kid.
"Meditating."
"What's that?" I asked. He thought about that for a moment.
" I was leaving this place." He said very calmly.
"No you didn't. I was watching the whole time. You were sleeping siting up." He had a lot of patience dealing with an obstinate little kid. I walked over to where he was sitting. He

had a bong on the table with some weed and some cashews. I had never been over to their house before because my mom didn't want me going over there.
I looked into the living room and he had tie dyes and tapestries hanging all over. You could smell incense and home cooking.
"So what were you really doing?" I asked again. "I know you were sleeping cause I yelled and you didn't wake up."
" I told you I was meditating."
"What's meditating?
"I told you, I left this place for awhile."
"While you were sitting here?" I asked him.
"Exactly." I thought about this for a second.
"I don't get it." I said, and I really didn't.
"Well, did you ever want to go somewhere and you can't? Or did you ever not want to be somewhere you were stuck at? When you meditate your body stay where it is and your mind and spirit goes to another place. It doesn't happen over night. It takes great practice over long periods of time. I have been meditating longer than your alive."
"What's your name?"
"Peter, My friends call me Pete. What's yours?"
"David. Are you old?"
"Older than you. I am twenty two. Are you old?"
"Hell no, I'm brand new." He laughed at the honesty only a little kid has.
"Would you like to learn how to meditate?"
"Yes." I said without hesitation. The thought of being to what I would later describe as projecting myself somewhere else was very appealing to me, even at that early age. He moved some of the cushions around so I could sit down.
"Sit here crossed legged, Indian style, and put your hands on your knees. Get comfortable. I sat the way he was, facing him.
"Now you have to deeply concentrate. You have to close your eyes and try to turn off the voice in your head."
"What voice? I don't have a voice in my head. He smiled again.
"Everyone does. Just listen and you will hear it. The voice in your head talks so much you don't even notice it. It's the

voice that tells you everything, what you want, when to be home, wonder what's for dinner. You must turn this voice off that is the first and most important part. This should be easier for you because you are so young your mind is not polluted with thoughts that you have accumulated over the years. This is much harder for an older person. So close your eyes and breathe in deep through you nose and out through your moth. Breathe slow long and deep. When you push the air out, push it all out and hold it out for a couple of seconds. Now this next part is very important, this will help you turn your voice off. Whenever you breathe in think, IN. Whenever you breathe out, think OUT. Whenever the voice talks to you only think IN or OUT. Do you understand?"
"I think so. In and out."
"Exactly. Now close your eyes and sit very still. We will meditate together.
I closed my eyes and tried to do exactly like he said. I sat there for a little bit, maybe five or six minutes then opened my eyes and looked at him, Peter was sitting motionless with his eyes closed. He didn't open his eyes and said to me. "Shut your eyes and breathe." I did so and tried for about ten more minutes. I opened my eyes.
"This isn't easy. The voice in my head keeps talking." Peter opened his eyes and smiled.
"You did good. You stayed quiet with your eyes closed longer than the grown ups I teach the first time.
"Does it really work? About what you said leaving your body?" I asked. I was really interested.
"It does, but you have to practice."
"Can I come over and practice again some time?"
"DAVIIIIID!" My mom walked out of the house and screamed my name for dinner.
"I gotta go." I turned around and jumped off his porch.
"David," Peter said. "Good to meet you. Come over anytime."
"Thanks. Good to meet you too."
I ran home and my mom was giving Peter stink eye. She didn't want me hanging out over there. Peter didn't see her though. He went back into a trance.

6

"Wake up." Was all I heard, it sounded like it was in my dream.
"Come on Lover boy, wake up." I looked up and there were my two pals, Steve and Gary, standing over me with big smiles on their faces.
"You have fun last night?" Steve asked pulling me out of the bed.
" You are a regular Casanova. She woke up the whole neighborhood." Gary said laughing.
I looked to my left and the beautiful girl I took home, Marie was gone. It was the first time I had ever slept with a girl, and at fourteen I could easily say I was in love.
"Come on out, breakfast is getting served." Gary said as he went back to the kitchen. Steve sat on the edge of the bed.
"Where'd she go?"
"She slipped out around six. Mom saw her leave. You have fun?"
"Time of my life." I said still in a dream like state.
"Good. Get up." Steve split and I jumped up and put my painter whites on. I left home at fourteen and went to live in my friend Gary's house. Steve was Gary's Brother and Gary's dad had a painting business. The first day his dad was going to work, he saw me sleeping on the couch, woke me up and put me to work painting houses. I did that for the next few years. I learned a lot staying with them, my first trade, a good work ethic. I soon realized the bills never stop coming, so I can never stop working, ever. Great house filled with great people. All love in that house, all the time. It was one happy family.
I walked into the kitchen and Gary's mom Cindy Lou was doing dishes. Gary's dad Gus, was at the table finishing his breakfast. "Let's make this quick, we're wasting daylight." He loved saying that, he hated wasting any part of the day.
I grabbed my plate and sat down and started eating my eggs. Everyone was looking at me and smiling.

"What?"
Gary looked at me with concern. "So you had fun last night?" He asked me.
"I love her." I said. The room was quiet for a second then they all started laughing, but in a good way.
"I am sure you do. And I am sure she loves you also. There is a big lesson here you need to learn right now. We don't come in girls." Everyone was silent looking at me. I felt a little uncomfortable talking about this in front of Steve and Gary's 's mom and dad. Gary could see my discomfort.
"Don't you worry about what anyone think's. We've all had this talk. It's simple math. If you come in girls you will get a baby. You don't need a baby."
Steve looked at his mother at the sink.
"She doesn't need any grand kids, not yet anyway." Cindy turned away from the sink and looked at me.
"Better listen to the man." She said.
Everyone was quiet looking at me to see if I got it. I started realizing how important this conversation was. Gary continued. " You don't need a baby, she doesn't need an abortion, and the sooner you get this lesson the better you her and everyone will be."
"But I love her. I want to marry her.' I said believing my own words. The all broke out laughing again, everyone except Gus. He wasn't laughing. He leaned in real close.
"Somehow you ended up in my house. That means you are my responsibility. It is up to me to teach you the lesson's my son's learn. You have to be responsible in this life. Responsible to yourself and who ever you deal with. You say you love this girl. I think it's a little soon to determine such a thing, but for the sake of argument let's say you do. Well even more than ever you should take your time, get to know each other. Bringing a child into this world is the most important precious thing two people can do, and should not be taken lightly. A child is not for eighteen years. A child is forever. You and the girl might not last, but the child will. Respect is everything. You have to respect yourself and your girl to make the right decisions. You want to be a man? Well the first step to being a man is being responsible for your own

actions. To take accountability for everything you do." He leaned back.

Steve and Gary got up, put their dishes in the sink and went outside to the truck.

"You got it?' Gus asked me. He was a very good man.

"I think so. I know I'm not ready for a baby. But I do love her." Gus stood up and messed up my hair.

"Of course you do. You're going to be fine. Just be aware of your actions. Try to always see past the next five minutes. Hurry up we got work to do. See you outside in five." Gus got up and left. I woofed down the rest of my eggs and toast and brought my plate to the sink. Cindy took it and motioned to the shelf.

"She left something for you." On the shelf was a folded piece of paper. I picked it up and unfolded it. Inside was hand drawn heart with the words 'call me' inside it. I jumped up for joy.

"Take it easy kid. It's all going to be O.K." I kissed Cindy on the cheek and ran out of the house.

7

"I'm going to Hawaii."

"What do you mean you are going to Hawaii? When are you going to Hawaii?" My dad was in shock. I had just come back to Miami to finish school and now I was dropping out again. He floored the accelerator in his Porsche 911. He loved those cars. And he always floored the accelerator when he got pissed off.

"Less than a week. I just have a few loose ends to tie up, pick up my new surfboards then I'm leaving."

My dad thought about this for a moment.

"You got money huh? How'd you get money like that?'

"You know how. I've been making moves for a while. Doesn't matter anyway, I'm going." He hit the pedal harder careening in and out of traffic on I-95 like Mario Andrettti.

"What about school?"

"They're not teaching anything in that building that's going to really help with life. Not my life."

"How would you know, you didn't live life at all yet." My dad really wanted me to be an Attorney like him. It just wasn't going to happen. I held up a picture of a wave breaking on the North Shore. A perfect cylinder barrel with a surfer inside the tube. He looked at it.

"This is what I have to do now. I'm 17 and I have been surfing since I'm ten. I gotta make my way and figure it out. I'm not asking you for anything. School's not going anywhere."

My dad looked at the picture. "You will get more life experience out in the world anyway."

"What 'd you say?"

"You heard me. Hey, I left you in California didn't I?"

"That wasn't a choice situation."

"For who?" We both smiled. Choices, life is full of them.

He dropped me off at my Friend Ernie's house where DCB was shaping surfboards in the back. No big goodbye with my Dad, just a firm handshake, then I didn't see him again for a few years.

I got out of the car a block from my buddy Ernie's house and walked the rest of the way smoking a joint. I felt an incredible feeling, like magical. It was the feeling of impending freedom. I was just about to really be on my own. And the excitement was not having a clue of what was coming my way. The excitement of the unknown, there is nothing like it.

I waited for what seemed like an eternity at the front door of Ernie's house. The music was blasting loud enough to be heard for miles. That combined with the sound of a planer wailing as it cut foam for surfboards in the back it was no wonder they couldn't hear me.

The door opened and Ernie stood there covered in foam dust from head to toe. He looked at me for a moment then smiled this shit eating grin.

"Wait till you see these. Get in here."

He pulled me inside by the shoulder and I went into the living room. Ernie's house was always buzzing. There were about ten surf rats in the back skating on a homemade ramp.

Behind that was the top secret shaping room where DCB was in the back shaping his up-sting down-wing surfboards. He would shape foam fins himself then glass them in. They became short light really space age looking surfboards that could really work well when you knew how to work them. This is Florida in the late seventies and these boards were in. I was almost seventeen and on my way to Hawaii. I was like the conquering hero in my neighborhood.

Gary was sitting next to me eating Bar B Q mackerel that they had just caught that day spear fishing. But that's another story. These guys grew up swimming down with nothing but a Russian sling to where the big sharks are and spear their dinner and bring it back. I always found that crazy. For sure the wounded fish sends out a distress signal. Next thing you now, you're the bait.

Gary handed me the bong with full bowl of some of our first green weed. It was all called Sinsemilla back then. Then it was Krypto. There wasn't forty flavors of weed like today, and for certain no over the counter shops. I used to say as a kid, "I hope I see weed become legal in my lifetime." Wow, it did.

"Wait till you see your sticks. They are so sick." Gary was completely faded. I hit the bong and sat back. Ernie and DCB walked in with my new sticks. They leaned them up against the wall in front of us and sat on the couch. We just stared at the boards in silence.

DCB was like a shaping God to us. No one could make a board like him. No one was allowed to watch him make a board because it was all top secret. We sat there in awe staring at the boards he made and they were beautiful. Two boards one six foot tall and one five feet eleven inches. Up sting down wing bat tail surfboards for smaller waves and a round tails for big waves. These were the best for Florida waves, especially in Miami where it doesn't get too big. Really good small wave boards. And they looked really cool from any surfers standpoint. DCB was way ahead of his time. I saw him surfing twenty five foot waves at Tres Palmas in Puerto Rico on a Five foot one Diamond tail surfboard. If you know anything about anything then you know that is a really little surfboard to be surfing such big waves. Generally the bigger the waves the bigger the board you need. Either way you cut it the two boards we were looking at were amazing.

"Wow. Thank You" I was in shock. It was kind of surreal. I was on my way to Hawaii, about to turn seventeen and I have two new custom made sticks.

"You are gonna rip it up on these." DCB said.

"You are gonna be the ripper." Gary said.

" You are gonna get killed." Dana said as he walked in with a Six foot nine inch Sam Hawk Rhino Chaser. Which is what they would call a big wave surfboard, also a Big Wave Gun, A spear. Dana was one of the older surfers at the house. We all surfed and skated, trained karate and were vegetarians. It was a tight knit little crew.

"Those little boards will be good till it gets about three feet. Three feet hawaiian will be like nothing you have ever seen before. It will have a lip as precise as a guillotine ready to take your head off. You are going to need some length underneath you to get in that wave." He held out the gun. Lightning bolts on the sides with a kamikaze red ball on the deck and the bottom, it looked like a Rhino chaser.

"You're gonna give him your gun? Really?" Ernie was in shock.

"You aint going to Hawaii are you? He is. There will never be waves big enough for this board here. Better off it sees some life." Ernie handed me the board. It was hard for me to even hold up I was so skinny. Everyone laughed.

"Put it in the barrel again for me kid." Dana said.

"You bet I will." I was stoked.

We gorged on fresh Snapper, Wahoo and a big Grouper that Ernie had speared that day we, got drunk and stoned on Jamaican beer and Colombian weed while we packed up my surfboards. This was my going away party. Stayed up most of the night then woke up the next day and got on the plane to Hawaii.

8

Landing in Hawaii is a trip. With those girls dancing around, putting lei's on everybody, everyone excited because they're on vacation. Saved up all their money to spend a week away from their lives and get loaded. On vacation.

I wasn't on vacation. I was there on a mission. I wanted to set myself up good. I had a friend living there already named Chris that I knew from when I lived in Leucadia. Chris could play the guitar like Jimmy Page from Led Zepplin. But that was all he could do. He just smoked weed and played guitar. He kind of went with the flow. He was staying at some hippie commune with some girl he met named Malia. Sounds Hawaiian.

I planned on finding Chris thinking maybe he would be into renting an apartment with me. Money was tight and I had to make something happen quick. I grabbed my boards and went to find some lodging. I didn't know anyone else on the island. Someone had told me to go the YMCA and I could rent a room for cheap day to day while I figured it out. It took a minute haggling with taxi drivers before I found one who would take me with all my boards a shit.

The YMCA was packed, there was about ten people waiting for a room. No one wanted to share with anyone. There were double rooms available to split but no singles. There was a big German traveller sitting waiting to get a room. He looked about twenty years old and was about six foot six. He looked like a mountaineer with his backpack and mountain boots. I walked up to him.

"How old are you?" I asked him. He looked up at me from his little drawing pad. He had the whole knap sack backpack across Europe thing happening.

"I am twenty four." He said is his heavy German accent.

"You got a drivers license?"

"Yaah I have international Driving license for car and scooter."

"Perfect. Wanna share a room?" he looked at me like I was from Mars.

"Look Colonel Klink. The only rooms they have are a double I'm gonna rent a room then a car and you are gonna drive me to see my friend. Then you can use the car all day. Deal?" I held out some cash and he liked that. He looked like he was on some starving student program.

The next day I woke up at the dawn and walked through Ala Moana Park and went surfing at magic Island which is across from Ala Moana Bowl, probably one of the most famous Surf spots in the world. It's the wave in the opening credits of the original Hawaii Five-O television show. We would go home just to watch that wave when we were kids.

I walked through the parking of the Rock n Roll clinic, a local night club in Honolulu. As I was walking through the parking lot I saw all these rolled up match books. They were around the backs of some cars all over the ground. Ten here, twenty over there. I kicked one and a half a joint came out. I picked it up, found some matches next to it and lit the roach. It was the best weed I had ever smoked in my life. I picked all the 'crutches' and smoked some and stashed some for later.

I can't explain the feeling of walking through that park to a wide open wave field. A Wednesday in Honolulu, everyone was either at work or I school, so I had the surf to myself. The waves were two to four feet, just over head and perfect hollow south shore. If you grew wave starved like I did in Florida till you moved to California then Hawaii, like I did, this was absolutely surreal.

I surfed all day standing in Barrels till my arms felt like jelly, then I got out and found my stashed half joints and went back to the Y. I found Gunther waiting for me by the room.

"You said we would get a car? I would like to do some sight seeing." He said.

"Take it easy Mein Furher. We will." I was beat I passed out till the next day. Gunther was huffing and puffing but tough shit I was beat, and I was a kid so I had that ten foot tall and bullet proof attitude to begin with, almost an invincible innocence., and I had the money. So I just didn't give a shit. I was in Hawaii and I had surfed, whatever else happened I did that. I fell asleep with a huge smile on my face.

The next day I came out of the car rental place with my huge German roommate and the keys to small compact car.

"Get in the front Eichmann, you drive." Gunther looked at me coldly and got in the driver's seat. We got in and Gunther put the keys in the ignition. He didn't turn them, instead he turned to me and looked me in the eye.

"I do not appreciate how you keep referring to me with these...these nazi names. I would like you to stop this."

"Take it easy Turbo. The truth is that probably your Grandparents burned my Grandparents alive...or somebody's Grandparents alive and I'm not holding that against you. Lighten up Adolph."

He looked at me crossed eyed then turned the key and took off. I figured right away everyone drives fast when they are pissed.

We found the hippie commune Chris was staying in no problem. Gunther was great with the directions. He was definitely a traveler. As soon as I walked in to the place I could see Chris gardening with a bunch of hippes. Dirt heads really, like they looked like they had been camping for the past month. With no shower, or bathroom. I walked up behind him, he didn't even notice. They probably drug the food or something.

"You seem pretty absorbed in that. What you planting?" I said. Chris turned around with a smile cause he recognized my voice.

"I'm gonna put in some Basil and Oregano." Then he looked around and said in a whisper," Then I'm gonna come out and plant some baby weed plants in between them."

"Good plan."

"You ready to get out of here?" I asked. Chris looked around. A really cute Hawaiian/ American girl walked up. I could see why Chris was living in the commune.

"This is Malia." Chris said. She looked at me like I was a piece of meat. "Malia this is DL." She held out her hand and gave me this really firm handshake and looked right in my eye..

"Pleased to meet you."

"Likewise."
"I'm going to go with DL for a little bit, and I will be back later."
"Don't forget dinner is at eight." She said. "You can't miss it." I thought, for certain the food is drugged.
We took off and went to the car. Gunther was standing next to it reading a map.
"Who's this?" Chris asked.
"Our Driver."
Nice."
We pulled into the parking of what I would later find out to be Sunset Beach North Shore Hawaii. Not much of a parking lot back then, this was in the late seventies, about 1979. I was seventeen and standing where every surfer dreams of being. We grabbed my two boards out of the car and told Gunther to pick us up by Sundown. He pulled out of the parking lot to go sight seeing.
I walked out to the beach with Chris. The waves were about three feet North Shore perfect tubes. A guy came out of a house on the beach carrying a surfboard so I walked over to him.
"Where am I?" I asked him. He could see my excitement and he smiled. He pointed at the different breaks.
"That's Sunset Beach, that's Stones own, then Rocky Point, Log Cabins and down there is Pipeline." He took off towards Pipeline. I paddled out at Rocky Point and had the best surf session of my life. I stood in barrels all day with my friend Chris and only two other surfers inn the water. We surfed till dark then got out and smoked a joint that I had brought with me.
"What are you gonna do? How long you plan on staying here?"
"Long as I can. Malia bought my ticket. I think she's kind of in love with me."
"I think she's in love with whoever."
"Probably. What are you gonna do?"
"Try to stay as long as I can also. Find a job. Apply for food stamps right away. Try to get a sponsor. I wanna surf in contests. Just surf every day. You think you can get her to

chip in on a place with me and we will all share it? Or you wanna keep living in that commune?"
"Let's get a place."
A group of Large Hawaiian locals had gathered for the sunset at the parking lot where we were waiting for Gunther. He came sliding into the lot and they all took notice at the big German tourist that probably needed a beating for kicking up the dust in their beautiful sunset. I knew it was time to go quick so we threw the boards in and took off. On the way back I thought how nice it is when a plan works out. Gonna find an apartment, get a job, make a life.

9

"You all right Braddah?"
I looked over at some big Moke who was watching me cough my lungs out after smoking a roach I found while I was walking across the parking lot of the Rock n Roll Clinic to go surf. It was about 6:00 A.M. and this became my morning ritual, scavenging roaches in the parking lot on my way to surf. I had learned enough already to keep to myself. No unnecessary conversation with anyone. It can lead to trouble. Hawaii can be vicious. I absolutely came here with innocence. It takes a few times of actually giving the money and waiting all night for the guy to come back with your concert tickets, or your bag of kind bud or whatever, and he doesn't show and you feel exactly like that cartoon character who's head turns into a lollipop with the word SUCKER on it before it sinks in. Some people just aint no good. It takes actually really getting ripped off before you lose the trust gene. Once you lose the trust gene it isn't coming back.
I had rented an apartment with Chris and Malia at the Kapiolani apartments. Since Chris had no Money he slept on the couch and Malia and me each got a room. That didn't last too long and Chris went back to the mainland after a couple of months. Malia got a job and had her own friends so I didn't see her much. She wasn't really giving me the time of day any

way. I tried to get it once or twice but she wasn't having it. She was hella cute and had guys with shit going on trying to get at her. I had three surfboards, a skateboard and not a lot else. I was buying some weed, Buddha sticks from Thailand and re selling them to the tourists at night skating around Honolulu. I saw my first Hookers there. I didn't even know why this beautiful girl was standing next to these other beautiful girls there all made up when it was as hot as can be.
"Hi." I said as I came to a screeching halt on my skateboard trying to impress her with my skating abilities.
"Hi yourself." She said with a smile.
"What's your name?" I was amazed, not many girls gave me the time of day.
"Sheena. What's yours?"
"David."
"What are you doing David. You want to go on a date? Would you like a little company?" She said and came a little closer. She was really cute. I was in shock. She was probably a couple of years older than me, but not much.
"Yeah that sounds good. I mean we could go to the beach or something." I still had no clue.
"How much money do you have David?" She said as she reached down and gave my crotch a little rub with her hand and a smile. All of a sudden it dawned on me like a lightning bolt.
"You're a hooker?" I asked.
All the other girls laughed and Sheena turned and left. I kept skating in and out of the tourists in Honolulu on the sidewalk. That's what I did when I wasn't surfing. Got stoned and skated.
I was skating around and this really beautiful young Hawaiian girl was standing with a couple of friends. I skated up.
"Hi."
"Aloha." The really cute one said. She was gorgeous to be exact. Light brown skin, long black hair, skinny, just like me.
"What's your name?"
"Nature. What's yours?"
"David. Wanna smoke a joint?"

"Sure. This is my sister Alicia. Come on."
We went into the girls bathroom and smoked a joint. All three of us were in the stall and it was getting kind of smoky.
"Wanna make out?" Nature asked Me. "With both of us."
She didn't have to tell me twice. We got into a kissing and groping frenzy all three of us. After about three minutes there was a loud knock on the stall.
"WHO SMOKING IN DEAH?" The security guard was outside. Nature opened the stall door and she walked out then Alicia walked out then I came flying out on my skateboard, He tried to grab me but I slipped out of his grasp. I skated down the block and waited for a minute. Nature came walking up.
"That was close." She said with a smile. Man she was gorgeous.
"Wanna go to my house I don't live far away."
"I can't." She said. "My brothers are already on the way to come get me."
"Brothers?"
"Yeah. I have five brothers. I'm the only girl. Three are coming to get me. We live over Makaha side."
It was like somebody dropped a bomb. Makaha, five brothers, and I was already in love. She held out a piece of paper.
"Here is my address and My Mom's number. Don't call past eight." She held out a picture of her. It was one of those wallet school pics. "Here is a picture of me so you don't forget about me." She held out a pen and paper.
"Write down your address and number."
"I don't have a number. But I can write down my address."
"O K Hurry up my brothers are going to be here any minute. I flipped my skateboard over and used it as a desk and wrote my address. I stood up and handed it to her. She read it then looked at me.
"Talk to you soon David." She gave me a kiss and turned around and skipped back I watched her go until I saw a beat down old pick up truck with three big Hawaiian dudes Looking at me with stink eye. I slammed my skateboard down and took off.
Didn't get a lot of sleep that night. Thinking about Beautiful Nature, and her Five Brothers on Makaha side. Oh Boy.

Nature sent me a letter with no stamp using my address as the return address. I thought that was pretty clever. I took the bus out to Makaha to visit her. The brothers all gave me stink eye at first, but then they loosened up. They had a skateboard ramp set up and I skated on that most of the day. One of the brothers got me some real good weed then made sure I smoked almost all of it with them. They let me know in plain English that they didn't like Haolie's, white guys, main landers or anyone who is not from there or trying to get at their sister. Nature was really cute but I didn't make the trip to Makaha again. I was thinking about the North Shore.

10

The days turned into weeks then turned into months of the same. I met a cool Rastafarian Jamaican guy named Clive that would front me Buddha Thai sticks to sell to the tourists. Life was good. Waking up early to go surf. Coming back to eat, smoke, skate around Honolulu selling weed that I got from the Clive. Then out to surf again. I was usually so tired at the end of the day it wouldn't matter what was on T.V. I would pass out by about eight o'clock wake up and do it all over again.
The only bathroom in the apartment was through Malia's room, which was a pain in the ass each morning when I had to take a piss. She would have to let me in whether she had an over night guest or not, I paid half the rent. I always went in and out as fast as I could anyway, I wanted to get in the water before the sun came up. I got in a couple of surf contests, didn't do so hot, the competition was fierce. Surfing against kids who ad grown up here surfing every day in perfect waves was tough. These guys were also riding Island boards, not Florida boards made for smaller waves. I was still having the time of my life though. I learned early on, the worst day chasing your dreams is better than the best day doing anything else.

I was walking through Waikiki after yet another fantastic Surf session. I had been through the entire summer season on the South shore. The South Shore is called Town and the waves break best in the summer. The North Sore of Oahu is called Country because it is exactly that, Country. Waikiki is buildings sidewalks Hookers and night clubs. The North Shore is pick up trucks, Hawaiian red necks and big waves. The home of the biggest most powerful and famous waves in the world. Pipeline, Sunset Beach, Rocky Point, Log Cabins, Velzyland. I had been looking at pictures of these surf breaks my whole life. I was already thinking about how was I going to make the move there. I never really met anyone when I was in Honolulu. I spent most of my time surfing or hustling the tourists. I could talk like a Hawaiian guy within a month. After growing up in Miami hearing all kinds of languages and dialects and imitating them it was easy. That was always the trip for me in travelling. Not just travel there, but become one of the locals.
"Where'd you get that board?" Some blonde guy walked up to me.
"DCB made it for me." I held the board over so he could that t was signed to me under the fiberglass. He leaned over to read it.
"To DL don't break your neck. DCB. Yep he made this for you. I know DCB."
"Cool. My name is David."
"You look like a Hippie with that hair. I'm Cooper. Wanna smoke?"
"Sure." So we went off to smoke. This was Geoff Copper. He was about 23 when I met him, about six years older than me. He was buck ass wild. He smoke Cocaine, smoked Heroin when he could get it, did mushrooms on the weekend and smoked tons of weed all day long. He is from Cooper city Florida, about twenty minutes from where I grew up. When he was fifteen and just a regular wave starved kid from Florida one of his rich uncles died and left him a bunch of money. And a generous allowance every two weeks, and bonuses when he turns 18, 21 and 25. So what would any red blooded fifteen year old surfer do with all that money? Drop

out of school and move to Hawaii post haste. It was now eight years later. He grew up with all the surf stars, Buttons, Michael Ho, Mark Liddel. He did drugs and partied like a mad man with his friend Robert who's dad owned a pig farm in Haleiwa. The two of them were more than a handful, nothing and no one was safe. Robert was related to one of the most powerful families around who just about ran the Island. So to say these two Psychos were connected would be an understatement. They were out of control. One other thing, Copper could surf. He could surf Pipeline at forty feet. He became my big wave guru. No matter how hard we partied at night, we were up every morning before the dawn and paddling out at sunbreak to catch the morning glass.

11

I spent the rest of the summer hanging out with Cooper. We both had a bond from being from Florida. He knew a bunch of the same people that I knew.
It was an insane summer. Hanging out with Surf stars Buttons and Mark who were Cooper's buddies all the time. Taking a boat out in the dark of dawn to surf the sunrise at Kewalo Basin also known as Point Panics because of all the sharks, then hanging out in Waikiki selling weed to the tourists, then an afternoon surf. It was an awesome way for a kid to spend his summer.
By the time it was over we had stolen so many mopeds from the moped rentals and had enough run ins that it was time to move to the North Shore. Time to go Country. This is what Cooper was doing since he was fifteen. I could see this is what I wanted to do. Cooper had an inheritance, and he did a good job of running out of that the first week partying harder than anyone I had ever met. He would then start borrowing all over town and get credit with every drug dealer around. By the time his check got there it was almost already gone. Me, I had to make shit happen, which wasn't hard in Waikiki. I had a good weed connection and the tourists looking for

weed was non stop. Country is a little quieter. I really had to make things happen.

Cooper rented a house on Mamao street three houses off Kam Highway on the North Shore of Oahu. The beach right by our house, a three minute walk, is called Backyards. They call it Pipeline training ground. That's where I surfed the most. To the right was a little cove called Freddy land, after that was Velzyland, and insane right. On the left was Sunset Beach, one of the most famous breaks in the world. Most of the big name surfers were there on any given day.

A normal day consisted of waking at the dawn, surfing most of the day, then scavenging or scamming for food or weed. I really had to use my wits just to keep eating and smoking. If you are clever like I was you would figure out where all kinds of food grows on trees. There's food all over just got to look.

I had a little money saved up when I first moved to the North Shore. I bought my first car there. A 1965 Volvo. I bought it from Jackie Dunn. He was in the Pipeline underground. He was in the crew of people that could really surf that break huge but never really got famous doing it. It was a rusted out Volvo that had been on the north shore for years that I got for fifty dollars. It had a kamikaze red ball and the words Surf Nazi painted on the back of the trunk. It had a stick shift and it was a bitch to learn. The North Shore is not the place to learn to drive a stick. I was stalling the car everywhere, at every light.

One time I stalled at a light and three cars back was a truck full of mokes in it. Mokes are like Hawaiian red necks. They are usually huge. I stalled and the two cars behind me hit each other, not too hard, but then the moke hit them. The Moke driver who was about twenty five and at least four hundred pounds got out and started waddling his way over to me. I was turning the key in the ignition and the car was not starting, jus turning over.

"Wow. He's a big boy." Cooper said totally amused. Everything amused Cooper.

"IMA GONNA SMASH UP YOU FACE LIKEA PIECE A HAMBURGER." The moke said as he was walking up, which wasn't easy for him. He was huge and he had to get past the two cars in front of him and not get hit by oncoming traffic. He was hitting the cars with his hand.

"This is gonna be good." Cooper sat back to watch.

"You're a lot of help." I said, trying to get the car started. Cars were honking.

"It's Big Marvin, remember him? He beat the shit out of the fire department last summer for putting out a house he set fire to. He is gonna crush you. Get the car started, like no kidding." Cooper said.

"I'm trying." I looked in the rear view and Marvin was less than ten feet away. I was turning the key in the ignition and the car was just turning over.

"Don't give it any gas. Just turn the key. Wait till it grabs. I looked in the rear view Marvin had three more feet to waddle and he would be at my window. I turned the key, the engine tried for a second then started.

"Don't flood it. Ease it into first and let the clutch out easy." Marvin reached my window and lifted his giant hand to smash me. The Volva took off just as Marvin was swinging down. He smashed out my back window as we took off.

"COOPA! GONNA GET YOU COOPA! YOU AND DAT HIPPIE! YOU GOTTEM ONE BEEF NOW COOPA!"

"Great. Now we got Big Marvin after us." Cooper said. He wasn't too happy about this. Big Marvin was in the Hui. That's like the mob on the North shore. They all wore black surf trunks. Some people called them the black shorts. They definitely ran the island and you didn't want to mess with them. It took Cooper weeks to patch that up and get Big Marvin off our ass.

The days started to run into another on the North Shore. It was absolutely quiet. It was late summer going into fall. The waves weren't too big yet so I was surfing ever day backyards or Velzyland. Cooper was the ultimate party animal and always had been. He was famous for getting loaded and wrecking cars. He was friends with all the surf star and all the drug heads. With his best friend Robert who's dad owned the pig farm in Haleiwa they spent every day surfing then getting loaded. And I mean getting really loaded. This was about 1978 so for Cooper to be freebasing cocaine and smoking it in joints like it was nothing, I would say he was a pioneer of that shit. I never liked these joints too much so I stayed away. I liked psychedelics, mushrooms, acid, mescaline, so we tripped a lot.

There was a cow field up the block from Velzyland and for a while we were having mushroom juice parties every three days. The house was a real party house, as most houses were on the North Shore. It doesn't matter how big and gnarly the waves were, when were tripping, the waves weren't as critical, it was more fun, not life and death. We would get high and walk down to the Pipeline sometimes when it was big and watch the Pros surf it.

I had a room, Joey Muck had a room, Cooper and his girl had a room and he kept renting the last room to a revolving door of girls that could put up with him for just about a month before they ran out of there. It didn't matter to me though. He was my big wave guru. For me whatever he did was cool, he rode Pipeline at 40 feet. Truthfully, Cooper could rip in any size surf.

One day we were sitting in the living room waiting for the swell to come up. When there are no waves there was not a lot to do. Except try to get high, skateboard around, which wasn't the best because the roads sucked on the North shore. I looked out the window and some guy was walking up the walk. He had real long hair and he was looking down as he walked, so we couldn't get a good look at him.

"Someone's here."

There was a loud knock on the door.

"You expecting anyone?" I asked Cooper, he looked at me like I was crazy. We didn't get too many visitors. Whoever it was knocked again louder. Cooper was always worried about bill collectors and people he had ripped off, there were so many people, he was always waiting to show up, so he went to the back of the house.

I opened the door and standing there was my previous big wave guru Clyde from California.

"What are you doing here? How did you find me?"

"I got your info from John. You called him two weeks ago. Cooper is real easy to find, everyone knows him. The South

Shore is breaking about twenty five feet. Closing out everywhere. I have been staying in a house on a break called China Wall. It's holding the waves good. It's a great left breaking for over a mile."

By now Cooper had come out of the back room. Clyde had some great weed so we all sat down to smoke and plan the surf trip to the South Shore.

We were pretty stoned when Cooper's friend Robert pulled in our driveway.

"Robert's here." Cooper and Robert were literally two of a kind, bot totally scandalous and the best of friends. Robert walked in carrying two Surfboards.

"Hey Coopa. I got em two more boards in the truck. Go and grab 'em."

"Where'd you get them?" Cooper said with a smile. He already knew the answer he just wanted to hear it.

"Some haolie tourist surfers stopped to check the waves, left 'em on dey car. I think the saw me unloading them but they didn't say anything. Must have not wanted them." Robert and Cooper both found this totally amusing. The truth is those guys were probably on the island for only a few days and left heir boards on their car while they all walked about three hundred feet off the road to check the waves. This is a no-no in Hawaii. Someone better stay with the boards. Like a whole lot of other places on the earth, it's your job to not get ripped off, and the locals job to rip you off. They probably took one look at Robert at six foot seven and three hundred fifty pounds and figured it wasn't worth the ass whipping he would have given them. Smart choice. We made a plan to leave at four in the morning, that way we would get to the break before the dawn.

It's always easy waking up to go surf. In fact it's hard to get to sleep because you are so excited. I could barely sleep at all thinking about twenty five foot waves. We piled into my car and drove to Haleiwa to pick up Robert at the pig farm. After attaching the boards to the roof rack Robert got in and we took off. We only drove about a block when Robert pointed ahead.

"Pull over by that bush." Robert said. I did exactly what Robert said. In fact everyone did exactly what Robert said. Robert got out of the car and reached over the seven foot bush. You could hear the branch snap as he took off one of the top colas of his neighbors weed plant. He got back in the car with a big smile.

"Let's go. Drive to the seven eleven." Robert handed the bud to Cooper who examined it.

"You think he will know you took it? Your neighbor I mean?"

"I hope he does." Robert said. "In fact I got one job for you this week Hippie."

"Cool." I said already dreading it. I knew if Robert had a job it was scandalous.

I said not thinking it's cool at all. Any job with Robert means you could easily end up dead or in jail.

We pulled up to the seven eleven and Robert handed me the bud. "Go dry this out in the microwave oven." Microwave ovens were a new thing at this point. I went inside and the guy behind the counter was as big as Robert. He was clean cut, more like a college football type. Robert was much greasier.

As I walked past the guy he eyed me pretty suspiciously. Here is this long haired hippie kid at four in the morning going straight to the microwave oven. I put the bud in the oven and set the timer for two minutes. After about a minute the whole store started smelling like fresh weed. The big guy behind the counter came over to me and he was not too happy.

"What you doing? Huh? What you got in that oven? GET OUTTA HERE."" He told me. I grabbed the bud and high tailed out of the store. The guy sprayed some cleaner inside the oven. I got back in the car and handed the bud over to Robert.

"This isn't dry. It's too wet to smoke." Now Robert wasn't too happy.

"There's a guy behind the counter as big as you and he told me to beat it." Robert got a big smile on his face. He loved a confrontation. He looked at Copper.

"I'll be right back." He said with a smile.

"I bet. Listen, lets not go to jail before we get to surf." Cooper said.

"Let's go hippie." Robert said to me and we got out of the car. I walked in the store first and the big guy looked at me like I was crazy, until he saw Robert right behind me. Robert walked up to the counter held out the bud to the guy and got right in his face.

"You mind I dry dis bud in your oven Braddah?" Robert said to him in his kindest menacing voice. The two of them were eye to eye at six foot seven. The guy behind the counter thought about it and caved in.

"No Braddah. It's all good." Robert handed me the bud.

"Hurry up." I went and dried the bud and in a few minutes we took off to the south shore, smoking kind bud the whole way.

We drove through the island in the darkness for about two hours. My car didn't have a radio, so it was quiet. We pulled into a really rich neighborhood. As we got closer to the break, the waves got louder. It sounded like bombs going of one after another.

We pulled into a cul de sac and parked. We all jumped out of the car and walked over to the edge. There was a ledge leading down to the water, about twenty feet off the ledge was a big table rock. There were three Hawaiian kids in the water. They were taking off next to the ledge making a bottom turn then coming up over the rock then dropping in again on a twenty five foot face and riding down the line for over a mile. A twenty five foot Hawaiian face is about three body lengths over head. The space between the ledge and the table rock was just wide enough to make a bottom turn then pull it back up and over. Any mistake and you would fall and then get chewed to hamburger meat against the ledge. Or had your body crushed against the table rock. The Hawaiian kids were ripping it. We stood there and watched for a minute. The sun was barely coming up.

"Didn't I tell you?" Clyde said.

"Yeah." I said. I was definitely a little intimidated by the size of the waves. It was a point break which was good, not a beach break. A point break is peeling down the line, A beach break is a lot heavier, pounding closer to shore, becoming faster and more hollow. Still these waves were rolling in at twenty five feet then peeling down the line for over a mile till they were just over head. They were perfect tubes. I waked over to the wall next to the house, it was a really rich neighbor hood, and took a piss. I turned around and Cooper was standing there with a lit joint, he handed it to me.

"You can do this." He said. It was always tough to read Cooper, He could easily be sending me to my doom for his own amusement. He was totally twisted.

"You think?" I wasn't too sure. These were for certain the biggest waves I would have ever surfed by far. "It's really big."

"Yeah but it's a point break. Listen take that Local Motion Swallow tail. It's really thick and will give you some flotation. Come on we will paddle out together."

We grabbed our boards and waxed up. Robert was using one of the new boards he had just took off the rent a car. Joey Muck always used the same board and old lightning bolt spear. Clyde had some Florida board, Cooper always rode Dick Brewer or Owl Chapman boards.

We got in the water and the waves were rolling in like mountains. I made it passed the rock and sat in the line up. Copper took off on the first wave and was gone Clyde was sitting too far out to catch one. I let a few go buy and then I figured I better take the drop. One thing about surfing, you will conquer your fears or they will conquer you.

I took off on a monster wave at least twentyfive feet. I made it to the bottom and looked up and I was in awe I just stood there and looked up and watched it scream down the line. The wave broke on top of me and pushed me to the bottom. I was getting clobbered by it, dragged and held under. After being held down for what seemed like an eternity, I made it to the surface and grabbed a mouthful of air. I looked up and Robert was taking off on the next wave, which was another twenty five footer. They were coming in ten wave sets so I knew I was in for it.

I watched Robert come screaming down the face, he made a bottom turn, pulled up then he saw me in front of him about ten feet. He bailed off his board and got clobbered by the wave. We both were in the spin cycle getting thrashed. I got held about ten feet under until it felt like my lungs were going to burst. I shot through the surface and gulp a mouth full of air. Robert grabbed his board and got on it. I pulled on my leash and dragged my board over to me.

"COME ON HIPPIE. GET ON DAT BOARD." Robert was paddling towards me as fast as he could. I hopped on my board and paddled as fast as I could. Robert could really paddle fast, he came up behind me and pushed my board. A huge wave broke behind us and a fifteen foot tall wall of white water picked us up from behind and we stayed on our belly's and rode it to the inside. After it passed Robert paddled over to me.

"Listen Hippie. There aint no speed at the bottom. Stay closer to the top or you're gonna get killed. You gotta milk 'em Hippie. You can do dis Braddah. NOW PADDLE." That was the nicest Robert ever was to me. He probably didn't want to go through the red tape it would have been if I had drowned out there. Robert was a straight up criminal. A crankster gangster with no scruples before that term was even invented. Hell, it was probably invented for Robert and Cooper simultaneously.

We paddled hard and long to not get crushed by the next twenty footer that was coming in. It crashed behind us and we rode on our belly's for a mile then paddled into the calm water and started the long paddle to the line up. I could see the Hawaiian kids ripping it up. My big wave guru Clyde was still sitting out too far to catch a wave. He wanted to make sure he didn't get washed up on to the reef.

"'You likem dat board Hippie?'

"Yeah it floats me good."

"You start catching some waves Hippie and I give you dat board. You can do dis Hippie, you from da shore." Robert was all about the rep of the surfers from the shore. This was also one of the boards he just took off the surfing tourist car. He didn't have any attachment to it and he probably figured if I got caught with it I would take the blame. Either way I now had a new board.

"You just gotta push your self over that ledge of fear." Robert said.

When you are looking down the face of a twenty foot monster, paddling so hard with your chin pushing on the deck, you cross through a threshhold most men never cross. The threshold of fear and you have to attack it, live it, conquer it, master it then have none at all.

We were paddling like banshees as fast as we could. It's a tricky situation, navigating the oncoming sets and surfers. Diving under big walls of white water, getting beaten and pushed to the bottom, then swimming to the surface gulping a lung full of air grabbing your board and paddling as fast as to get over the next mountain of water coming at you.

We got back out to the line up. There were about six kids waiting to take off, totally ripping down the line. These were for certain the biggest waves I had ever been in. Thirty feet at the take off point and then you are ripping down the face of a twentyfive foot monster. It continually gets smaller until it is just over your head and you are standing in a head high tube. We got back to the line up.

"You can do dis." Robert said again.

"Yeah you just gotta take off. Push it over the ledge." Cooper said. "There isn't any speed at the bottom. Stay on the high line."

I looked out to the horizon and I could se a big set looming in. My big wave guru Clyde was sitting so far out there was no way he could catch a wave but I am sure that is what he wanted. He had just got to Hawaii. I let the first two pass knowing if I fall I don't want to get pounded by the next ten coming after it. I saw one coming in that was all mine. I started paddling as fast and hard as I could. There comes a time you just say 'I don't give a damn what happens to me I am taking off'. Looking down a thirty foot monster and paddling as hard as you can to get into it, is a soul searching deal. If the wave passes you by and you don't catch it you will be pummeled by the lip to the bottom possibly dragged against some rocks or coral heads. Whether you make it or not depends on your level of commitment.

I could feel it lifting me and I stood up and in one second I knew I had it. I remember what Cooper said, 'stay on the high line' so I held it up tight for a while. I came screaming down the face and stood in a tube so big I could have had some one on my shoulders. That day was a monumental day in my surfing career. I conquered a big thing that day, fear. I learned one of the things I could conquer was myself. I just had to want it bad enough. I surfed with my friends all day and then we went back the next two days while the swell was pounding. If you grew up surfing in the United States and reading surf magazines like I did then you remember the big swell on the South Shore. I think it was in the late eighties. A boat called the Tiger 5 was trying to get out of the Ala Moana canal and it capsized. It was big news back then. It was in all the surfer magazines.

When the swell dropped we went back to the North Shore. On the way back Robert looked at me.

"You like em dat board Hippie? You like keep em?"

"It's cool. I don't have any money though." I knew Robert was trying to get money out of me.

"Thats ok Hippie. You keep dat board. I got job you can help me with. You rode the board good today. Yeah you keep em Hippie. We figure it out later."

"Uh. OK Robert." I knew this was not as good as it sounds.

These guys were always looking for ways to get money to do drugs when they weren't surfing. Didn't really matter what it was they would do anything. They were always trying to get Heroin. Cooper was always talking about how the guys who surfed pipeline really big all smoked heroin. Brown rocks from Bali, China White, it always had these exotic names and had this crazy story and this elaborate scheme attached to get it here. At least a dozen times we went on a wild goose chase with no result after going up and down hotel street in Honolulu all night and either buying bunk or getting ripped off. This time Cooper was determined to find some Heroin. He called this big time Hawaiian Mafia guy he knew named Guy. He made arrangements to go to Makaha and pick up some China White. Supposed to be the cream of the crop of Heroin. Cooper didn't have a car and he had me drive him everywhere. I wasn't thrilled to go to Makaha. That's the west side of the Island. They don't like Haolies there. Foreigners.

Anyone who is not from Hawaii. But they really didn't like us in Makaha.

We drove to Makaha and parked outside a big house. Makaha was about an hour from the North Shore.

"You wait here. I'm gonna go get us some dope."

"Uh ok." He hopped out of the car and left me in the darkness outside a big house on Makaha side, in a neighborhood I have never been in, in a beat up rusted out Volvo with a red ball and the words SURF NAZI spray painted around it. I decided the best thing to do was lay down in the back seat.

It took Cooper so long I fell asleep back there. He slammed the door and I woke up.

"Come on lets get out of here." He said. I could tell there was something different about him. He was wasted like I had never seen him before.

"Did you get it?" I asked him I was just as eager as he was. It was this fabled drug I had never done but only heard stories about. This is what has been sailing across the seas for centuries. This is what built the railroads in the west. This is what they brought over on the Opium Clippers at the turn of the century. Heroin.

"Yeah. I got it." Except for occasionally scratching he nodded out in the passengers seat while I drove us back to the North Shore.

"Come on wake up. Cooper. WAKE UP." I had been shaking him for five minutes. He was out cold, sleeping more peacefully than I had ever seen. When he finally came to he was really wasted, he looked like he was bleeding out of his eyes.

"Lets go. We gotta get some tin foil."

"We just got home."

"Well we need tin Foil. I told you that."

"No you didn't." Cooper socked me in the face and we had a two minute, knock down drag out fight till he convinced me we had to go back to the store to get tin foil or we wouldn't be getting stoned. Everything was extreme with Copper. It was nothing to him or me to fight at a seconds notice or with no provocation we did it all the time. I guess that is the frame of mind it takes to ride forty foot Pipeline.

We got back from the store with some Reynolds wrap and we sat at the table like little kids.

"This is what the big boys do. The doo. Do the doo. Do da doo. Do da doo all da day." Cooper was happy like a little kid as he set up his little tin foil tube to smoke out of. He took outa little bag of light brown powder and poured a little pile on the foil. "This is called Chasing the Dragon." He said. He then lit a match and held it under the foil. Within seconds it started to move across the foil in a trail of smoke, which Cooper followed with the rolled up tin foil tube inhaling the smoke. He took a big hit and held it as long as he could. He let it out then fell deeper into the couch. I grabbed the tube and foil and without a second thought I did exactly what I saw Cooper do. I took a big hit. It tasted sharp and sweet at the same time. I held it as long as I could and let it out. The only way I could describe the feeling was euphoria. Bliss. I felt as if I had smoked thirty joints at one time, in one hit. I was completely penetrated. I could instantly feel the romance of the drug that caused such a stir over the centuries. It was exotic, faraway, and I felt no pain.

I think what happens to you in life, who you eventually become is greatly determined by who you are around, who influences you growing up. Who you emulate and want to be influences the choices you make. That's how I could grab the Heroin and try it without a care. I thought about all those times people said smoking pot leads to dope. I don't necessarily believe that. It definitely takes an open mind to try anything, but there are some things that take careful consideration. Pot might lead to dope if you are looking for it, or if it comes in your path in the hand of your big wave guru, your friend, or any other circumstance.

We smoked more heroin on the tin foil for about an hour. We passed it back and forth smoking it like it was a race. Robert showed up and that was pretty much it for me. Robert brought some coke over and him and Cooper cooked it up and smoked the rest of the heroin mixed with the coke themselves. Robert would turn into a monster licking his lips with his eyes bulging out of his head. He was over three hundred pounds so this was a pretty scary sight.

Robert kept telling me he had a job for me and him to do, but he wouldn't say what. Great. That's all I needed I thought, was to get more involved with this Psycho. Everyone on the North was afraid of Robert. He pretty much did whatever he wanted to do.

I woke up the next day late, not feeling too hot. I grabbed my surfboard and went for a surf. I never saw heroin again on the island. Cooper searched for it a lot, all the time in fact. He was an adrenalin junkie, whatever it was that gave him a rush he was into it. So when there were no waves he turned to his search for dope. And he was relentless.

12

"Roberts here." Cooper called to my room from the living room. I knew that tonight was the night. Robert had some job to do and he was picking me up at eight. They told me to dress in all dark clothing so I knew we were probably going to steal something. These guys were always stealing shit. Whatever wasn't nailed down. I ran out of the house and jumped in the truck.

"You ready hippie?" Robert asked looking me over.

"Ready as I'll ever be." I was definitely nervous. Robert was about twenty five and I was almost seventeen. He was huge and I was skinny. If it went wrong, whatever it was, I was pretty sure I would get the worst end of it.

We drove for a while in the darkness of the North Shore. Neither of us said a word. I couldn't tell if Robert was on a good one or not, I just took it for granted he was.

He pulled into a residential neighborhood on the other end of Haleiwa. We drove real slow and quiet. It was about three in the morning so everything was quiet. Robert turned his lights and we drove on the complete darkness for a few hundred feet. He turned the engine off and we coasted to a stop. Robert pointed to a big hedge.

"See that hedge?"

"Yeah."

"That's my cousin's house. He's got about forty weed plants about to bud. We gonna take um."
"You gonna rob your cousin?"
"Yeah. He nevah suspect me." Robert said with a grin. "I help him find the guy who did it."
I thought how Robert has absolutely no scruples at all. I didn't know if I believed it was Robert's real cousin or not. He said everyone was his cousin, until he crossed you or robbed you. That usually cut the family ties.
We got out of the car and hurried across the lot next to the hedge. Robert walked up to it and separated two hedges with his hands. We walked into the yard and there were forty of the most beautiful weed plants I ever saw. I heard a real low growl behind me and I froze. I could tell it was a dog. I turned real slowly and saw a big pit bull looking at me lowering his head and growling. I felt all the blood rush out of my face. I thought I was finished for sure.
"Sssshhhh Petunia. Come here pretty girl." Robert said in a whisper. Instantly Petunia stopped growling and walked over to Robert so he could scratch her behind the ears.
"You don't think it was important to tell me about Petunia."
"Oh yeah. My cousin got em one big dog." Robert said with a grin. He found the whole thing amusing.
We picked up the plants two buckets at a time and carried them out to Roberts truck. It took about eight minutes and we were on our way back with Roberts cousins complete garden. We drove to the pig farm and dropped them off. Robert sat there watering them with a source of pride. I sat there watching him and I had an ominous feeling this would not turn out right. Boy was I right.
The next day the shit hit the fan. Roberts cousin's plants missing was big news and his cousin put out a reward to anyone who knew who took them. I spent the whole day surfing and staying away from the house. That was probably not the best thing to do. When I got back to my house Robert his cousin and a few of his brothers were waiting for me.
I put my surfboard away and went into the living room. Robert called me outside to smoke a joint. I knew there was

nothing to do but play the cards out. I walked into the front yard and Robert was smoking a joint.

"Hippie come here. Lets smoke em one joint." Robert held out the joint to me. I looked over at his truck and the cousin and brothers were all standing leaning against the truck like it was ringside seating. I walked over to Robert and it became one of those times when everything turned into slow motion. Each step felt like I was sinking further. I watched my hand reach out to grab the joint. It seemed like it was moving so slowly. I took the joint and started to hit it and for one second I thought everything was going to be ok. Maybe they were just stopping by on their way home from extorting shopkeepers, or taking the purses from old ladies, or stealing surfboards. Either way I started to lighten up as I was hitting the joint.

"Why you take my cousins weed hippie?" Robert asked me as he was winding up with a knockout punch. He slammed me before I could answer while I was hitting the joint. I went flying across the front lawn and landed on the grass. I jumped up and ran straight at Robert who was swinging wildly. I knew there was nothing I could do but fight. I knew I was gonna get beat, I knew I couldn't sell Robert out to his cousin. I might end up dead in the pineapple fields if I did that so the only thing to do was fight as hard as I could and take my lumps.

Robert beat me up pretty good that night. I found out later he told his cousin he would fid out who took his crop for half of it. I guess he figured he was gonna get caught anyway, he might as well be the hero and get half than get caught and get none. Either way I had enough of Paradise for now. I packed up my stuff and flew back to Miami. Things were really starting to pop off there. It was the pre scarface era and Miami was the spot were most drugs started their journey into the US. Everyone was making lots of money selling, smuggling and dealing drugs. I decided to go back home and see what trouble I could get in there.

13

"I'll pay for it and you go first." I told Ronnie. We were beat from Painting houses all day in the Miami sun.
"Deal." Ronnie said.
We had been talking about getting a tattoo for a long time. Ronnie was a drummer in the best band in town. Neither of us had any tattoos so this was a big deal.
We walked into the local tattoo shop called Tattoo You, which was in our neighborhood. It was a one room hole in the wall. The flash, which is what the drawings on the walls of a tattoo shop are called, were stapled on the wall in the same way he got them. No color, no shading, only line drawings, no frames. I had never even been in a tattoo shop and I knew this was not how it was supposed to be. There were two guys in there drinking beers and watching football.
"I'll have that one." Ronnie pointed at a drawing after about looking at the wall for about thirty seconds. "On my arm right here." I don't think there was a lot of thought involved. He picked a skull with a dagger through it with a snake and a banner. It was a very traditional piece. In the banner he put the name of the band he was the drummer in, 'Death Before Dishonor'.
I looked all around and didn't see anything I would have put on me forever. Forever is a long time. I was always into art, my Mom being the Art teacher and all, so I figured if I like something enough to have it on my wall, then I might like it on my body, forever. I had been thinking about getting a tattoo for years. Drawing on my arm with a black marker then looking in the mirror thinking, "This could be real."
I called Gary up.
"Hey, could you bring down a few of those books on training. There aint nothing here worth getting."
"You guys are really doing it?" Gary was in dis belief.
"Yeah, Ronnie is in the chair now."
"What did he get?"
"Some skull and Dagger with a snake through it."

"You guys are insane." Gary was always the straight shooter of the bunch.

" I'll be right there." He said.

I hung up and went back to Ronnie who was wincing in pain. I found the whole tattoo thing fascinating. Watching the needle go in and out, leaving a permanent mark just seemed cool to me. About twenty minutes later Gary walked in with a pile of books. We started going through them and I wasn't having any luck. We opened a book on Japanese Kanji, which is the Japanese alphabet, with the translation of each. Each one of the Kanji's looked like a piece of Art to me, so we started looking at them and the translations of each one.

Gary pointed down at one. "This is one is you." I looked closer and read it. It said,

'Muga Mushin – Selflessness – When you are going into battle you are not thinking about your wife, or your life or your self. You are only content with killing your enemy.'

"This one is you." Gary said.

"You think so?"

"Absolutely." I always trusted Gary with just about anything. He had his head on straight early on. He is just one of those guys that doesn't make a lot of mistakes. Ronnie's tattoo was done and it was my turn. I showed the guy what I wanted and he started making a stencil. He was a little drunk by now so I ended up finishing the stencil myself. The guy was about 30, and we were about 16. He put the stencil on my arm and started tattooing me. Gary was standing over the guy's shoulder watching.

"He's fucking it up. He's fucking it up." Gary said. I pulled back and looked the tattoo guy in the eye.

"Check it out Bro. If you mess up this tattoo, I can guarantee you me and my two friend will wreck this place and everything in it, you included."

The guy just looked at me in sort of dis belief, or he was just wasted. I snapped at him.

"DO YOU GET IT?" The guy got it. He sat back and put the machine down.

"Can I have a glass of water?" He asked me.

"I think that's a good idea." I told him. He got up and guzzled two glasses back to back then sat back down and finished the tattoo. You could see how serious he was all of a sudden doing my tattoo. He realized how serious the situation he was in actually was. It just goes to show you that it doesn't matter how old a man is, once he is a man. When the guy finished I paid him for both and we all split. I knew right then I wanted to be completely tattooed, like Queequeg in Moby Dick. I wanted to be a tattoo artist, and I set my mind for that. One year later I was working in the oldest shop in the United States at that time, Lyle Tuttle tattoo on seventh street and market in San Francisco.

14

I was boxing as a little kid. My dad was a boxer in the Navy. He really loved boxing and took me to all the fights. He was always holding his hands up and teaching me moves for in the ring. He got me in a little kids boxing league when I was like eight years old at Uleta, the local gym. My mom was against it but my dad didn't listen to anyone.

He wouldn't let me play football, not in school anyway. He was afraid I would get hit hard and paralyzed. He did let me box though. In fact he promoted that in me. He felt this was something I could use through out my life, if for nothing else, to defend myself when necessary. It definitely helped me have confidence I got to admit that, but I did get in a lot of fights. I remember my Mom getting mad cause the other mothers would call up and say I couldn't come over any more after I beat the tar out of their kid. That's what kids do.

I started training Karate at sixteen. At eighteen all I wanted was to be a Karate teacher and have six dedicated students. This dematerialized as different things in my life started to take hold. Training became less and less important. I started to find that self medicating myself and doing art was what I was doing most. I was always a functioning addict. I always went to work or had a hustle, even when I was homeless or loaded Those years of training taught me a few things, like there is nothing I can't do or conquer. You start out thinking you will never be able to master back stance. You wonder if you can achieve a black belt with out ever mastering this. Then you make it your favorite stance.

I started reading about Samurai life style. Bushido, and great warriors like Miyamoto Musashi. I then adopted this lifestyle, at least on the serious man part, to whatever I did. I already felt that I was on a path of enlightenment, this just refined this train of thought. I took everything I went through in life as a life and death matter. I enjoyed being serious. I imagined that's how Samurai were. Serious.

15

"Did you get it?"

"Yeah, hurry up." I jumped in the back of the car and we took off.

" Let's see." Bobby Hunter said and stuck his hand out. He was the school bully and I didn't expect to see him in the car. I had stolen a little cocaine from my Dad's dresser drawer. I reluctantly handed it over. He inspected it, then put it in his pocket.

"Hey."

"Hey what? Relax, you're gonna get some." One of the girls in the front seat, Stacey looked back at me reassuringly. Like I better take it easy, he might bash my head in. It wasn't easy growing up skinny, everyone always wanted to try and take your shit, and I was never into letting them no matter how big they were.

So there I was, getting strong armed at fifteen by a sixteen year old kid, life went from excitement to doom and gloom in an instant. We drove into this deserted lot, just a bunch of abandoned cars in it, an old refrigerator, some bums with their shopping carts..

Cocaine was just hitting the streets when I was a kid, and I watched it chew some people up real bad. Chewed my dad

up, and a whole lot of other people. All kinds of people lost everything and then some, from attorney's to surfers and everyone in between. Basically whoever tried it..
Guy down the block from my house OD'd, and the kid around the corner, also a bunch of my sister's friends. People didn't know when to stop. They didn't know when to quit, till their heart was about to explode. Just like the rat in the cage they showed us on that movie in science class.
Back in the day you could buy ether kits and petri dishes to make base cocaine, over the counter at Vibrations records. Like it was no big deal. No one knew what they were really getting into. It was only a big deal when you lost the house, or the neighbor dies in your living room.
Lindsay turned on the car light and Bobby took out a small mirror and poured out the baggie of coke. He crushed it up and made some lines, taking the biggest two for himself which he snorted before he handed the mirror back. Lindsay and Stacey did the next two lines then I did my two. We sat there and waited.
"You feel anything?"
"I don't know. Do you?"
"Shut Up." Bobby said. "I'm rushing out." I looked up at him and he had his eyes closed and was kind of vibrating. I looked at Lindsay, she looked at Stacey and we got out of the car. We stood there and smoked a joint while Bobby Hunter stayed in the car. We were watching him search around the car.
"What's he looking for?"
"I don't know." After like ten minutes Bobby got out of the car and walked up to me.
"We need some more." He said to me, kind of menacing.
"I don't have any."
"Well you're gonna get some."
"No I'm not. Aint no place to get some more anyway. My dad lives in the Grove so we aint going back there and even if we did, he isn't expecting to see me till next week."
Bobby stepped up and grabbed me by the collar.
"We gotta get some more now."
"Lemme go." I said trying to rip his hands off of me.
"Let him go ROBERT." Lindsay said.

"Yeah, there aint no more, your wrecking our high." Stacey said.

"I don't like that shit anyway, I aint never getting it again." I said.

"Wanna bet?" Bobby said and he started shaking me violently. I started punching him in the face as many times as I could over and over. He was kind of dodging them while he shook me. He threw me to the ground and started this kind of temper tantrum. He picked up a big pipe and started beating one of the abandoned cars. Then he started after the bums who were in a corner minding their own business. I got up and Stacey handed me the joint.

"Crazy." Lindsay said as we watched Bobby argue and chase the bums around the lot.

" Did you feel it? Anything?" I asked them both.

" I don't know." Stacey said. "You?"

"I think so. My teeth got numb." Lindsay said as she was rubbing her teeth.

"Well I didn't feel shit. And if this shit does nothing but make you freak out I have had enough of it. I like going down anyway, not up." I said. We watched Bobby for another minute.

"Let's get out of here." I said. We all got in the car and Lindsay started the car. As soon as Bobby heard the car, he started running after us, with the pipe.

"Better hurry." I said " Here comes Bobby." Lindsay and Stacey turned around and looked behind us, Bobby was running at the car, screaming with the pipe in his hand. Lindsay slammed the car in gear and we pulled out of there. I looked out the back window and I gave Bobby the finger.

About four months later I got to school and everyone was on the front lawn in a circle talking. Lindsay walked up to me.

"Did you hear what happened? Bobby Hunter OD'd in his bedroom last night. He was cooking that shit up and smoking it. His mom found him." I stood there for a moment taking that in. Lindsay stood there waiting for a reaction from me.

"What are you thinking?" She asked me.

"I wonder what's for lunch today." I said.

16

"Shhhhh. Be quiet. Someone's coming." I was laying on a lawn chair after school with my new girlfriend Janice and I heard a car pull up in front.. We had skipped school and were behind a house making out down the block from where I used to live. I could see a uniformed policeman walking into the back of the house from the other side. We got up quickly and went out the opposite side of the house only to run into the cops partner. I was a pretty skinny kid and that cop picked me up by my collar.

"What have we got here?" he said as he held me up. Janice just stood there watching. The other cop walked up and grabbed her also.

"Shouldn't you two be in school?"

"Schools out." I said. " Let me go."

The cop looked at his watch. "According to my calculations school is still in session for another three hours." They dragged us over to the police car and went through our pockets.

"And what do we have here?" The cop pulled out a baggie from my pocket with some Blonde Lebanese Hash in it. Everyone had hash back then. They searched Janice and found two Quaaludes in her purse. Everyone had Quaaludes too.

"Don't say a word." I told her. This pissed the cop off greatly. He threw me in the back of the car. They put Janice in the other side of the car and took off to the police station. I was definitely more nervous about what my dad would do to me more than the cops. My parents were already divorced. It was just me and my mom at home. My dad had moved to Coconut Grove, but was still trying to control everything.

"My dad is a criminal attorney." I told the cop thinking this might get me somewhere. I had already been in trouble in my life enough to know whatever I say they will use against me.

"Yeah I got that. I recognize your name. Your dad beat the last two cases I was involved in. Let's see if he can get you out of this. Just sit back and enjoy the ride."

We rode the rest of the way in silence.

We pulled into the police garage and they pulled Janice away and walked her to the women's side.

"Don't say anything." I told her again as they took her away.

"Oh we got a tough guy." The cop said as he shoved me into the holding cell. I sat there for a couple of hours wondering what is going to happen next. After a couple of hours my dad walked in the cell. He was more mad than I had ever seen him.

"Don't you say one word." He told me. He seemed to know all the cops and he walked me out of there. We got in his car in silence and drove that way for a while. We pulled into the garage under his condo in the grove. I hadn't ever lived with him since he moved out about five years earlier and we didn't have the best relationship.

"You are going to tell me where you got that hash." He said.

" No I'm not. For what reason? It wasn't that guy's fault I got caught." We were walking into the elevator. I thought about running but he would have caught me. My dad was a beast, a savage. And I had already been to California on a surf trip, so I knew where I was heading. I just had to get back home and get the rest of my stash, sell it and get on the Greyhound bus heading west.

"Let me tell you how this is going to work." My dad said. "You are going to stay here until you give up the name of the guy you got that from. Then I am going to figure out what to do next."

"Aint gonna happen." My dad slammed me into next week after that remark. I got up and looked at him with disdain, then went to the guest room. My dad went to work every day and locked me in the house. There was nothing I could do, nowhere to go, so I just sat there. After two days my dad walked in the room.

"Your mother just found your stash and flushed it down the toilet." I was furious, that was my escaping money.

"This is bullshit. You get high and I know it. You are a hypocrite." My dad slammed me and I was on my ass again. I got up quick.
"We'll see how much you want to say in a day or two." He said as he walked out of the room. I sat there completely lost, not knowing at all what I would do next.
The next day he woke me up early. "Get up and get your things together."
We got in his car and he drove us to a big building in downtown Miami.
"What's this place?" I asked.
"Your new home for a while. Operation Fresh Start. It's a rehab for drug abusers."
"Oh yeah? You going too?" I asked him. My dad looked at me like he wanted to slam me again but instead he just got out of the car. I looked over and my Mother was pulling up to the building. Poor woman, she looked distraught. I walked up to her and gave her a hug, she held me tight.
"This is for your own good." She said almost crying. "What is?" I asked. "You going to this rehabilitation center." She said through her tears.
I looked at the building and thought to myself, the only place I am going is to California.
We went inside and sat down with the Director of the place. My mom was at her wits end. The director explained that if I didn't say I wanted to bet there, like signing up of my own free will then they wouldn't take me.
"Well that's not going to happen. There isn't anything wrong with me. I smoke some weed that's it. I don't even drink. Which is more than I can say for some of the people in this room." My dad glared at me.
"This isn't about me, it's about you. And I can promise you this, if you don't say you want to be here the only place you will be going is to a juvenile detention center. I will see to it." My dad said.
I looked at him in disbelief. What a hypocrite I thought to myself.
"But if you start the program honey I will come get you later and you can come home." My mom said with tears in her

eyes. I thought about the big picture. I had to get home so I could get my stuff and get out of dodge.

"OK, I will do the program." I said reluctantly.

"Good." The director said as he stood up. He handed me a clipboard and I signed where they said to. The director shook my dad's hand, who immediately split.

My mom gave me a hug, "Now do good honey and I will be back tonight to get you." I watched my parents walk out then go their separate ways. The director led me into the courtyard and introduced me to some kid with a clip board.

"This is Bill, he will show you around. Today is your first day so you don't have to participate or do the classes, that will all start tomorrow. Today is your orientation"

So this kid Bill, who was about seventeen was like the model prisoner there showed me the layout. He walked me all around, showed me all the classes and activities I would have to do, he introduced me to some other kids. He explained to me I could no longer use the TV or radio when I got home nor could I ever talk to anyone that I knew before I got to Operation Fresh Start, that I would have to make all new friends. At the end of the day they all sat in a circle in the courtyard and had a discussion.

"I'm so glad I didn't drink today." One girl said.

"Me also. I thought about doing coke all day and now I am glad I didn't." said another.

I saw my mom pull up and park across the street with the other mom's.

"So how was your first day David?" Bill asked me. " What do you think?" I smiled and stood up.

"I think I like smoking weed. I don't think I am out of control at all with it. I don't have a drug problem I don't do drugs. I think as soon as I get home I am going to break out my stash and have a good smoke then I am going to figure out what to do next. Tell you what I will not be here tomorrow. I will be on the way to a better place, but if I am here tomorrow, I will go through the whole program." I turned around and bolted for the gate. I ran through it and jumped in my mom's car.

"How was it?' She asked me.

"Let's just go home." I had to be cool so she just left before the director or that model prisoner came running out. She took off and in my rear view I could see Bill running after the car. My mom didn't see him.

We got to the house and I ripped the fridge open and started eating good food. My dad didn't eat like I did so I hadn't eaten in like three days. I picked up the phone and started dialing friends to get me out of there. Every time I picked up the phone my mom would run into her room and pick up the phone. I loved her and revered her. She never abandoned me. And I wasn't a walk in park growing up. As soon as anyone of my friends picked up the phone I would say, "If I hang up, you hang up and I will call you back. Can you come get me?" No one was able to come get me. My mom figured out I was trying to run away and called my dad.

"So you think you are going to run away? Believe you me Sonny Jim, I will come get you right now and have you locked up. You have to promise me you won't run away."

"I promise." All I was thinking was I promise myself I will. My mom seemed a little relieved. No matter how mad I was I couldn't take it out on her. Since my dad me and my mom and we had a special bond. When you are a little kid and watch your mom cry every night, you end up not liking the person that made her cry. My dad made her cry.

I know I couldn't reach any of my friends like this so I went to sleep and set my alarm for three in the morning.

I woke up just before the alarm went off and turned it off before it rang, didn't want to wake my mom up. I was laying in my bed wondering who to call. I was thinking f I can't reach anyone, I would just walk out of there and figure out the rest tomorrow, as long as I didn't wake up there and have to go back to the rehab.

All of a sudden there was alight knock on my window. I jumped up and moved the blinds and saw my friend Big Al at my window.

"Let's go up coast. The waves are hitting good. North swell." He said. I ran to the front door and let him in. I explained the whole story to him.

"God sent you here to rescue me." I told him.

"God sent me here to take you up coast and go surfing, I know you have gas money. I don't know about that other shit." Big Al said.

It took me and Al about an hour to quietly get my stereo and records, my three surfboards and my clothes out of the house without waking my mom. I remember looking at my house as we drove away as if it was for the last time. I left my mom a note on the table, 'Don't worry, I will be ok. I Love You.' It said. I knew she would worry, It's what mom's do. I also knew it was time for me to go. Some things you just know.

The next day we went by the high school and I sold two of the surfboards and my stereo and all my records. This was now my escape money. I got some weed from a friend of mine and had Big Al drop me off at the greyhound bus station.

"You sure you know what you are doing?" Al asked me.

" I think so." Al gave me a hug and split. I sat in that station waiting for the bus to pull in. This was a big deal for me running away. I was two days from my sixteenth birthday, embarking on what I saw as the beginning of the adventure of my life. The bus pulled in and the driver walked into the station.

"All aboard for Tallahassee, Mobile, El Paso and Points West." He yelled.

Points West. I like the sound of that I thought. The West is the Best. Jim Morrison says so.

I got on the bus with more excitement in my heart than I had ever felt before, the excitement of the unknown.

17

I turned sixteen on the bus to California. I had sold two of my surfboards and my stereo and records. I think I had about six or seven hundred dollars. I also had about two ounces of Blonde Lebanese hash. It was worth way more in California than in Florida. The bus ticket was forty five dollars so I was doing good. My friend gave me two ounces of weed for the trip so I was set weed wise.

Forty five dollars for a ride across the country, I thought this was the best deal happening. Three days and four nights and I will be there. I got on the bus around six at night and was tired as hell from all the shenanigans I had recently gone through, so I passed out.

I woke up somewhere in Louisiana. Forty five bucks to get across the country was a good deal, but I could see already I will be very happy to get off the bus. The people that were going all the way across the country were mostly sitting in the back of the bus. I was tired of sitting up straight. As soon as we pulled into the next stop and the back three seats were empty I moved all my stuff over there and sat down. I controlled those three seats for the rest of the ride. The bus was getting ready to pull out and new people were boarding. Some worker guy was walking to the back. He looked like he worked on a fishing boat or something. He walked right up to me thinking I would move.

"Excuse me." He said as he tried to squeeze in the seat.

"Excuse you for what?"

"I want to sit there."

"Can't."

"Why not?" He looked confused. He was from the sticks. I was from the big city. I learned early on you have to take what you want, aint no one giving it to you.

"Cause I'm already sitting here."

"In all the seats?"

"That's right. I'm going all the way across the country and I am sitting in all the seats for that ride. There's plenty of other seats. Go sit in one of those."

He looked at me for a second in disbelief, I looked him right in the eye, he could see I was ready to go, he didn't want any, he then shrugged his shoulders and turned back around and found a seat closer to the front. I used to try people like that when I was younger, kind of challenge myself. I had already been training for years so I was full of confidence I just had a lot to learn. A couple of the men and women in the back snickered, we were all getting a little friendly in the back of the bus.

We boarded the bus after the dinner spot on the second night, somewhere in Texas. I was pretty stoned and tired, but way excited. It was my birthday, which I kept to myself. Turning sixteen and heading West, I was filled with excitement.

We went through small town to small town for a while. Local people would get on the bus and ride for twenty or forty miles then get off again. There was nothing around there by my standards, maybe anybody's standards. Just a lot of open fields.

We pulled into a stop and a few people got on the bus. I was sitting next to the window looking out, so I didn't see this really sexy kind of drunk lady sit down on the back seat. She must have been about twentyfive, no more than thirty.

"That seat's taken." I said.

"By me Darlin." She said with a drunken smile. She was real cute and real drunk. A big cowboy made his way to the back of the bus and tried to sit in between us, there were three seats in the back. Before this Cowboy could sit down, this lady lays down across the seats and puts her head in my lap. She looks up at the guy.

"This seat's taken Darlin' gotta find one up front." The cowboy looked at her then at me, shrugged his shoulders and went back to the front

The bus took off and the lights on the bus went out. It was as dark as night on the bus, couldn't really see anything. I could feel my fly being undone. The drunken lady started giving me a blowjob. One of the men sitting in the seat in front of me and on the side of me looked back and smiled. After a few minutes of that she sits up.

"Come on." She grabs my hand and we went into the bathroom on the bus. It was really small but we made it work. We made a pretty good racket for a while, but you could only hear it in the back few seats. We came back out and all the people in the back were smiling at us. We sat there for a while and drove in silence. We pulled into the next stop. It was real dark, not much around at all.

"This is my stop Darlin." She said. She was very cute. It was surreal.

"It was REALLY good to meet you. What's your name?" I asked her.
"Alice. What's your's?"
"David."
"Good to meet you David. You made my night."
"Believe me. You made mine."
She got up and walked off the bus shaking her ass the whole way down the aisle. Everybody watched, even the ladies. As soon as she got off the bus everyone starting joking me about it.
"Well it is my birthday." I said.
One of the men looked out the window.
"Here she comes again." Everyone got quiet. She walked all the way to the back again, shaking her ass the whole way. She stepped up to me.
"I thought this was your stop."
"It is." She said. "I was hoping you might want to get off for the night. You can jump back on in the morning, or afternoon, whatever the case may be."
She was really cute, I thought about it for a second.
"I really can't. There are people waiting for me. I have to show up on time."
She handed me a folded piece of paper.
"If you are ever in West Texas again Sugar, You better give me a call."
She turned around and shook her ass all the way off the bus again. Everyone watched he go, even the ladies. I slept like a little kid that night on that bus, not a care in the world.

18

The bus pulled into the bus station in downtown San Diego a day and a half later, and I was very ready to get off. I grabbed my surfboard and walked out of the bus, I was the last one out. My two pals Johnny and Louie were there waiting for me with big smiles on their faces.
"Wow homeboy, you really made it." Johnny said.

"How was the ride?" Louie asked.
"Brutal." I said. Louie took me by the arm. "Your dad's been calling Bill's house. Said if you are here he's gonna beat the shit out of every one of us. How could he know you were here?"
"I don't know. He's just trying everywhere he thinks I might be. I came here last year so he figures I might try to make it across. He's a million miles away. Don't worry about it. I'm not." We jumped in Louie's truck and took off.
I rented a room in a house from an old surfer dude from Miami named Carlo who got me a job on a construction site he was working on picking up debris. We would wake up at the dawn and go surf or an hour, then go to work and work all day, then surf in the afternoon until dark. I lived in Encinitas California, which is like Surf city. There were a bunch of guys from Miami all living in a big house down the block. They had big parties there every weekend. The town was full of kids, a beach vibe. You could stand there with your surfboard on Pacific Coast Highway and stick your thumb out with a joint in your mouth and someone would do a three lane maneuver to pick you up.
I was surfing as much as I could, ten hours a day on the weekends. I was the youngest one there from Miami, so everyone kind of watched out for me.
I met these two California surfers, Kimo and Wally that used to hang out at the house all the time. They were telling me about Mexico and how it was uncrowded and the waves were perfect. I wanted to go and I had the gas money. We made an arrangement for them to pick me up at four am the next day which was Saturday, I had the day off.
 I didn't tell any of the older guys what I was doing, I woke up real early and waited outside. I fell asleep on the porch and some of the guys woke me up on the way out.
"What are you doing out here?" Johnny said.
"Nothing. Must have fell asleep."
"Let's go surf." Johnny took off down the beach. I was disappointed that Wally and Kimo didn't show up. I walked down to the beach with my board and when I got there I saw Wally and Kimo sitting watching the waves.

"Why didn't you guys pick me up?" I asked them not too happy.
"Over slept homeboy. Happens."
"Is it too late to go?"
"Never too late. You still wanna go?"
"Hell yeah. Pick me up at my house, I'm gonna grab some money." I ran back to my house and grabbed about forty bucks. Wally pulled up and I jumped in the truck and we took off. Kimo had a cigar box full of weed and we smoked like fiends all the way to the border. Wally pulled off on the exit just before the crossing.
"Gimme that." Wally took the cigar box of weed. "That too." I took one last drag and handed him the joint. He took it and jumped out of the truck and stashed the box in a pile of garbage.
"What did you do that for?"
I asked him. He jumped in the car and we peeled out of there.
"They frown on that sort of shit down there. It will be there when we get back, don't worry Tiger."
We crossed the border and drove for a while. We pulled up to a beach with no one at it and perfect four foot peaks peeling along for a quarter mile in both directions. I learned later this spot was called A frames.
I had one of the best sessions of my life that day. Certainly the best one I had ever had up till that point. I stood in tube after tube and got barreled all day.
We got out of the water beat tired and drove into town happy. We ate some tacos and got back on the road to go home. Wally saw a stand and stopped the truck.
"What's here?"
"Fireworks." Wally and Kimo jumped out of the truck and went inside. The store had all kinds of Fireworks. Some looked like little sticks of dynamite, some looked like big sticks.
"Look at this." Kimo was holding two big bottles of tequila.
"Look inside."
I looked in the bottle real close and saw a worm at the bottom.
"What's that?"

"That's the worm homeboy. You eat that and you get real fucked up. You see visions and shit."

"He aint lying," Wally walked up with all the fireworks he bought, enough to blow up a Toyota.

"Let's get out of here." Kimo and Wally walked out with their goods. They moved some blankets and towels around and stashed the Tequila and Fireworks under the surfboards and stuff.

"What are you doing?" I asked.

"We can't just take this stuff across the border. They don't like that shit. For one you aint even old enough to drink.

"What if they catch us?" I was starting to get a little worried.

"They won't catch us. Just don't say a word."

We got back in the truck and took off. When we were waiting in line to cross the border I was thinking how bad this will be if I get in trouble again. The car in front of us moved and we pulled up to the border patrol officer. He leaned in the window and looked at us real close.

"What are you boys bringing back from Mexico today?"

"Just some good memories of some tasty waves and a sunburn." Wally said with a smile.

The officer looked at three sunburnt kids in the truck, then looked at the boards in the back, then looked back at us and smiled.

"Have a good day fellas."

"Yes sir. Will do."

We pulled out of there and started laughing. I immediately thought that I just completed a smuggling venture. I was excited more than ever with this thought. We pulled off the exit and Kimo jumped out and grabbed the cigar box. It was right where we left it. We smoked like kings al the way back to Encinitas.

We turned on our block and I saw Johnny and Louie on the corner talking. We pulled up to them.

"Have you seen…" Johnny stopped his sentence as soon as he saw me.

"Where have you been?" Johnny asked me. We got out of the truck.

"Mexico. Got tubed all day." I said.

"We thought you drowned. We've been combing the beach looking for you." Johnny said.
"You're a dead man." Louie said as they both starting chasing me all around the truck. They weren't as mad as they were relieved I wasn't dead. We were laughing as they tackled me. We went up to the house and had a barbeque. Some girls came over, typical beach life style. I didn't stay up cause I was so tired.
I woke up to Johnny and Louie standing over me.
"Come on get up." Johnny said as he ripped my blankest off me.
"What are you doing? What time is it?" I asked him.
"Get up." Louie said. "We gotta go."
"Where we going?' I asked rubbing the sleep out of my eyes.
"Mexico."

19

Time just went by. Miami was so far removed from me I barely thought about it at all. I was making my way in the world. I had a place and a job and I was learning that the rent comes every month like clockwork. Being on my own taught me responsibility.
I had been living in California for almost five months. I hadn't called home even one time. I rode my bicycle from my house in Cardiff by the sea, I had moved twice, to the big house my friends were renting in Encinitas. Then we were all going to pile into the truck and go to a big party in Solana Beach.
I got to the house and all my friends were waiting. We smoked a few joints then we all went outside to leave. As were getting into the truck , a rental car pulled up quick, the door flew open and the light inside the car came on. I could see the hand inside putting the car in park, it was my dad's Rolex that he had been wearing his whole life. My eyes went wide.

"It's my father." I said. Everyone ran back into the house. My dad came running up trying to grab me but the truck was between us.

"I'm not going back." I said. "If you make me I will just run away again."

"I don't know what to say." He was a little shaken. "Where are you going?"

"To a party a few towns over."

"Can I come?"

"Are you gonna make a scene? Try to take me back? Beat up my friends?" I looked at the house all my friends were looking out the kitchen window.

"No." We stood there for a moment just staring at each other. I can only imagine how hard this was for him. It was not easy for me.

"You can follow us." I wasn't sure if I got in his car if he wouldn't just keep driving and try to take me back. He got in his car and everyone came out of the house and piled in the truck. There was about six of us in the bed of the truck. We picked up a couple of girls along the way, who also piled in the back with a bunch of blankets. My dad stayed real close to the truck the whole way there.

We got to the party at a big house in Solana Beach. There were about four hundred kids there. Cars were parked up and down the blocks for miles.

We went inside and there was a band playing in the living room and the dance floor was full. The floor itself was going up and down ten inches in both directions. My dad was amazed.

"Looks like fun." My dad said.

"It is. Here being a kid is EVERYTHING."

"I see that. Does this happen often? Parties like this?"

"Only every weekend." I said with a smile. I had relaxed. I could see he wasn't going to try anything funny. I think he just wanted to see that I was ok.

The next day he met me at the beach and watched me go surfing. When I got out of the water he was waiting.

" I would have never found you."

"You did find me."

"I was walking up and down the beach for days with binoculars. I looked at every surfer. Once the wet suit is on you all look the same." He took out his phone and dialed a number, then handed me the phone.
"Tell your mother you are ok. She is worried about you." I took the phone and listened to it ring.
"Hello."
"Hi Mom."
"David? David how are you? I have been worried sick."
"I know mom, I'm sorry. I had to go, it was time." She was silent for a moment.
"I understand. How long will you be gone?"
"I'm not sure. I'm ok mom. I have a place and a job. I'm going to be fine."
"Am I ever going to see you again?" She started to cry.
"Don't cry mom, I will come see you in a couple of months. I love you."
"I love you my son." She hung up. I know this was very hard but this is what happens. Children grow up and move out. I just think she didn't think it would happen so fast. I gave the phone back to my father. He took it and reached into his pocket. He took out his wallet and gave me all the money in it, about three hundred dollars.
"You don't have to give me that I am fine dad."
"I see that. You are growing up. Take the money, you might need it." He looked me in the eye. He was way intense.
"You are on your own. Take care of yourself. I handled those charges, you won't hear about them again, juvenile anyway. Stay out of trouble, stay in touch and let us know how you're doing. Your mother and I love you very much." He gave me a hug, shook my hand, turned and walked to his car and left. It was a little sad but exciting at the same time. I was really on my own.

20

I heard a loud knock on my door then it flew open.

"GET UP. We're gonna be late." Louie said. "If we are late one more time they are gonna fire us. You for sure." I jumped out of bed and threw on my work clothes, grabbed my tool belt and ran out of the house. I jumped in the car and Louie handed me a joint. I took it and he peeled out of the driveway. I was on my third room for rent in eight months since I had been away. It seemed to be the pattern. Stay a month or two, then get a story about how someone is coming home from vacation or they are remodeling or some horse shit but I always had to move. There were a lot of transient kids in this area.

We go to the construction site and Johnny was already on the roof working, he gave us the finger.

"LOUIE." The foreman called out from the office. Louie ran inside, the foreman glared at me. I picked up a broom and started sweeping right away. That was my job, cleaning up construction sites. Seemed like a good job when I took it. Paid the bills, but now it was starting to seem like if I don't make something happen I would end up doing this for years. I had been virtually broke since I got here, moving around all the time was taking its toll on me. I had it going on when I was in Miami. I wasn't surfing all the time, which is what I loved to do. But I was learning valuable lessons in life. Like surfing is not paying my bills. As much as I love it, I knew I had to figure out a way to find a balance.

Louie came out of the office and I knew I got canned.

"You don't even got to say it." I said.

"Sorry kid. See ya later." He handed me two days pay and and I split.

I got home and went in my room and lit up a joint and looked at my stuff. I didn't have much, a surfboard, a skateboard, a backpack full of clothes and an army jacket. I thought about how I don't want to go back home, not yet anyway, and I felt like I had to do as much as I could to stay around here.

I had a friend that had also moved to California from Miami named Pauly, about my age that had been living in Thousand Oaks California for about a year. Pauly had a job delivering fruit and vegetables with his own truck. He didn't surf or anything, he was just one of the kids from the neighborhood

that got high. Pauly had a cousin named Josh and they were always together. And they were always getting high.
I figured I would hitch hike up the coast. Hitch hiking was pretty safe back then, this was the mid seventies. A lot of things weren't even invented yet, or at least blasted across the front page. Serial Killers, crack, gangs, guns in school, there was none of that, it was a different time. There was no social disease the doctor couldn't take care of with a shot of penicillin. Weed was pretty scarce and when you got it, it was Colombian or Panamanian, qua-aludes were big, coke was just coming out of the closet. People had no idea. All they knew was it felt good at the time, then they would wake up in the morning and ask. "Where's the TV?"
"You don't remember? You gave it to the man for that last gram."
"Oh."
I started packing up all my stuff. It was still early in the day so I figured I could hitch hike up to Pauly's place in Thousand Oaks in just a few hours. I knew it was somewhere between here and LA. I had Pauly's address from Josh, who was up North of San Francisco. At least I would have all day to get there. And embarking on a new adventure always excited me. I always love adventuring into the unknown, anything can happen, and usually does. Better than sitting at home I always thought.
I wrote those guys a note let them know I was splitting and skateboarded to I-5 which is the highway which ran up and down the coast. I had never hitchhiked on I-5 before, but I was unafraid, I never worried about anything.
I stood there for about an hour before I got my first ride.
"Where you headed?" The guy asked me.
"Thousand Oaks."
"Throw your backpack in the back and get in, I'm going that way."
I jumped in and we drove for about an hour without saying anything. He seemed harmless enough. He was an older guy in a beat up old Impala. He had this big radio on the front seat and a whole bunch of construction stuff on the back seat. . He had a pretty big ghetto blaster between us on the seat. He

kept changing the dial, adjusting the volume. Then he started with a bunch of stupid questions.
"You got a girlfriend?"
"No."
"You like girls?"
"Yes."
"Why don't you have a girlfriend?"
"I don't know. Just don't."
He reached over and started messing with the dial again. I knew something was up.
"You like getting your dick sucked?" He asked me as he put his hand on my leg. I grabbed the wheel with my left hand and started punching him in the face with my right. I pulled the wheel hard to the right while he was holding onto it with both hands. His nose started bleeding but I kept hitting him as the car cut across all the lanes to the side. Other cars where hitting their brakes to avoid hitting us. He slammed on the brakes and I jumped out with my skateboard. He took off with my backpack still in the car. I threw some rocks at his car as it pulled away but he didn't stop. Fucking freak, that was one of my first incidences with a real idiot.
At least I had my skateboard, no clothes though, that asshole took my backpack. I rode my skateboard up to the next off ramp. I was about an hour away from Thousand Oaks I figured. I got off and called Pauly, who quickly came and picked me up in his fruit delivery truck. There was a whole network of kids from Miami that had moved out West. They all wanted to find the guy and kill him. It's in our Miami blood.

21

Pauly pulled up happy to see me. I jumped in and we took off. He handed me a joint.
"Where's all your stuff?"

"You don't want to know. Some freak on the highway, gave me a ride then had some other ideas." I took a big hit and handed the joint back to Pauly.
"For real?"
"Yeah, I bashed his face up pretty good though."
"I got some clothes for you. You're almost about my size." Pauly said.
We drove along for about twenty minutes.
"We're almost there. Marcus is pretty fucked up. I'm just warning you, he gets a little intense."
"What do you mean?"
"I mean they were doing pretty good when they first got here, moving about a key of blow a week. Having it driven out from Miami, then hiring drivers to do everything, deliveries and pickups basically carry it the whole way. He never even had to touch it all. He just made the connections and now he sat back and collected."
"So what's the problem?" I took the joint back all the time thinking, 'why can't I get a break like that?'
"Everything was fine until he figured out how to cook that shit. Now he sits around smoking free base cocaine all day long. The kitchen is like a lab and he is smoking his profits as fast as he makes it."
"Wow."
"Tell me about it. I rented a room in his condo, I get up at like three in the morning to be at the market at four and this guy is up all night partying. I gotta find another place to live."
We pulled up to Marcus's condo and got out. I could smell the coke as soon as we got out of the truck. I knew I didn't want to stay here long. We walked in and Marcus was happy to see me.
"David. Great to see you." Marcus said with the pipe in his hand. He was sitting in front of a table with a pile of coke on it and all kinds of bottles and petri dishes and shit.
"Good to see you Marcus. Thanks for letting me crash."
"First month is free while you get on your feet. Least I can do for a homeboy. Wanna hit?"

Marcus handed me the glass pipe and Pauly looked at me cross eyed. "I'm going to bed, I gotta get up early. You working with me or what?" Pauly said a little pissed off.

"Yes I am." I said.

"Then don't party all night. You're going to work either way so get some sleep." Pauly slammed the door as he went to bed.

"Don't mind him, he's just pissed he smoked up every bit of savings he had and has to go back to delivering fruit. I did the delivering gig for a while, till I got this rolling, now it rolls itself." Marcus held up this little torch and lit the pipe.

I had never smoked cocaine before this was my first time. I took a big hit and handed back the pipe. I can easily say I never ever felt that same rush again like I did that time. It blew my head off. And I instantly wanted more. I ended up smoking all the money I had in my pocket and owing Marcus two hundred dollars by the time Pauly opened his door to go to work. He took one look at me, I was totally freaked in a chair in the corner.

"Take these." He handed me four valiums. I took them and drank some water.

"Let's go." Pauly said. Marcus was loading another hit into his pipe.

"And don't forget you owe me two hundred bucks, D." Marcus called out with a laugh. He just wanted Pauly to know how in debt I already was. Pauly looked at me like I was an idiot.

We got in the truck and I could feel the valiums taking effect and they felt good.

"Feeling better?" Pauly asked me.

"A little, thanks."

"I told you he was way intense." Pauly said.

"It aint just him, that shit is intense." I was starting to feel a little better.

"Tell me about it. I just got out of debt. Now I am saving for my own place. Do your self a favor and stay away from that shit. He will keep giving it to you till you owe him about a thousand bucks, then he will cut you off."

We pulled into the fruit stand and as Pauly jumped out he looked back at me.

"Try to get a little rest, these guys will load up the truck, I check it on the way in, the truck, the rest is up to us."
"What do you mean up to us?"
"I'm trying to build up a route, get some customers. I gotta beat the other guys there and beat their price."
"Sounds risky."
"Everything's a risk these days."
Pauly jumped out of the truck and I tried to close my eyes. At least the valiums were kicking in. He woke me up about an hour later.
"Let's go."
Pauly was smooth, every restaurant he stopped at bought his stuff. We were done by three o'clock. He handed me a hundred for the day. He made about five hundred.
"Now don't blow it with Marcus and his shit. In about a week I'm moving somewhere else, you can go also I bet they have another room.
"Ya think?" I said enthusiastically. I knew had to get out of there. Before I was dead.

22

We pulled up to Marcus's condo. "Remember what I said." Pauly warned me. Good advice can always be given, but it isn't always taken. Soon as we walked inside Marcus offered us a hit. Pauly said no and went in his room, I didn't have a room to go to, I was sleeping on the couch, and who was I to refuse. This pattern went on for about three days and nights. Friday came and Pauly woke me up for work and I was actually sleeping. We got in the truck and Pauly looked at me with a smile.
"He cut you off, huh?"
"Yeah. And now I fucking owe him a thousand bucks." I said all pissed off.
"Don't worry about it, he's not. He's making about ten grand a week. He just has a thing about giving it up for free after a little while. You're better off."

"I know. I don't even know why I was doing it. Like it was calling me. I don't even like rushing out. I like going down better than up."

"Yeah, me too. That's the drug. That's what it's geared to do, makes you think about nothing else, don't want nothing else. Shit aint no good."

I fell into a routine. Waking up early and delivering fruit. Pauly and me moved out of Marcus's condo and into a big house that a guy named Kevin was renting rooms out of. We each got a room and kept delivering fruit and vegetables. There wasn't a lot going on except work. Kevin didn't work, he sold weed and had a good clientele. A lot of cute girls were always coming in and out. I didn't trust him though he was shifty.

I still owed Marcus that thousand dollars. I hadn't paid him anything. I started going up North to San Francisco and meeting Jeff on the weekends. I would buy real good hash or some ounces of good weed and bring it back. There was always a concert to go to, a lot of times it was the Grateful Dead. I really dug going to those shows, it was like a big drug party. I realized I didn't like coke and I was getting more into other drugs like psychadelics, LSD, Mushrooms, Peyote, anything that would expand my mind. I would ride the greyhound back and forth up and down the California coast. It was my method of travel for a long time. It always seemed safe.

"How was the trip?" Pauly asked me. I just got back from San Francisco with some Nepalese Temple balls. I had built up a little clientele so I not only worked delivering fruit I was dealing also.

"Awesome. Got some insane hash. Nepalese Temple balls." We went inside and I broke it out. Pauly was visibly impressed. I was always getting the best, most exotic smoke I could find. I was into the hippie drugs, like weed, hash, mushrooms and acid. I never got into drinking at all, I stayed away from Coke after that episode at Marcus's and I never saw Heroin too much. It was never around. And I wasn't looking for it.

We sat in the living room and smoked till we were way stoned. Pauly looked at me with a grin.
"What you got going on now?" I asked him. I knew something was up.
"Come here, I wanna show you something." We got up and went to his bedroom. He looked around then unlocked the door, which I found strange, he never locked his door and besides, we were in the house who could be there without us knowing it? He slipped in his room with me right after him and in the middle of the floor was a pile of weed, a bunch of pounds all bagged into half pound bags.
"Where'd you get that?" I reached over and picked one up, open it and smelled it. "Not bad." I said as I started rolling up a joint.
"Marcus fronted it to me. He got a hundred pounds delivered from Miami. Kevin is on the way back, he took a sample to a guy and hopefully we will get rid of it in one shot."
"I don't trust him, he's shifty." I said.
"I know I got that. That's why I need you to go with us if we go do the deal. I will pay the thousand back to Marcus that you owe him."
"Deal." We sat there and smoked for about an hour until Kevin showed up. This guy was a snake and I knew it. He always had a story and was always in a rush.
"I got good news and bad news." He said. Fucking shifty motherfucker he was.
"The price was a little steep for the first guy but I called another friend who liked the price and will probably take it all. We just gotta bring him a sample."
"What about the first sample?"
"I smoked it with him and left him the rest to see what he could do. This is how it works Pauly. You gotta get it out there so somebody sees it who wants it."
Pauly looked at me and I looked at him like, 'I told you so.'
"Ok." Pauly said reluctantly. He took an ounce and bagged it up.
"You think this guy might want to buy some Black Nepalese Temple balls?" I held up a ball of hash. Kevin's eyes bulged at the sight of it.

"Absolutely. No doubt about it." I grabbed my backpack with my scale, ledger, and three ounces of hash inside it at the bottom in a separate bag, then all my clothes on top. I had just come back from up north and did not have time to unpack.

We piled into Kevin's beat up Volkswagen bug and took off. It was just getting dark.

We drove about a mile and Kevin kept talking about the people he knew and connections he had. People that know people and have connections like that don't talk about it.

"Uh oh." Kevin said.

"What? I asked.

"We got a cop behind us."

"Is he pulling us over?" Pauly asked.

"Not yet. I'm gonna make a right on the next block, I have a taillight out."

I knew right then it was all bad, I just had a bad feeling. He made the right and the cop turned on his lights.

"Shit. He's pulling us over. Listen, I picked you two up hitch hiking."

"No you didn't." I said.

"Yes I did. You have hash on you and he has weed. You better stash it, but If you get popped say I picked you up hitch hiking. I'm on parole."

"If I get popped I'm not gonna say anything." I said, I knew that much. Pauly stashed his ounce in his sock. I had four ounces of hash, a scale, and a ledger of who owed what in the bottom of my backpack, so there was no way I could dig it out without making a scene. The cop strolled up to the car and leaned in the window.

"Good evening. The reason I stopped you is because you have a tail light out. Do you have any weapons or drugs in the vehicle."

"No sir." Kevin said.

"License and registration from you driver, I.D's from you two." We handed over our I.D.'s and Kevin handed them all to the cop, Kevin's hand was almost visibly shaking.

"Sit tight gentlemen, I'll be right back." The cop said with a smirk. He then strolled back to his car like he had all the time in the world. Truth is, time starts to slow down when everything is going bad, as soon as you know it is all going south, it all becomes surreal as you start watching it all happen in slow motion.

It seemed like an eternity while we waited for the cop to come back, no one said a word, just total silence. I could se in the rear view mirror the cop walking back and another squad car pull up and two other cops get out. I knew I was screwed.

"Here he comes. Be cool. Let me do the talking."

"The cop is the only one's gonna be talking." I said

"Shut up." Kevin hissed at me. He was visibly nervous. The cop came up to the door and opened it.

"Everybody out." We all got out of the car. I was last and I left my bag on the back seat.

"You three stand right there." He stuck his head in and smelled around and stuck his head back out. "I smell marijuana." I could see other cars go real slowly with kids in the cars watching us. The other cops walked up and searched us. The cop pulled my backpack out of the back seat.

"Who's is this?" Nobody said anything. Kevin looked at me with a glare. I didn't say anything. Kevin spoke up.

"I picked them up hitch hiking. I never saw that bag before." The cop looked right at me.

"I'm going to ask one more time. Who's bag is this?" Nobody said anything and the cop unzipped the bag and started going through it. He was pulling the clothes out and placing them on the hood. Then he got to the scale, ledger and bag with four one ounce balls of black Nepalese Temple ball hash. Three stripes, the best there is. The cop took out one ball, broke it in half and smelled it. He looked at me, "Look's like Heroin."

"It's not." I said. The cop grabbed me and spun me around and threw some handcuffs on me. "Tell it to the judge." They walked me over to the squad car and put me in the back. That must have been enough for them because they didn't even continue to search Kevin's car. They let them go and took me off to jail. All in slow motion.

23

I sat on the bench in the San Diego courthouse with Pauly. I was waiting for my hearing on the hash charges. They got me for possession with intent to distribute on account of the scale and ledger. I was not too sure of what was going to happen, the public defender I had didn't look to interested in my case when he talked to me.
The lobby was full of all kinds of people, mostly from the street on drugs or violence charges, Two weeks into being eighteen and I am thinking I am going straight to the slammer. I couldn't stop my leg from shaking. There was no one to call. I wasn't going to worry my mom with this shit.
Some guard walked up and opened the doors to the court with a key and everyone got up and walked inside.
"You ready?"
"This sucks." I was totally bummed. We started to walk in and the cop who arrested me walked past and smirked at me. " I have a ninety percent conviction rate."
"Good for you." I said. Fuck him, thinks he is going to intimidate me? I was shaking.
We walked inside and took two seats in the back. The cop went up and sat next to the prosecutor and whispered something in his ear and they both laughed. I thought 'great, I 'm screwed.' I looked over at the public defender, his desk was covered with files he didn't look very confident.
"If this goes south I am gonna run out of here and you pick me up around the corner."
"Are you crazy? That aint gonna work. You won't even make it out of the court"
"Wanna bet? Fear is a great motivator."
"So's a paycheck." Pauly motioned to the cop at the door. He looked like a linebacker for the Chargers. He definitely looked like he could catch me.
"ALL RISE." The judge walked in and everyone got up. Pauly pulled me up. "Don't be stupid." He said. "Just relax."
"I'm trying."

They started calling people by name and they would step up one at a time and stand between the two tables. The prosecutor would read the charges and the judge would ask them if they had anything to say. Sometimes the cop would speak, but mostly everyone was just taking whatever deal the court offered. He was handing out one to three years in jail like it was nothing. I thought I was doomed.
The called my case and the cop got on the stand, I sat at the table next to the public defender. The guy was completely over worked with a pile of cases in front of him he could barely see the judge.
The cop starts telling this fairy tale of how we were weaving in and out of traffic, so he pulled us over. All lies I'm telling you.
"Your honor, I pulled the suspects over for weaving. After I pulled the suspects over, I saw in the backseat a backpack with a plastic bag sticking out of the zipper. At that time I suspected there was narcotics in the backpack so I made entry and found the contraband." The cop lied. The Judge thought about this for a moment then looked down at me, visibly shaking, long hair, Birkenstocks, my best button down surf shirt, sitting at the desk across from him.
"And what do you have to say about this officer's testimony young man?" The Judge asked me. I sat up straight and said quietly,
"It's insane that he swore to tell the truth, then lied like the devil to lock me up. I don't understand. Why would he do that?" You could hear the court sort of laugh quietly. The Judge thought about this for a minute.
" I don't know, I'll ask him. " He turned to the cop. " How did you know there was contraband in the back pack?"
"Uh excuse me?" The cop was dumbfounded. "I saw the plastic."
"That could have been a sandwich, couldn't it have been? Officer?"
"I guess so." The cop said still astounded the Judge was siding with me.
"' know so. Case dismissed." The judge said it so quick it took me a second to react. Then I jumped up and ran out. I walked

to the nearest pay phone and called Gary to see what was happening back home. I had burned out California for a minute I thought.

"Oigo." Gary always answered like a Cuban. Oigo means, "I'm listening."

"What's happening?' I asked.

"I hear you are getting in all kinds of trouble out there. Guess the West aint the best after all." Gary said.

"Maybe it just needs a break. Whats happening at home?"

"You wouldn't believe it if I told you."

"Try."

"Work has been going crazy. Guys that were humping bails now own boats. Everyone and their mother is smuggling. Making money hand over fist."

"My room still empty?"

"And you got a job waiting for ya. I gotta warn you though."

"What?"

"It's about a hundred degrees in the shade."

I got on the next Greyhound Bus and headed back east. Home.

24

"Here's five hundred. Go buy all the food you want, get cases." Frank said. He went back to the truck to use the phone and talk to his partner Doug. I walked into the local Vegetarian food market. I bought cases of everything, Soy Milk, Tofu, chips and Candy. Bread and Cheese and whatever I thought would be good for the guys that didn't eat the way I did. We had boxes of food, which is the smartest way to go out on the open sea.

We loaded up the truck and headed for the Marina. There were other boat Captains and crews packing up their boats also, and everyone heading out around dusk, also like usual.

We headed out into the blackness of the ocean. There is always an exciting feeling on the way out of the Harbor. Anything can happen and I was well aware of that. I never worried though, I was only thinking about the money I was going to make.

We got out into the open ocean at the meeting spot and there were already two boats waiting. We got the news that about forty miles further out to sea was a Colombian freighter with twenty thousand pounds welded into the hull of the boat. The Colombians would not break the seal until there were enough boats to unload the weed at one time. We had to wait on the water for two more days while other boats arrive. Good thing we brought over a weeks worth of food.

On the third night we got the news tonight was the night. There were about ten boats there ready to unload. We could take about five thousand pounds, but some boats could only take a thousand. We pulled up to the freighter and got in line. We were the third boat back. Frank was looking at the time.

"If these guys don't hurry up, we are going to get fucked. The sun will be coming up when we are trying to get back. That aint good."

I thought about this for a moment. "Pull up on the other side." I said to Frank.

"For what? Are you crazy? We will lose our place in line."

"Trust me." It was hard for Frank to trust me. I was younger than anyone else there by a few years.

"I have a plan. You wanna get out of here quick, right?"

"Yeah." Frank said reluctantly. He undid the line and called out to the Captain behind us.

"Save my place OK? I gotta check something out."

"Not a chance." The other Captain called back as he moved his boat up into position.

Frank looked at me with a glare. "This better work or it will be your last ride."

"It will, hurry up." Frank and Doug were both pissed.

We pulled up on the other side of the boat and the Colombians started waving us off, and yelling that we should get back in line.

"Then I guess you don't want this." I held up two big bags of food. The Colombians eye's lit up. I knew they would want the food. They have been on the open sea for over a month. FOR SURE they would want a bunch of American food. They started waving us over. They reached for the bags. "Not until we're loaded." I said. I threw them the lines and we tied up. We were now loading bales as fast as we could, same as the first boat on the other side. We pulled off of the freighter right after the first boat and headed for the Miami coast. We rode in silence for about an hour. The tension is thick on the way back the boat loaded with thousands of pounds of weed. It's a real adrenalin rush. We got about three miles from the coast and I picked up the handset.

"This is Spike, This is Spike. I'm about two miles from the exit. How's it look?"

"STOP YOUR BOAT. HE'S ABOUT TWO OCLOCK, WAY UP THERE. LIKE A STAR." The voice had so much fear in it I couldn't even tell which friend was talking to me it was one of the fishing boats watching the coast guard helicopter. Even if the boat is painted gray or blue to avoid detection like ours was, when it is moving in the water, the oxygen that is moving from the propellers creates a trail that can be seen from the sky. That is luminescence. The oxygen glows like a light and it makes a white trail behind the boat which can be seen from the sky. Frank stopped the boat and looked into the sky.

The ocean sky is covered in stars. There are no city lights out on the ocean to brighten them out. It's wall to wall stars like a carpet, with shooting stars every five minutes. We were all looking and looking and all of a sudden one of the starts made a slight move.

"He's got us." Frank said. One star that was way high in the sky looked like it started moving. He made a slight turn and it was obvious he was bearing down on us.

"Let's get out of here." I said. We sat there waiting for what seemed like an eternity until the helicopter was right over the boat. All of a sudden they turned the daylight on us and we could see everything. The bottom of the helicopter above the deck looked like a ship out of Star Wars it was so close. We had about twenty bales wrapped in burlap with a red, green and red stripe on them sitting right on the deck in the open. The hull was completely full with fifty six bales, over six thousand pounds total.

I sat with my head buried in my knees. Frank turned the boat hard right and left trying to lose them but they stayed right on us. I saw my friends watching this whole thing from the fishing boats and I knew my other friends were listening to it on the CB radio at the stash house. We tried to lose the helicopter but after about ten turns we straightened out and headed back out to sea. The helicopter turned off of us and went after another boat trying to get in the cut. We headed back out to open ocean. I could the sky getting slightly brighter as the sun started to come up. I knew this wasn't good.

There were about ten boats trying to make it in that night, ten crews with ten families counting on this. Only one boat made it in that night we learned later. One guy went up north and was arrested in Ft. Lauderdale, two guys tied the steering wheel so their boat would go around in a circle, jumped off and swam to the shore, where they were promptly arrested. One guy who was listening to this giant clusterfuck on his radio, jumped into his 15 foot Donzi speed boat, drove it out to his boat and traded boats with the drivers and drove his load in. Everyone else that night got busted on US soil. Except us, we went through something else.

We pulled up to one of the Bimini which is one of the Bahamian sitting in the ocean less than a hundred miles off the Miami coast. Frank had a friend there named Speedy. He radioed ahead to let Speedy know we were coming and we wanted to park our boat in his boat garage until later that night when we would try again. We needed gas, food and a place to chill and rest for the day. We had been up all night and the adrenalin rush was wearing off. There was a whole network of workers running these islands and the Florida coast. Frank had been in these waters for years and everyone knew him, even the cops.

Everyone had a boat garage. It's just like a car garage except on the water. You could drive in and park your boat and close the door behind you. We needed to find a stash place quick. We had all those bails on the deck in the open and the sun was starting to lighten the sky. Whatever it cost to stash us and the boat would be worth it, better than getting busted or waiting out on the open ocean all day till nightfall hoping no one would discover us.

As we approached the island we could see a jeep waiting on the shore with three guys in blue uniforms. The jeep was blue and we couldn't make out the BDF on the door because it was a little too dark still. Chances were good the US coast guard also radioed ahead, and the chances were also good that these guys were waiting for us. The sun wasn't up yet so there was still a chance we could make it to Speedy's. On top of it all we were running out of gas, we had to do something. There was no guarantee they were there for us, and even if they were, there was a chance we could buy them off.

As we pulled into the channel, which was not much wider than our boat, we ran out of gas. Two of the men fired M-16's over the boat. I don't know if you have ever been shot at, but when the bullet is travelling twenty feet over your head, it sounds like it is travelling right by your ear. We all hit the deck. The guys on the shore started yelling at us to bring the boat here.

"We ran out of gas." Frank yelled back. They fired more shots.

"Get in da water and bring da boot here mon." The guy yelled back in an Island dialect. Frank jumped in the water, it was only waist deep and took a rope and dragged the boat to shore. Soon as we got there, two of these island cowboy cops jumped on our boat and they seemed very happy. They had on Blue Cop uniforms that they looked like they slept in. They were all checking the bails and slapping each other on the backs, happy as kids.

"Who is da Captain?" No one said anything . The main cop started punching Frank in the face. Frank just stood there taking the hits. One after another, right in the face. The other cops were laughing.

After three punches I said, "We are all the Captain." The main guy looked at me and smiled.

"That's good." He said with a smile. "Now I'm da Captain. An ya'll in trouble." They all started laughing. I looked at the bails of beautiful Gold Columbian weed. Gold with white hairs. This is years before Green Weed, 'Sinsemilla' hit the streets, this is back in the day.

A little ten foot boat with an outboard motor and six more cops all with different assault rifles pulled up all talking fast, kind of arguing. I have no problem to say at 16 years old I was pretty nervous. These men were like half cop half and half Pirate. It was obvious they were arguing about whether or not to keep the boat and weed and just kill us. I grew up in Miami surrounded by Jamaicans and Bahamians so I could understand a little of what was being said. I knew it wasn't good. The sun was coming up and about twenty people were walking to the dock and pointing at us. I think that probably saved us, too many witnesses.

The tied up our Forty foot Cigarette boat a with our nearly six thousand pounds of Prime Colombian weed to their ten foot outboard and towed us into town. Things can change real fast out here, and human life isn't worth as much here as it is at home. I sat on the boat wondering if I would ever see home again. I went from going to make ten thousand dollars in one night, living a high sea adventure, to our boat and weed being confiscated and me not sure if they will kill us or put us in jail forever or what.

"Look at that." I said to Frank and Doug. The whole town was coming out and walking toward the dock. They knew the cops would make us unload our own weed. They had seen this before, probably more than once.

We pulled up to the dock and at gunpoint they made us unload our boat. I was bummed out and a little worried about my immediate future. I figured as soon as they thought they didn't need us any more they would kill us. I picked up one bale and walked toward the one room building that they were storing it in.

"Give me one. Change my life mon. Ya loss it enyway. Give me one." The islanders were asking me to give them a bale. I figured why not, we lost it anyway. There was a little turn where I was out of sight of the boat and the building we were walking to. On the next trip I picked up two bails and headed toward the house. At the turn I let one go and an Islander picked it right up. This became the routine. Each time I would grab two and leave one at the turn. No one had any idea what was happening until we were done and the counts didn't match. The cops were yelling and screaming up a storm, boy they were pissed.

" You gave away some bails." Frank asked me.

"Yeah." I thought he might be mad.

"How many?"

"I don't know, many as I could. Maybe 16."

Frank smiled, "Good for you." Fuck em, we lost it anyway. At least some one will make out." I was relieved but still a little worried.

"What happens now?" I asked.

"I gotta try and negotiate a deal so they will let us go." Frank said.

"How you gonna do that?"

"Give them what they want, money." Frank stood up and was immediately pushed back into the chair. We were then handcuffed to the chairs all three of us side by side.

Frank finally got to talk to the Police Chief. They had a very long intense conversation in the chief's office. There was a glass window and we could see the whole thing. Frank was sitting and the Chief was talking over him. Like a negotiation not an interrogation. After a while the Chief pushed the phone to Frank, who dialed a number and talked for about two minutes and hung up. Then Frank came back out and sat back down.

"What happened?' I asked him, I was definitely getting more and more nervous.

"I made a deal. We have three days to get twenty five thousand dollars here and they will let us go. With the boat, just no weed."

"Better than being dead. You got this covered, right?" Frank could see I was more than a little shaken.

"Yeah. I called my mom, she knows where to get the cash she is making arrangements to fly it here." I felt a little relief. I needed a joint real bad.

"How do we know they won't kill us and your mom too when she gets here?"

"We don't." Frank said. "I don't know, I just know. I've been in these waters for years. He's heard of me, the main guy. Kind

of like honor amongst thieves or something. It wouldn't be right. He made a deal. Cop or not."
I thought about this for a moment. There was a white Jamaican guy sleeping in the corner. Everyone seemed to know they guy and was real polite to him.
"What's that guy's story?" I asked Frank motioning to the sleeping guy.
"That's Montgomery from Jamaica. He flies planes except he isn't the best pilot. He's crashed about ten times. Walked away from every one. I've known him for years."
"Sounds like a good pilot to me. Walked away from ten crashes. I bet anyone can fly a plane. It's all about the landing, especially when you weren't planning to land."
"Yeah well He's buying his way out of here also. He's waiting on his money to get here so they cut him loose. That ought to put your mind at ease. If they kill us they won't have a chance to do this again." Frank smiled and sat back down. I looked over at the Jamaican guy, not a care in the world. I relaxed a little.
I guess it was a good thing I gave those bales away because they brought us lobster dinners with Brown Becks in the Coca Cola can every night. I didn't drink but Frank and Doug did. The girl bringing the food in each meal was way cute. Each time she gave me my tray I asked her the same thing, "Can you bring me a joint?" She looked at me like I was crazy the first few times, then one day she was handing out breakfast, scrambled eggs with fresh baked bread and a small salad. She looked me in the eye.
"Is under da bread, mon." She said very quietly. I waited for her to leave. They unlocked our hands so we could eat. I looked under the toast and there was a big joint and a pack of matches.
"I gotta use the toilet." I called out. "It's an emergency. Frank and Doug looked at me like I was crazy then went back to eating their breakfast. One of the cops walked me over to the bathroom and I went inside. I knew the routine, the cop wasn't going to wait for me there wasn't any where for me to go. I waited a moment then sparked up the joint and smoked it as fast as I could. I must have took too long cause the cop

came back and opened the door looking for me and walked into a room full of smoke. He looked at me crosseyed for a second then started laughing. He grabbed me by the collar and threw me back into the room. The smoke had now poured out into the whole place.

"You couldn't have saved me some?" Frank asked me. "If I could have I would have. I knew I was gonna get caught. Had to finish it quick." Frank understood. He wasn't mad. After that all the cops treated me a little better.

On the third day Frank's Mother showed up with twenty five thousand dollars in cash. That was about the tenses moment. Wondering if they would just kill us anyway. Amazingly enough they kept their word and let us go, with our boat.

We were driving back three days later, a load lighter, but alive. I crawled into the hull and scraped up some weed, rolled us each a joint and we all smoked. After a few minutes we all started laughing.

"You gonna go again?' Frank asked me.

"Soon as you're ready, Captain."

25

"You think this is a good idea?' I asked Gary. I was a little worried. I had only been back in Miami a week and I was already getting back on the boat to go pick up a load of weed for ten grand. I had no problem with that. It was who I was going out to sea with and how not prepared we were that was freaking me out. The captain was a beer drinking redneck named Joe. We never got along too good. I had been away about a year and the guys who were loading bales when I left were boat captains now, making five times the amount of cash in one evening that they were previously making.

"Shouldn't we get some more food? What if some thing happens?' I was skeptical to say the least. You can't even visualize the slightest bad result. You might get it. But I hadn't totally learned that lesson yet. The sea is unforgiving.

The sea is a monster ready to swallow you up. Sometimes that's a lesson you have to learn yourself. Going out to sea, over and over making ten thousand dollars in one evening, and having the biggest adrenalin rush night after night, kind of makes you lose sight of how dangerous smuggling really is.
"Everything will be fine. You guys are only going about eighty miles and back. There's a boat right off Bimini waiting for you. It's all set up. Don't worry about a thing." Gary said. Famous last words.
"Joe has done this a lot. He's a pilot."
"Then why aren't we flying?"
"Very funny, tough guy." Gary said. I wasn't kidding. Joe was this big guy who was about ten years older then me. Just a beer drinking redneck from Miami. I was already on my path to enlightenment. Birkenstocks and tofu sandwiches, I had a job cooking at the biggest vegetarian restaurant in town, training karate five nights a week in the dojo, trying to get into a routine. One look at this guy and I knew my routine was about to get screwed up.
"Come on. You'll be right back." I got in the boat and we shoved off the dock. Joe was driving the boat with me riding shot gun. A thirty five five foot Corsa with two outboard motors. This was for sure the hey day of smuggling ventures. Everyone was doing it back then.
As we got further and further away from the dock I looked around and saw nothing but the blackness of the sea. I knew somehow this wasn't completely thought out. We didn't even have a gallon of water.
"Don't you think we need food? Maybe some water?" I asked Joe. He looked at me like he was crazy or something, like I was supposed to be scared or something, but I wasn't. Which pissed him off further. Like I said, he was way bigger and older than me.
"We'll be fine. We're only going out for a few hours. Not even an all niter. Could be fun to go to Bimini and bang some of them Bahamian whores." He chuckled when he said that. I couldn't stand him. I knew this wasn't going to work out. I looked back at the dock and watched Gary drive out of the

parking lot. The sun was setting behind us. In front was nothing but black.

"What if something happens?" I said again.

"Don't say that. You'll jinx us. Nothing is going to happen. We're gonna go about fourteen miles off Bimini. JT will be waiting for us with about forty bails. Load 'em up, head on back. Collect our dough."

He guzzled a whole beer in one shot and threw it in the Ocean. He's a litter bug to boot. I was hating him more every minute.

"How much you making?' He asked me.

"How much you making?" I answered him.

"I asked you first." What a child. A big ass grown man getting drunk during the operation. What a stupid little child in a big ass grown man's body.

"I'm making ten grand. You?'

"Twenty five." He beamed with pride when he said that. "I'm the Captain."

"Time will tell about that." I said under my breath.

"What did you say?" He asked me with that stupid menacing sort of humor he had. He thought it was funny to try and scare people. Guys like that were always around growing up. Especially if you grew up skinny like I did. All the jocks always like to pick on the skinny guy. That's cause they got no heart. Well most of them anyway.

God, did he make me sick. This guy couldn't be the Captain on a boat in the bathtub as far as I was concerned. All the Captains I knew were way more together than this guy, and he was a pilot. Amazing.

We cruised about fifty miles an hour, which is fast in the water, in case you don't know. Seventy is flying on the water. Everything is faster on the water. Anyway we were clipping along real good and I started to think everything was going to work out fine when BOOM. We heard a small explosion in the compartment holding the motor. The boat had a drastic loss of power.

"What was that?" Joe asked me.

"How the hell do I know?" I said. Here was that ominous feeling again except it was in no way unsure, now it was solid. It was an absolute surety in my mind that this was a bad idea. This mission was ill prepared. The boat was chugging along about five miles an hour.

"There's no power." Joe said, bewildered.

"You think you better take a look, or what? You are the Captain." I said dripping with sarcasim. I was such a smart ass when I was younger.

"I guess." Joe said and for the first time I saw a look of worry on his face, which scared the shit out of me. I figured I better take it easy on him. I jumped off my seat and started to take off the cover covering the motor.

"Come on big guy. You can fix it." I said to Joe trying to boost his confidence. We took off the cover and looked at the motor. It was still light enough to see it. Joe took out a flashlight and started looking around.

"Look right there, that hose blew." Joe pointed to a hose that had blown off the motor.

"Can you fix it?"

"I don't know. We don't really have any tools."

"You are an idiot, not a Captain." Joe looked like he was going to hit me but he knew what a bad idea that was. If he did when we got back my brothers would have whooped his ass, and he knew it. Looking back he could have easily have thrown me overboard and made up any story he wanted. That's what I mean about the ocean, anything can happen and no one would know.

Joe was digging around in the hull and took out the flare gun kit. It had a used flare casing in it. Joe took that out and looked at it.

"I think I can fix it."

"I doubt it."

"Have some faith." I gotta admit he was pretty positive. He took an empty flare gun casing and duct taped it to the broken tube, which gave the motor compression again. We started chugging along at twenty miles an hour, then thirty, then forty.

"I told you I could fix it."

"Good. You fixed it. Now take us back."

"We're fine. We can make it." He said full of pride.

"No we can't. The boat is broken. At least we didn't get the weed yet and we can go back and fix the boat."

"It's fixed."

"Not enough to pick up a load you dumb redneck." I had decided diplomacy was now out the window with this idiot. I knew for sure we don't want to come in with a boatload of weed and have the boat break again. I knew I had to reason with this lunatic or I might be really screwed.

"Listen. It's not your fault. The boat broke, that was an accident. Amazingly enough you fixed it, temporarily. It needs a correct fix before we risk our freedom trying to take a load of weed in."

"Look, we're almost there. Thirty miles to go and we should see JT. We're already more that fifty miles off the coast. Might as well pick up the load."

"You don't get it. This is our freedom you are messing with."

"That's what you signed up for."

"Not in a broken boat."

"It's not broken." He said very matter of fact. He was an idiot. I thought I was gonna lose my mind talking to him. I was getting nowhere except further out to sea. There was nothing I could do. He was way bigger than me and there was nothing around us but the blackness of the ocean. There was probably a bunch of sharks just swimming around waiting for him to throw me overboard. I sat there steaming in my seat.

We rode that way for a little while cruising around fifty. The blackness of the ocean was in every direction. We didn't even have a radar device. I knew he didn't know where we were. All of a sudden he slowed the engine down.

"What?" I asked him.

"I think we're here."

"What makes you think that?"

"Cause we been cruising long enough at fifty we should be here. I'm gonna signal for J.T."

He picked up the light and started swinging it around like an idiot. After a minute he stopped and we looked around for a signal. There was nothing but the black all around..

"Look around."

"I am." I was and I couldn't see anything. There was nothing in any direction.
"Call him on the radio." I said.
He leaned down and picked up the handset from the CB.
"JT. This is Big Dog. Over" He waited a second. "J.T. You out there?" Over?"
The radio made a crackling noise like it was trying to receive something. I knew we were fucked.
"We're fucked."
"Shut up. No we aint." I could see Joe was starting to panic a little, which only compounded the fact that I was already feeling, which was that we were really fucked.
"Big Dog. You out there? Over?' The radio made another crackling noise then it stopped again. Joe grabbed the receiver.
"J.T. Where you at? Over?" Nothing but silence. This is about the moment real panic sets in.
"Are you sure we're in the right place?"
"It's what the map says."
"Then where is he?"
"I don't know. He's supposed to be here."
"If we're in the right place." I'm sure he was sick of hearing my sarcasm, but I knew for damn sure this could now be considered a failed mission. The only thing I was concerned with was getting home alive and free. I no longer cared about the money we were supposed to make.
"Try the radio again." I knew all my friends were listening to the radio also, Everyone waiting for the load to come in so they could unload it and make some money. I figured they might hear the mess we are in.
"Big Dog.......You out there?.... Over." This time I could hear a little fear in Joe's voice. Not good.
"Big Dog?......This is J.T. You out there?" Not a sound. The radio crackled a little like it was trying to receive a transmission, but then there was nothing. We both sat there in silence in the darkness of the ocean. I know my mind was spinning the worst possible scenario, even if I was trying to think positively. The ocean can be a scary place.

"Turn on the boat and lets cruise around a little. Maybe he will see or hear us."
"Yeah. That might work." The fact that Joe was no longer aggressive really scared the shit outta me. I just wanted to get home alive at this point.
Joe turned the boat on and we started cruising real slow, just looking in every direction for a light or a sound or something.
"What do you think?" Joe asked me.
" I think you are the Captain." Joe glared at me. I didn't care. He was an idiot as far as I was concerned. My job was to load and unload bails, no more no less. It's the Captain's job to get us there and back.
"Maybe we are not in the right place. Maybe we didn't go far enough" Joe said, his anxiety more obvious every minute. Which only increases my personal fears.
"I'm gonna cruise about twenty miles further East." He said.
"Yeah. Good idea." Better off to just agree with him. Having the Captain scared shitless aint no good.
Joe turned the key and the boat tried a couple of times then stopped.
"Great. Yeah you fixed it all right." So much for agreeing with him.
"SHUT UP."
Joe took off the cover and looked at the engine with a flashlight. He pulled the accelerator on the carb and primed the engine.
 "That oughta work."
I just sat there with my arms crossed pissed off and scared at the same time. Not good.
Joe turned the key and the engine turned over smoothly.
"See I told you I fixed it." I didn't say anything. We started cruising real slow in the darkness of the ocean, maybe about fifteen knots, I think that's like twenty miles an hour in sea talk.
"Look all around."
" I am looking around you dumb redneck. The smartest thing to do would be to just drive the boat back home and fix it."
"The smartest thing to do is pick up the load and take it back and collect our dough. And maybe bang some of them

Bahamian whores on the way." Joe chuckled again at that thought. GOD I hated this guy.

We cruised that way for about an hour in the darkness looking for the other boat. We were probably going in circles for all we knew. Joe slowed the boat down.

"LOOK. Look over there. I see a light." Joe said all excited. He thought he was going to save the day, dumb bastard.

I looked in the direction Joe was pointing. I didn't see anything.

"I don't see anything."

"Over there." Joe pointed all excited. I squinted trying to look into the darkness in the hopes that there was really a boat there. I couldn't see anything. Joe picked up the handset on the C.B.

"Big Dog. You out there? Over." Silence.

"Big Dog? Over." Nothing. Joe was staring out into the darkness. Me also. I couldn't see a thing.

"OVER THERE." Joe pointed. "There it is again." I looked into the direction Joe was pointing but couldn't se anything.

"I didn't see anything."

"It was there I'm telling you." Joe said all excited. "I'm gonna head that way. It's gotta be him."

Joe turned the boat back on and we started cruising about twenty miles an hour. I was totally at a loss on how I felt. In the one hand I was definitely hoping this was Big Dog and we were going to pick up our load, get home safe and get our cash. On the other hand I knew just how difficult that can be even with a boat that works perfectly. Sometimes we have to out run the cops. To say the least I was more than a little worried.

"Take it easy. You don't want the boat to break again."

"I told you I fixed it." Joe said with a smug grin on his stupid face. Then just to be an asshole he increased the speed. First 30 MPH then 40 MPH then 50 MPH then BOOM, the empty flare cartridge that Joe taped on the broken hose shot off the hose and out into sea. The boat immediately slowed to about one mile an hour.

"Yeah you fixed it all right. Fixed it real good."

"SHUT UP."

Joe cut the motor and took out his flashlight to look at the motor. The hose was now blown in two spots, one near the motor and the original hole was twice as big.

"Now what, Mr. Captain."

"Keep talking and I will be the only one on this boat trying to figure it out."

"You come back without me and I think you know what will happen. My brothers will kill you."

Joe didn't say anything at that. He knew I was right. I also knew he had fifteen years on me and out weighed me by about a hundred pounds. It was a tense dismal situation. We were now drifting quietly deeper into the open sea.

"What are we gonna do?" I really wanted to know.

"You are gonna get on that radio and start doing a mayday distress call. Do it over and over. Our guys are listening someone will hear us. We gotta wait till morning to have enough light to fix the boat."

"With what tools? And what food? I told we should bring provisions. We always bring provisions. You are an idiot."

"Just shut up. I gotta think."

I knew we were in a world of trouble so I shut up. No sense in aggravating the situation. We were drifting who knows where. The boat had no compression at all, the sea was too deep to put down and anchor and wait so all we could do is drift. I fell asleep in my chair.

I woke up the next day with the sun beating on my face as hot as can be. We were no longer drifting. We were now tied up to a little atoll. An atoll is like a real small island in a chain of Islands. Its like a circle shaped like a ring, with not too much on it. The tallest plant on this atoll was knee high crocus plant, so there was no shade at all. The whole thing was about as big as a football field. I looked around in every direction, nothing but water. There was another atoll next to us with just as much nothing on it. I could see Joe walking towards the boat from across the atoll. I was definitely hating him with every fiber of my being, but I knew for sure I need this idiot to get out of here. As he reached the boat I could see this was taking a toll on him. Just a beer drinking redneck he was starting to turn red already from the scorching sun. He was probably gonna go into the heebie jeebies when all the beer starts sweating out of him.

"Aint nothing on this whole island taller than two feet. No shade anywhere. We gotta stay inside the hull to keep out of the sun till help arrives."

"Yeah? And when is help going to arrive smart guy."

"Just as soon as you get on that radio and start doing a mayday distress call."

"What are you gonna do?"

"Gonna have a look at the motor, see if I can fix it."

"Like you fixed it last time."

"Better shut your trap or else I'm gonna shut it for you."

I don't know why I did what I did, but at that moment I just had this terrible feeling I was never getting out of there so I stood up and socked Joe in the face as hard as I could. I figured if I was gonna die, I might as well blast the guy at least one time who got me there. Joe took that hit and I jumped out of the boat and started running. I ran for a minute across the atoll. I could hear Joe chasing me so I started zig sagging left and right. He chased me for about ten minutes but he couldn't catch me. Fear is a great motivator. He got tired before I did and collapsed on the sand. I walked over and looked down on him. He was huffing and puffing and so out of breath I thought he was gonna die.

"You shouldn't have hit me." He said. I could tell he felt bad.

"Fuck you. We're probably gonna die out here cause you are so damn greedy. I figured I better blast you one first." He held his hand up.

"No one's gonna die out here. Help me up."

I grabbed his hand and he faked like he was gonna blast me so I ducked.

"I should knock your block off. Listen, we gotta keep our cool or we ARE gonna die out here." He said it real serious.

We started walking back to the boat. Things looked pretty bleak from where I sat. Broken boat, no weed means no money coming my way. Might not even get off this island alive.

We walked back to the boat in silence. The sun was beating down like the Sahara desert. The ocean is like a huge reflecting frying pan and the boat, the island and us are like eggs and bacon on a hot skillet. No breeze, way humid, and Joe was really starting to stink. Had to be the alcohol pouring out of him.

We climbed back into the boat.

"Get on that radio."

"What do I say?"

"Mayday. Say that over and over. Also boat in distress. Those guys are all listening. Someone is bound to hear us. I'm sure they are looking for us. We were supposed to be back hours ago."

"Where are we?"

"I don't know." Joe said and the way he said it I could tell he was almost defeated. I am sure he was feeling the pressure more than me. Not only was he the Captain, but he was a beer drinking, Coke snorting Cigarette smoking, pothead. And we had no pot. Me on the other hand had been a vegetarian for years, no alcohol, no meat or dairy. I was used to fasting every now and then. I'm not saying I didn't feel the pressure cause I did for sure, just not as much as Joe. Not only was he responsible for the boat, the load and my safety, he had a family at home, a wife and daughters, that I am certain did not know what he did in the smuggling world.

I picked up the handset.

"Mayday mayday mayday.....This is Corsa in distress. Can anyone hear my mayday? Over." We both listened intently. Nothing. Then a big crackle. Then nothing.

"Mayday mayday mayday this is Corsa in distress. Is anybody out there?" Another crackle then nothing.

"We're fucked."

"Don't say that." Joe was messing around with the motor. "Just stay on that radio."

What an idiot. My depression was compounding deeper every second. I clicked on the handset.

"Mayday mayday mayday. This is Corsa in distress. I am stuck out in the ocean with a big dumb redneck. Can anyone hear me." Joe through an empty beer can at me.

"Quit screwing around."

"I'm not screwing around. You are a big dumb redneck and we are stuck out in the ocean." Joe threw a wrench at me. I ducked.
"Stay on that radio. Someone will hear you." I picked up the receiver. Before I could say anything I heard something. It was the sound of a boat. I came racing out of the hull. Joe was standing up watching the boat cruising our way.
 "Hand me that flare gun."
"Why? We should flag those guys down. They can help us." Joe looked at me like I was insane.
"The only thing those guys will help themselves to is cutting our throats and taking this hundred thousand dollar boat. Now give me that flare gun quick. We gotta make them think we are just waiting for a drop off."
 I handed Joe the flare gun and he stood on the deck holding the gun up. A twentyfoot boat with one outboard motor and six Bahamians in it went cruising by real slow about a quarter of a mile away. They were for sure scoping us out.
"Great. That's all we need." I said.
"Just relax. They don't want to get killed. They don't know this boat is broken. They don't know we don't have guns."
"Or food. Or money."
"Exactly. Just relax yourself hippie and stay on that radio. You know those guys at home are looking for us."
I got back on the radio and continued my distress call. Over and over and over. This went on for days. Every day the Bahamians would cruise by slowly. We always heard them coming, so Joe was always on the deck holding out the flare gun. By the third day with no food and water my energy was completely drained. Joe's also. We would spend the day inside the hull, out of the sun, until we heard the Bahamians, then Joe would jump on deck with the flare gun and look as tough as can be. Beer bellied redneck with a flare gun must have looked tough to those Bahamians, because they never got too close to the boat. Probably didn't want to get shot.
On the morning of the third day I got a hit.
"Mayday mayday mayday this is Corsa in distress. Can anybody hear my mayday? Over"

We heard a big crackle, then silence, then, "Yes I hear your mayday. Over."

Joe sat up straight. He grabbed the maps.

"Who is this? Where are you? Can you call the coast guard? Over."

" My name is Fred Whitney and I'm on a ham radio in Delaware. Yes, I can call the coast guard and anyone else you want. I'm in a wheel chair so that's all I can do or else I would come save you myself."

Joe held up the map and frantically pointed where he thought we were, which was south east of Andros Island.

"Can you call Dana at this number and tell him we think we are south east of Andros Island. Here are the coordinates we think we are at." I read the coordinates to Fred and for the first time I thought I might get out of there. Within an hour a Coast Guard Jet came flying overhead. He spoke over the radio just as clear as can be.

"Corsa in distress, this Coast Guard Rescue CJ-4 flying over head. We are dropping a case of provisions for you until the chopper arrives which will be in an hour. There is a rope attached. Pull the rope. DO NOT get in the water. There are sharks all around the boat. Over."

They dropped a steel waterproof suitcase in the water about 300 feet from the boat with a rope attached that came directly across our boat. I thought that is one good pilot. I pulled the rope till the suitcase got close to the boat and pulled it up. Inside was fried chicken, ice cubes, fruit juice, chocolate, bread, cheese, and some first aid stuff. We were shoving everything in our mouths at the same time, eating like we hadn't eaten in weeks, not days. When were done I looked at Joe.

"Helicopter will be here soon. Tomorrow we will come back for you."

"I aint staying here." Joe said.

"Yeah you are. You are the captain, remember."

"Doesn't matter. I aint staying here. My wife and kids are probably worried sick."

"If you leave and no one is here to watch the boat, those Bahamians that have been passing every day are gonna take the boat."

"Let 'em. I aint staying."

"Frank is gonna be pissed. Those guys are gonna steal the boat."

Joe was ignoring me at this point. I was right and he knew it. He had to stay with the boat. Or else there wasn't gonna be no boat.

In about an hour a Coast Guard Helicopter came and rescued us. They dropped down a basket and I climbed in first, then they lowered it and Joe got in.

The chopper pilot turned and looked at both of us. "What were you guys doing way out here? There's nothing out here."

"We were going diving, but the boat broke and we drifted." I said hoping he would believe me. I doubt he did.

"You guys drifted about a hundred miles over night. Lucky for you that guy heard your mayday. Else you might have died out here."

He knew we were out here to smuggle. If we had already picked up the load he would be taking us straight to jail, not the Coast Guard Rescue station,

Inside the Helicopter was a panel of all kinds of gauges and switches. One of them said DAYLIGHT.

"Whats that? The Daylight." I asked him.

He turned back around and looked me square in the eye.

"We put that on people who are smuggling drugs into our country at night. We get over them and turn it on and all of a sudden its daylight. No where to hide."

"Oh."

He kept staring at me for a reaction but I didn't give him any. I knew we were scraping back to freedom by the skin of our teeth.

When we got back, Joe had hell to pay. Him and Frank got in a huge fistfight for leaving the boat while we all watched. It wasn't my fault so I didn't get in any trouble.

The next day Frank and a few of his buddies took another boat out there, fixed the first one and brought it back. I knew

I would go again, I needed money to get out of Florida. I wanted to go back to California. I figured if I stayed in Florida I would keep smuggling cause it's what everyone did. Simple math was I knew if I stayed home sooner or later I would be dead or in jail. Those are the odds, and it's a sure bet.

About a month later Joe went out again. I told Gary I would never go out with that asshole again and I am sure he felt the same way about me. This time Joe went with a real cool friend of ours named Jungle Johnny. Johnny had a Panther tattoo on his shoulder that said JUNGLE JOHNNY over it. He had survived three tours of Viet Nam and now spent most of his time gambling and partying. And to support those habits he smuggled. Johnny was way cool, always relaxed.

When Johnny and Joe went I was one of the guys waiting in the house to offload the bails. Everyone is always intently listening to the radio. AT 9:30 P.M. we got a radio transmission that everything was fine, they were waiting for the drop off. At 10:30 P.M. one hour later we got another Transmission. It was Johnny saying they were taking on water.

That was the last thing we ever heard from them again. Three days later Dana had to go tell Joe's wife that Joe was a smuggler and we lost him at sea. I waited in the truck. It didn't go over too well. She had no idea Joe was a smuggler. About a year later we heard they were locked up in a Cuban jail. After three trips and thousands of dollars spent to find them, it turned out to be another guy with a Panther tattoo on his shoulder.

The Ocean commands respect. If you aint careful, it will swallow you up.

26

"Wake up Mon, we gotta get movin." Montgomery said. "Gotta be in the Bahamas by nightfall or else they gonna make me do maneuvers again. An I HATE doin maneuvers so GET YA RAS ASS UP."

I had moved to Jamaica to continue my smuggling experience. I went from boats to Planes always and only filled with weed. I figured same reward less risk, but what did I know. I was just another dumb teenager living my adventure.

I had gotten busted in the Bahamas with a boat load of weed a while back, and while I was in that Bahamian jail I met a guy who had crashed ten planes and walked away from every crash. He was a real tall skinny white Jamaican guy named Montgomery. Monty for short, but yo had to know hm real good to call him Monty. Not too many people did. He was as cool as can be, I mean cool like the Fonz, in a Jamaican sort of way. When you meet some one in jail, you know they are cool, well usually they are, truth is you never really can tell these days.

Educated in Europe and America, he used to fly for one of the big airlines like Pan Am before he got into smuggling full time. His parents owned this really cool hotel that was carved into the side of a mountain outside of Kingston. He invited me to come live in Jamaica and work for him when we were in the Bahamian jail so I had finally took him up on it.

They gave me my own room on one side of the hotel that was kind of in renovation. We didn't smuggle all the time so I spent a lot of time by myself adventuring around. There was always something to do. In the mornings I would take a cab, the same cab driver would pick me up every day and take me to one of the two places that had surfable waves on the island. The closest and best spot was right behind the Donald L Quarrie elementary school. Donald L. Quarrie was a famous Jamaican track and field guy. I think he went to the Olympics or something. Anyway the waves broke perfect behind this school. From two foot to twenty feet it broke perfect and like Pipeline. There were a handful of kids that surfed there, no more than five, and they ripped. At lunchtime or recess all the kids would come out from the school and watch us surf. The wind would turn onshore by noon so I would go back to the hotel and see what trouble I could get into. They had a furniture factory near the hotel so there was always a bunch of guys there working, cooking breadfruit and akee and salt fish, and smoking tons and tons of weed.

"See my mom on the way out, she got some sandwiches for us an HURRY UP." Montgomery said laughing all the way down the hall. I put some clothes on and hurried down the hall, grabbed the sandwiches and jumped in the back of the truck with six other guys. We drove up into the Hills to where Montgomery had his own airport.

When I say airport I mean a big hangar to store planes and a make shift air strip to take off and land planes. We got there and everyone jumped out of the truck and got to work. Gotta get the plane ready, gotta load bales, gotta make sure everything is straight. Montgomery had a special seat made which was an extra gas tank. There are no seats in the plane, we would stuff it full of weed and and then me and Harold would get in and they shut the door behind us. This is straight smuggling at it's finest. Adrenalin is pumping, we got 'Record Breaker' painted on the door and the music is Blasting as we take off.

It's about four hours to the Bahamas in a non pressurized cabin, which is no fun I can tell you. It feels like your sinuses are gonna break out of your face. I was literally pushing on them as hard as I could.

We came in so low over the houses in the Bahamas I could see the dials on people's watches. We hit the ground on a very bumpy make shift airstrip. Montgomery was cursing out loud trying to keep the plane from flipping over as it ran down the airstrip. We had stopped on a field surrounded by Australian Pines with nothing on it but a panel truck.

"LETS GO BOYS MOVE THAT SHIT. WE GOTTA GO. TWO MINUTES." Montgomery walked casually over to the wing to fill up his zippo with jet fuel. He smoked these specially rolled tobacco cigars he had made just for him and he loved how jet fuel smelled when he lit them.

We unloaded that plane in less than a minute and got in shutting the door behind us.

"BETTER HANG ON." Montgomery screamed over the roar of the engines. 400 feet is not a lot of airstrip to take off in, even for a little Cessna plane. He held the break as long as he could then let go. That plane started screaming down the runway.

All three of us looking at the two hundred feet tall pine trees in front of us.

"Come on.......COME ON. We gotta get up to speed or we never gonna make it." Montgomery said very very seriously. As we got so close that it was getting scary, the wheels came off the ground and we barely cleared the Pines. Me and Harold rolled to the back of the plane and where held there with G forces until we leveled off. We turned around and made a real big circle as if we were just arriving from Jamaica.

"This is the Record Breaker arriving from Jamaica requesting a landing field. Over." Montgomery turned back to us.

"This is the moment of truth."

"What do you mean?"

"If he knows we have been on the ground already." Montgomery's attention went back to the radio.

"What? Ok Leveling off at fifteen thousand feet. Yes sir." Montgomery covered the mouthpiece with his hand.

"He's making me do maneuvers. But I can tell we're all good."

We did maneuvers for an hour before he let us land. Maneuvers are like maintain this altitude for this long and that type of shit. They knew we were probably on the ground already but they could not prove it. His flight plan would never show it. So they always made him do a bunch of maneuvers before we landed.

We always stayed in a classy hotel and Montgomery walked around like a king. Full of class he always tipped big. Money came to him in big suitcases so he handed it out almost as easily. Before we would go back to Jamaica, every time he would buy sneakers and soccer balls and clothes and toys and whatever else people needed or wanted on our way back to the hotel.

He had gold tips on his cowboy boots and a twenty five thousand dollar Rolex on his wrist.

"Ya see dis watch." He held it up to my face. "When a mon see dis watch on my wrist in a meetin he knows I mean bizness, ya unnerstan? Dis watch is serious bizness."

We landed at a commercial airport after we unloaded the weed but the plan was to build a new airstrip for clandestine landings. We scouted around until we found a good spot and for the next week I spent every day cutting down crocus plants and leveling the field. Every now and then Montgomery would come out and check on our progress then back to the hotel to relax. Montgomery didn't do the grunt work.

Smuggling was a big deal in the late seventies. Especially in South Florida, the Bahamas and Jamaica. If you were in any way cool just growing up you would get offered a chance to unload a boat, or go on a ride if your balls were big enough. I have always been a climber. Got somewhere to be, even if I'm not sure exactly where that somewhere is.

All the guys in the network that came to build the airstrip were really into getting loaded. Crack was not invented yet, but free base cocaine was really hitting the Bahamas hard. These guys would work in the hot sun all day then go to house and buy based up cocaine and smoke it in bent beer cans right in front of the house. They wouldn't even make it twenty feet. The entire curb in front of the house would be covered in Bahamians and smugglers all smoking cans. All I was into was weed so I would walk back and forth with Harold and watch him freak out smoking that shit. Fortunately for me I was into going down not up, or else I would have fallen into that trap.

We got the airstrip built, they guy showed up and paid for the weed we brought and we got ready to go back to Jamaica. Harold went and a big back of rocks to take back and when we got back to the hotel he stayed in his room for a week. I went back to Surfing every day waiting to go on a run again.

27

"So you really thought this through?"
"Absolutely. We gotta branch out. We canna keep doin the same route. The DEA is gonna get on our ass. We gonna go meet dis guy and see what dis place has to offer."

We passed through security, which was almost nonexistent back then and got on a Pan Am plane to Caracas Venezuela. Montgomery had set up a meeting to see if it could work to fly to Colombia first pick up a load then drop it off in the water for a boat to pick up. Doing drops like that was always pretty damn scary. Gotta strap your self in with this little hook and a cable around your waist and as the pilot would fly down low over the water. We would break a cylume so it glowed and strap to the bales and throw out six bales at a time. The boat would pick them up and we would repeat the process until the plane was empty. Then the boat would drive to Miami and unload the weed into a million dollar house.
We landed in Caracas and a real big fat guy Named Carlito picked us up from the airport with one of his workers, I never found out that guys name. He drove us through town to his house. Everywhere we went everyone waved at him and he waved back. We stopped to get some food and they gave it to him free. He tried to pay but they would not take his money.
"He must be really important." Montgomery said impressed.
We got to the guys house and his wife came out with Coffee con Leche, and the nicest pastries you ever ate. Fresh hot from the oven. We sat there and tried to have a conversation but we didn't speak Spanish and he didn't speak English. We used a lot of hand gestures. He drew a map of the way were going to travel to show us the airstrip he wanted us to land at. It was in the Guarjira peninsula in Colombia.
Montgomery got up to use the bathroom and when he came out he sat down with a grin.
"You should go wash up."
"I'm good.'
"Lissen mon, I wan ya to go wash up. Den you gonna see why we ok."
I got up and went in the house and on every picture was the guy in full police uniform. Pics of him in the Academy and arresting folks and all kinds of Cops shit.
I came back outside and I looked a little spooked, Montgomery just looked at me and laughed. He looked at the big fat guy who picked us up.
"You Policia?"

The big guy said something in Spanish to his friend and they both laughed real heard. Then he leaned in to Montgomery and pointed at himself.

"Me es Numero Uno Policia. Polica Capitan." He beat his chest and laughed REALLY loud.

"Told you we were good. Carlito is the Chief of Police" Carlito looked at me and laughed some more.

Montgomery relaxed. I was beginning to like this situation.

We woke up the next day early and got in a Jeep that had a back cover on it. It was Carlito driving with Montgomery in the front seat, There were two of Carlitos henchmen in the back so I had to lay down in the back of the Jeep.

As soon as we left Venezuela we hit the desert, or what I would imagine the desert to be. There was nothing but sand rocks and cactus for as far as your eyes could see. The road was bumpy as hell and I spent the next five hours being beaten up and down side to side in the back of that Jeep. Carlito would drive like he was on the highway and there was literally NO road.

After about two hors on the road we pulled up to this little building. Literally in the absolute middle of nowhere, with about six Guajira Indians standing in front. I don't know how they had ice cold coca colas, but they did. I really needed to smoke some weed.

"I really need to smoke a joint Monty. Can you ask this guy?"

"You better chill out wit dat mon. You shoulda brought some wit ya."

"How the HELL was I gonna bring some with me?"

"In ya pocket mon."

Montgomery was not a smoker so he really could care less. He didn't party much at all, and to be honest I don't think he was in dire straights as far as money went either. He was more like an adrenalin Junkie, Smuggling REALLY was an adventure for Montgomery.

The Guajira Indians were as cool as can be. I showed them how to flick a bottle caps from your fingers and they were amazed. We got along great after that despite any language barrier.

Totally chill, they didn't have anything and they didn't mind at all. They ate Goat three times a day. Goat meat, Goat cheese, Goat milk, there was not a lot out there. And me being a vegetarian all I could have was some bread and goat cheese. Three days of that and you are ready to have ANYTHING else. We drove about three more hours and we got to a village where the Indians lived at. The next day we were going to look at airstrips. Carlito motioned for us to get in the Jeep and go with him.

We drove about ten minutes and we pulled up to a big barn.

"What are we doing?"

"I dont know. Me think he wanna show us something."

Carlito got out and opened the barn door and there was about thirty thousand pounds of Colombian weed stacked neatly in bales all the way to the ceiling. Jamaican bails usually came in any shape or size covered in brown tape that is stuck to itself. They would just put the bail on a spindle and put tape all around it. Colombian bails were always perfect. Burlap bags with a red green and red stripe on them. This barn had some beautiful gold Colombian weed with white hairs. Sweet Santa Marta Colombian. This is years before green weed hit the scene.

My eyes lit up like a kid in a candy store. Montgomery saw that.

"Dont freak dem out mon. Me dont think dey smoke."

I started looking in every pocket I had. Montgomery started laughing.

"You dont got no paper, have you?" He laughed even harder.

I picked up a brown paper bag and started crumbling it up and un-crumbling it over and over, basically just softening it out. Then I took about an ounce of weed, cleaned the seeds out of it and rolled a one ounce joint in brown paper. The Indians all lined up to watch me smoke it like it was a big show. Not one person there smoked weed except me. I sat back and smoke that GIANT spliff like it was nothing. The Indians were totally impressed. I took a big bag for my stay and we went back to the encampment.

They were getting ready for dinner, they had a big fire going and everyone was doing some task to help the tribe. There were goats walking around and I was petting one. The Indians found that amusing as this goat was dinner and I didn't know it. There was a Y about six feet tall made of sticks that was stuck in the ground. They put ropes around the goats back feet and pulled all of a sudden yanked it up through the Y. Then they cut the goats throat and caught all the blood in a bowl. I stepped back and bumped into Montgomery.

"They dont waste anything here. Try not to get to friendly with their dinner." He said.

I walked over to the edge of the fire and smoked another brown paper joint.

We slept under this big overhang in hammocks. About twenty hammocks fit under the overhand. The hammocks were real thick and you could swing the sides over and cover yourself up completely, which was necessary as it was as cold as can be at night in the desert. Carlito snored so loud it kept everyone up all night except him. Didn't matter though, Carlito is the MAN in these parts so everyone just joked him in the morning.

We got up and went looking at three different airstrips, each directly on the edge of a cliff that led out to open Ocean. For somebody that has landed on all kinds of makeshift airstrips, this set up didn't look so bad.

At the last air strip Carlito took out a pen and paper and wrote down some things and handed it to Montgomery. He read it and the smile left his face. He looked back at Carlito who was anxiously waiting for his response. Montgomery smiled and said OK which made Carlito jump for joy.

"What's he want?" I asked. Montgomery handed me the piece of paper. In badly written English it said -.44 .357 9mm Browning S &W.

"He wants us to bring him guns when we come pick up the load." Montgomery did not like this at all.

"What did you tell him?'

"What you think? I tell him we comin back next week wit his guns. You wanna get home or not?"

We drove all night back to Caracas and left the next day. The planes were bigger and nicer back then, or so it seems

anyway. I settled into my seat, buckled up and looked at Montgomery.
"So when we coming back?" BMontgomery looked at me as if I was completely stupid, then he smiled.
"Never. If we come back here that chief of Police is gonna kill us both, take our plane, money and the guns we bring him."
I thought about that for a minute.
"An besides. I dont work wit cops. Evern if dey dirty."
It was a long plane ride back to Jamaica, when I got there I looked around at my room. I had been living in Jamaica for about a year. I had a little saved up, not much. I thought, some times you gotta know when to get out. Don't wait till the last minute or till you have to leave, or are asked to leave or are arrested. Sometimes its best to pick up pack up and move on, see what other adventure is out there. So that's what I did. I went surfing one more time. Gave my surfboards to the dreadys that surfed the break that I had made friends with. There was a big twelve tribes dance the night before I left. I had made quite a few friends in my time in Jamaica and they all came to say goodbye. It was hard to go but I was ready. There is no excitement like the excitement of the unknown.

28

I got back to Miami and got a job painting houses to stay alive and kill time while I waited for a smuggling job . A lot of guys were still smuggling, some got arrested, some got killed, a few got rich. Not many. I wanted to move to California and I needed money to do that. I had to get on the right boat.
Smuggling was much sketchier than when I started. The cops had confiscated boats and were now using them to catch the smugglers. So they now had boats as fast as us.
Big boats with big motors that were not previously in the cops budget. It was always a contest who had the biggest fastest boat around. Now the cops were in that contest also. They would hang out at Rum Runner bay, which was this bar

on the water that all the rich smugglers hung out at making connections, showing off their boats. The cops would be there taking pictures and writing down numbers.

They Cops now had a helicopter that would go back and forth up and down the coast looking for anyone who dared cross our coastline in a boat full of weed. The guys I worked for never took loads of coke. I got a job on a good boat for fifteen grand in one night to bring back a boatload of weed within a couple of weeks.

We were on our way to the store to stock up for the trip. This was a good boat with a good captain that knew what he was doing. Fat Freddy was the Captain and had been smuggling in these waters for a long time. I grew up at the same beach he did so he knew me most of my life. I did my first couple of jobs with him when he had one boat, now he had six. Freddy was always over prepared. He would take me to the big vegetarian store in town and give me like six hundred dollars for food for an over night stay.

"You never know what can happen." He would say. Tell me about it.

"How come no one in our crew runs coke. The payoff is bigger."

"So is the punishment. And not just with the law. With the world."

"What do you mean by that."

We had just pulled up to the Store. Freddy turned off the motor.

There aint nothing wrong with weed. Hell, it will probably be legal one day in this life."

"You think so?"

"Sure. Just like prohibition."

Freddy handed me six hundred dollars.

"Go get some supplies. And hurry up, we are leaving by sunset which is in about three hours. We still got a lot to do. Gotta get the boat ready."

 "Aye aye Captain." I saluted him. He saluted back. I was always goofing around. It was cool to be about ten years younger than everyone else. Made me feel special.

Guys were getting busted left and right. It was a big decision to go out again. Just one more time, just one more time was all I kept saying in my head. So few guys got in and made dough and got out. Almost none. Sooner or later it catches up with you. I felt good about this trip. Just one more time I kept repeating in my head. Just one more time.

There was a reason Freddy was so successful and that is cause he was respected and that was because he was always prepared. He always took care of everyone along the way and they respected him for it.

We left the dock at sunset, drove out to the meeting point and met a Colombian Freighter. There were already a few boats there unloading. We filled our load and turned back for the coast.

"We gotta really hurry huh. To beat those other guys."

"No we're good." Freddy was totally relaxed. He looked at his watch, lit a joint and handed it to me.

"It's good to give those guys a head start. Gives the cops someone to chase. We aint in no rush. Guys who rush get busted."

We drove back at a good pace. Not too fast. Freddy got on the radio and as we pulled into the intercoastal a boat pulled in front of and behind us. These are our escorts. As I passed the boats that were watching out for us my buddy Gary held his hands in the air in Triumph. The only thing I could hear in my head repeating over and over was, 'just one more time just one more time'.

We pulled up to the million dollar home and there were five of my friends in there, all dressed in black, al ready to make money. Everyone is happy as hell and trying to be quiet at the same time. We unloaded all the bales in the house, no furniture and plastic on all the carpets. I am certain the owners had no idea who they were renting to.

We drove the boat to the marina cleaning it with a dust buster on the way. The marine patrol could be waiting for us you never know.

I walked out of the marina and Freddy was waiting for me in his truck. I got inside and there was a brown paper bag on the seat.

"That's for you." Freddy said as we took off. I opened the bag and it was full of stacks of twenties.
"It looks a little heavy."
"It is. I owe you fifteen grand, that's twenty five."
"Why's that?"
"You aint going again. Like I said I been doing this for a long time. It's amazing I am still alive and free. How old are you? Sixteen?"
"I just turned seventeen."
"Exactly. I don't know if I'm doing this for you or me. I know you wanna get out, go back to California. Here's the money. Sooner or later you are gonna get jailed or killed. Or maybe never come back from sea. I guess I just want to see at least one person run this scam and then move on to better things. Take the money and go to California like you want. This is getting washed up for everyone. It aint gonna last forever."
We pulled up to my buddy Al's house where I rented a room. Freddy held out his hand. I shook it. He was a good man.
"Don't let me hear about you getting on any other boats either, I mean it."
"Aye aye Captain." I saluted him and he saluted me back.
I never saw Freddy after that day. He got all tangled up in a big sting operation and ended up fleeing the country with the cops on his tail. Last I heard he was somewhere down in Central America with a wife and like six kids. That doesn't sound so bad really. I don't think he can ever come back stateside though. See at least someone got out, and not just me.

29

"It will work I'm telling you. Just pick me up at the airport." Zack hung the phone up on me and I stood in the phone booth thinking this is never going to work. I had made it back out to California and I was living outside Los Angeles near Vista. A lot of my Miami transplant friends had moved out there. Everyone had a hustle. Qua-aludes where big and cheap. A great seller. I wasn't into Qua- alludes but I was into money. Zack was gonna get on a plane with a backpack full to the top with Qua-aludes. Like I said airport security is not what it used to be.

"I told you it would work." Zack said as he got in my truck. I had a badass 1962 Chevy pick up. Drove it out from Florida. Slept in it many a night.

"What's the plan?" Zack always had a plan. He was definite climber. He's got somewhere's to be.

"What would you do if you just landed in LA with a backpack full of Qua-aludes?"

"Sell them. But I bet you got that sewed up." I said.

"You can bet we're gonna sell them. We're gonna clean up...at the ROLLING STONES CONCERT." Zack held up two tickets for the Stones at the LA forum. He was so proud of himself. I gotta admit I was a little impressed.

"It's tomorrow night. We gotta unload half of these at Marcus's. The rest is ours. They cost about twentyfive cents a piece when I get them in bulk. You can have them for fifty cents. We can sell them for a dollar all day long."

Zack lit up a big joint. He was so proud of himself. He had it all figured out, or so he thought. We met up with our friend Jeff who was also really killing it in California. We all grew up together in Miami. Jeff was as smart as can be. He was bringing keys of coke from Miami to Marin County and doubling his money. He was making eight grand a week at eighteen years old. He had a forty year old girlfriend. Jeff came down from Marin to see the Stones and nothing more. He had a pocket full of mushrooms, some good weed and a bunch of paper trips. Hippie drugs.

I was dating this Swedish girl named Marie who was going to art school at Otis in Los Angeles. Marie was a gorgeous blonde girl with blue eyes. We both came out here from Miami. She was on a path of getting it together and I was a long haired surfer on a path to getting high. She lived in the dorm across the street from Macarthur park. Which is right around 7th street, where all the action was. All kinds of transients hung out there all the time. That mixed in with a bunch of arty kids and I had a steady flow of customers. I was going back and forth every week on the greyhound bus getting weed and selling it at the school. That was my gig. I had no direction at all, none except getting high.

I met Zack the next day with Marie in front of the LA forum. Jeff showed up and we started to walk in. Zack had this big bag of Qua-aludes wrapped up in a t shirt.

"What are you gonna do with that?"

We looked at the gate and they were checking people who were smuggling in beers. They don't want people bring in beers, they want to sell beers.

"Gimme that." We all got close to each other and I took the bag of ludes and put them in my pocket. I had these army pants on with pockets down the sides so we walked right in. They didn't even check me.

Soon as we got inside Jeff pulled out a bag of mushrooms and we got swamped. He was pulling them out and pricing them.

"25"

"40"

"10"

It went like that until they were gone. Took about five whole minutes. My girl Marie just stood next to us, kind of oblivious. She was an art student working on a degree. She came to see the Rolling Stones with her boyfriend. Her boyfriend came to make some dough. I was an up and coming drug dealer.

Zack went off tell sell his ludes. He was a lude head.

"Don't take any, we came here to sell them Don't eat any."

"I know." He was already wasted, probably popped a couple for breakfast.

"Lets all meet back here in an hour." I said.

We all split up to go walk around. The forum was filling up fast we were on the field just checking out the carnival of people. Jeff had a bunch of paper trips, but the way he was swamped over the mushrooms he was a little sketchy about trying to off the trips.

We walked around and got back to the meeting place an hour later and there was no Zack.

"He probably got busted." Jeff said.

"Don't say that shit. It might come true." I said.

"He probably did. He was wasted. You saw that."

"I now. Listen, wait here and I will go over to the other side. If he doesn't show up in 30 minutes come get me."
I made my way through the crowd with Marie. She was way excited.
"The concert is about to start. Lets go up to the front." She said.
"Soon as we get Zack we will."
We got to the spot and waited for a few minutes.
"There he is." Marie pointed. "He's wasted."
Zack was stumbling in our direction.
"Ludes." He mumbled to anyone who would listen.
"Ludes. Anybody want ludes?"
He was asking everyone and anyone as he passed them. He was holding his rolled up shirt with the bag of ludes in it. Or what was left of it.
"Lets get out of here. He hasn't seen us yet." She said. She was scared.
"I can't do that. Relax. It's gonna be ok."
Zack saw us and made a beeline straight for us. If I had enough sense at that time of my life I would have realized by now Zack probably had some cops on him. But these are the lessons you learn the hard way. Like to look beyond what your eyes can see.
"You're wasted."
"So what. I sold almost all of them." Zack looked around.
 "Where's Jeff."
"On the other side, let's go."
We stared walking towards Jeff and Zack stopped.
 "Let me put these back in your pocket. And I got a wad of bills also. We all stood real close and Zack put the bills in my hand and I stuffed them in my pocket. About a thousand dollars in one's fives tens and twenties. Then he gave me the bag of ludes that he had wrapped up in his shirt and I stuffed them in my other pocket. We turned to walk to Jeff and two construction type looking dudes walked up on us and grabbed us by each arm.
"You both are under arrest." They said as they flashed their badges.
The cop looked at Marie then asked me.

"Is she with you?"
"Never met her before." I said.
The cop looked at Marie with disgust.
"Get out of here. These guys are going to jail."
I looked at Marie and said quietly,
"Jeff." Marie turned quickly and walked over to Jeff.
Everything started moving in slow motion again, just like it always does when you are getting busted. The cops puled the bag of ludes out of my pocket and four people walked right up to buy some, after all the cops just looked like concert goers.
As they were walking away I could see Marie with Jeff pointing at me and Zack.
Jeff took all the paper trips out of his pocket and through them in the air.
"FREE ACID!" He yelled and the crowd went into a frenzy trying to grab a hit. Jeff grabbed Marie's hand and got away from there fast. Jeff was as smart as could be and he knew they could be following her to him.
As they escorted us in handcuffs into the locker room of the Los Angeles Rams, I could hear the loudspeaker.
"LADIES AND GENTLEMEN.....THE ROLLING STONES."
The roar of the crowd was deafening. Nightmare. Actually the nightmare was just beginning.
We got into the locker room and there was a line of everyone that had gotten busted so far that day. There was about forty guys in a line and maybe five girls off to the side. Every cop had a desk and was processing their violators. We could hear the Stones jamming in full blast. Living nightmare. Two months into being seventeen and I am busted with what I think is a real bust, that I will really get in trouble for. I had done some Juvenille hall shit, not much. And had gotten busted before with hash and completed probabtion, so I knew the drill, but now I got caught with a bag of pills and money IN MY POCKET. I thought the end was here.
I knew enough to keep my mouth absolutely shut. My dad had taught me well in that respect. He was a criminal attorney in Miami. He got it quick that his son was more of a

criminal than a student so he advised me in that manner. KEEP your moth SHUT.
"Cops speak a different language than you." He used to tell me.
"Just keep your mouth shut tight till your atorney shows up. You are only going to make it worse by opening your mouth. And don't trust any of them. They are doing their job, which is to lock you up. Do yours, be smarter than them."
The cops walked us over to our own table and started emptying my pockets. Everyone started looking over at the pile of crumbled up bills and all the ludes.
"We got the dealers of the night. WE GOT THE DEALERS OF THE NIGHT!" The cops started screaming as they were high fiving each other and slapping each other on the back.
They counted all the ludes and money. There were 411 ludes left and $983 dollars. They put everything in evidence bags and put us in this line. Everyone had to take there clothes off and the cops would then check the clothes, make you bend over, hold you balls up and cough, look in your mouth and hair then they would give us our clothes back. There was a young Mexican kid who had taken too much of something. PCP maybe who knows? Anyway when he took his clothes he had an erection and all the cops started joking him about it.
"What are you doing? Getting excited?? You getting off in the locker room?"
The guy went into full freak out mode.
"I jerk off. I jerk off. I jerk off." He kept saying that over and over, louder and louder. I felt bad for the guy. They gave him his clothes back and he rushed them on. The cops hand cuffed him and he freaked out further.
"You've got my hands. GIVE ME BACK MY HANDS. YOU HAVE TAKEN MY HANDS."
He was trying to bring his hands from behind his back but they were handcuffed tight. Poor guy. He was absolutely freaking out.
They hand cuffed us all together in a line and walked us out to the van that would take us to Glasshouse which is what they called the jail in Los Angeles county. I have no idea why

they called it Glass House. I didn't see any glass. Only steel bars and concrete cells.

They cuffed me to a real big guy who was totally wasted on my left with Zack on my right. The guy probably was wasted on the ludes from Zack.

We were in the last row of seats all cuffed together with our hands behind our backs. The big guy immediately slumped over on me almost unconscious. They put the Mexican guy who was freaking out in the back behind us. He was totally gone at this point.

"I want to be in a seat. I need to be in a seat." The Mexican guy said freaking out.

The big guy turned back.

"Sit down and shut up."

""Fuck you Gaylord. Fuck Gaylord. Fuck you Gaylord." He then spit on the big guy except he didn't have any spit. He tried spitting on him over and over.

"When we get to Glasshouse I'm gonna break your arms." The big guy said.

"Fuck you Gaylord fuck you Gaylord Fuck you Gaylord." The Mexican guy kept repeating.

I turned back and looked at the guy.

"Listen dude. You are freaking out. Try to breathe and listen to your heartbeat and relax.

"Fuck you Gaylord Fuck you Gaylord Fuck you Gaylord." He then spit directly in my face. Well I have a split in my two front teeth which lets me spit with accuracy. I spit in his left eye then his right. Now he was all messed up, handcuffed and he couldn't see. He started spitting in any direction he could.

"HEY YOU DUMB COPS THIS GUY IS SPITTING ON US." The big guy screamed out.

The cops came to the back of the van and ripped the Mexican dude out. They hogtied him, which means he is on his belly with his hands and ankles tied together behind him. They then laid him on his belly and we took off to Glasshouse.

As we left the stadium I saw Jeff on a pay phone outside the stadium with Marie next to him.

"I just saw Jeff on a payphone."

"Good. He is calling his Uncle Joe. He's a bail bonds man. We'll get out soon."

As we rode away handcuffed from the forum all I could think was this was not how I planned the night to go.

We rode to the Glasshouse in silence. No one person in the van made a sound, not even the Mexican who was laying on his belly hog tied in the back. When we got there the cops picked him up by his elbows and carried him over to the processing desk and dropped him on his belly. His chin hit the ground and split open making a pretty big pile of blood.

Immediately after that, they uncuffed us for processing and the big guy sprung to life and started swinging on the cops. I backed up as six cops swooped down on him and beat the living tar with their batons. One cop put him in the sleeper hold and held him there till he passed out. I had never seen that before, holding a guy till he passed out.

I had already been arrested before so I knew damn well to shut the hell up. Just get pics and prints and let the attorney figure it out later.

We got into this holding tank with about forty bunk beds and about two hundred guys in it. There were full on junkies, fiending for the candy cart, which would come by every half hour. They would stand by the bars and buy up all the chocolate bars and rip the wrappers off so fast and them chew them up it was amazing. Then bug everyone in the cell for spare change to buy more. I didn't even know what a junkie was. I for sure had never seen one.

"Junkies."

"What?"

"Junkies. Look at 'em. Trying to get that sugar rush. Any rush. Whatever's out there at this point."

This tall skinny black man was talking to me. He had a city bus driver uniform on, but the tags and patches had been ripped off. You could see that somebody had ripped them off violently. He looked all bummed.

"What are you in here for?" I asked him.

"Bank Robbery." I was shocked. He looked so normal. I think of bank robbery I think of John Dillinger, Bonnie and Clyde. Not the city bus driver.

"For real? You robbed a bank?" I was astonished. A real live bank robber.
"Yeah. I did it while I was driving my bus route. I figured they wouldn't think a bus driver on his route would rob the bank. I had been casing the bank for months. Used to park my bus down the block during my break. One day I just woke up and said, 'Todays the day' and on my break I took my shirt off, walked in as easy as you please and handed the girl a note."
"What it say?"
"One thing about them tellers is they gotta do whatever the note says. And you don't want them to have to read a book. Short and simple. Fill the bag with cash. Large bills. No dye packs. No alarm. Or I'll kill you."
"Whats a dye pack?" I was amazed.
"Exploding money. They give you a pack of bills that will explode with a dye that will cover you and the money also s you get caught and you can't spend the money."
"Wow. I can't believe it. You're a bank robber."
"It aint so uncommon. You'd be surprised. Probably five banks a day get robbed in Los Angeles. Maybe ten. Some of them are real shoot outs."
"How'd your patches get ripped off?"
"I guess some of these cops took it kind of personal. Like we all work for the city or something like that. I didn't even finish my route before they caught me. Don't know how they figure it out so quick. Soon as I saw them red cherries burning in my rear view mirror I knew I was sunk. I though about running for a minute but where the hell was I gonna go with a bus full of passengers? Man I thought I had the whole thing figured out."
" Can I ask you a question? "
"Sure kid."
 "Why they call this the place glasshouse?"
"I was wondering that myself."
The line for the phone was a mile long. I walked over and got in line. There was a sign over the phone that said limit calls to five minutes but guys stayed on till everyone started yelling. Which took about five and a half minutes.

I called Marie and she was as pissed off as can be. Zack called Jeff and within a few hours we were out on bail.
The next day I called my dad because he had covered the bail and he unloaded on me. He thought it was a different Zack and David, two weed smuggling clients of his. So as soon as he figured out that he was spending money and not making it he went ballistic.
I got back on the greyhound and went up north to Marin County. When I finally went back for court the public defender had beaten it down to six months of informal probation. Informal probation is almost like having no restrictions on you at all. You just gotta be a little extra careful. That's not so good for learning lessons, or not learning them. I spent the next few years getting arrested over and over. Using the jail like a revolving door, in a quest for the next high or the next scam or the next thrill.

30

"Wanna go up to Mendocino and harvest? We can take your truck you could make a pound easy. Maybe two."
"Hell yes." I was always looking for the next scam, the next way to make money, get high, without ever looking far enough to see the danger in it. It takes a while to see the danger as opposed to the rewards in things. Guess you gotta face the dangers head on a few times first. Some people even more than a few times. Like me.
Jeff had things sewn up tight. He was living in San Rafael with his girlfriend, who was WAY hot and WAY older than him. He was on a crew that was harvesting hundreds of pounds every year of outdoor kind bud. Green weed. Sinsemilla. This is when green weed was first hitting the scene.
It was the pot wars of the 80's. Humboldt was booming and all around that area was a war zone. The pot farmers against the cops, the city people against the cops because this huge cash crop was sustaining so many lives. Then you add in the

natural paranoia a farmer carries next to his .44 magnum and you have a seriously volatile situation.

The season before we lost the whole crop. This is after all of us taking two week shifts for four months at a time living out in the forest in a big tee pee. We had a car battery to power the TV. A bear claw bathtub that the water stayed in till it was black and had a compost heap the size of the house. Every night you could hear folks firing off guns, riding ATV's, hootin' a and hollerin' like banshees. Bunch of pot farmers.

We lost that first crop all right. We sat on the top of the ridge and watched the cops cut it all down.

But this year was different. We bought a parcel on a gated area that was cordoned off with some other growers. It's tons of work growing weed outdoors. First of all you have to always watch out for bears. They are the real predators out there. I carried a shotgun and Jeff had a .44 magnum.

"You are just gonna piss him off with that shotgun." Jeff would tell me.

"Then what good is it?" I asked.

"It's gonna get his attention while I blast him with this .44 Magnum. This thing would stop an Elephant."

That didn't make me feel any easier about the situation. There was weeks of digging holes, then carting water up and down hills while we set up water lines, then bringing out clones of insane Blueberry crossed with Sour Diesel, or gas, or glass, or sewage. They all had brand names even back then And Kryptonite. Everything was Kryptonite back then. Kryptonite was the biggest. Everyone figured of it could drop Superman it was great. So they named their weed after that. Krippy. Killer Krip. Krypto.

Jeff's Brother has it really together in the brains department and he set it up with the best clones around. No one had weed like us we had the best.

Jeff was into other drugs though. Like a bad science experiment I watched my friends demise in record speed. From the time he picked up opiates till he was dead was less than a year.

You can only become a junkie once, not twice. And you never see yourself becoming a junkie while it happens, it just sort of happens. Jeff was into smoking Heroin.

"There is something wrong about this." I would say to Jeff. He was definitely living a high life. He had made great connections from bringing keys out from Miami. Jeff and his brother were plugged into Grateful Dead family and we were going to every show there was in the Bay area backstage. These guys were tapers meaning they could sit in the taping section and record the concert. They would wheel in tanks of Nitrous Oxide, laughing gas, disguised as their taping equipment. They would have hash, weed, pills, acid and do it all at once. Mass Transit we called it. Jeff would be in the top row smoking Persian Heroin at 800 dollars a gram all alone. His brother didn't want any part of the opiate scene.

"Don't bring me down with your trip. This is my own money, my own drugs, my own life. You want some or not?" Jeff asked me. Of course I wanted some.

Misery loves company, although Jeff didn't seem so miserable. He was having a blast. I am certain he was unaware the monster of a junkie he was becoming. Like I said, you can't see it happening, it just happens. And when you realize it, usually it's too late. That's why you never see any old junkies. They all die. Or get locked up.

At first we would do Fentanyl. I am sure we thought it was China white Heroin, who ever sold it to us told us that. The smallest match head of Fentanyl and we would nod out for eight hours. We had no idea how deadly that stuff was. It's amazing we didn't die with the amounts we did, for weeks on end waiting for the plants to grow. By the time we went up to harvest the first truckload Jeff was so strung out it was insane.

"Hurry up. We gotta go." Jeff said already sitting in the truck smoking dope.

I jumped into the driver seat and started the three hour drive up to the crop. Jeff was smoking Persian Heroin on tin foil, chasing the Dragon, and nodding out the whole way.

" Can I get a hit of that?"

"Naah. You gotta drive."

"I can drive."

"Then drive."

Jeff was less and less into sharing his dope as he got further down that road. At first it was a social environment, he always shared his dope with me, but that soon went away and only despair and desperation remained. And a big dope habit.

We got up to the Crop and Jeff's Brother Sammy was standing there with the two other guys we did this with Tom and Harry. They had cut down and boxed up the first load to drive back in cardboard boxes. We filled up the back of my Chevy pick up with cardboard boxes of freshly cut weed, then we put a tarp over the boxes and covered the tarp with the smelliest compost from the heap. This was six months of rotting garbage and it stunk bad. We figured that would disguise the smell of freshly cut weed, which surrounded the truck for twenty yards in every direction. Seemed like a good plan at the time.

We said goodbye to Sammy, Tom and Harry and took off in the first truck of what would be fourteen trucks full of weed this season. And I mean we grew the very best weed at that time. And it smelled like it.

"You two be careful. Do the speed limit. Don't stop till you get on the highway. There's cops all over Willits. DO NOT stop in Willits. They are looking for guys just like you, who recently harvested. There's a war on." Sammy warned me.

"I got it."

It took about an hour to get off the mountain and to the road to town. We grew our weed at the same altitude as Afghanistan. All on the correct facing ridge to get the most out of the sunlight hours. This was stuff that Sammy thought up or knew, cause he is as smart as any one person could be. He had straight hippie hair down to his ass and smart like Einstein.

It was definitely a big responsibility taking back the first load. I looked over at Jeff and I knew I was going to be doing all the driving. He had run out of dope this morning and he was scratching. He looked beat up bad. Nose rubbed raw like it has been sandpapered, sweating profusely. He needed to get back and get loaded. "Take it easy. You are gonna lose the compost. SLOW DOWN."

Jeff was irritable about everything cause he was coming down so hard. Everything bothered him. The bumping up and down on that country road wasn't helping his ride a bit either.

We pulled into Willits about eight o'clock in the evening. It was quiet. I had gas and I planned on driving straight through.

"Pull over. I need some coffee."

"Sam said not to pull over. I think we should...."

"Pull over at that Quickie Mart. I wanna get some chocolate."

I Looked at Jeff and he was a mess. Any cop would look at him and know something was up. I thought about the junkies at glasshouse and that my buddy was strung out bad. We pulled into the Quickie mart.

"I need some coffee. With lots of sugar." Jeff jumped out of the truck. I looked all around, seemed quiet. I got out of the truck and went inside. Jeff was making himself a cup of sugar with some coffee and I grabbed a sandwich. We were standing waiting to pay and an old lady walked up to Jeff.

"Is that your Chevy Pick up out there?" She asked.

"Yeah."

"Cops are looking at it."

Jeff put the coffee on the counter.

"We are leaving." He said as he made a mad dash for the door. What I should have done is made a mad dash for the back door. But you never see this shit as it happens, it just happens.

I jumped in the truck and leaned over and opened the door for Jeff. Soon as he got in and shut the door, a man with a flash light flashed it on us and started walking over towards us. Jeff looked right at me.

"We are going to JAIL."

Once again everything started moving in slow motion. He walked up to the truck just as easy as you please. He pulled out his pistol.

"You boys want to step out real slow now." The cop said.

We got out of the truck and all of a sudden I really noticed the aroma of fresh cut weed. It was thick.

"Smells like you got some weed in there."

"No Sir. Nothing but compost." Jeff said. He looked bad.

"Mind if I have a look?"

"Not at all. If you have a warrant." Jeff said as calm as can be.

Now that pissed that cop off something fierce. Looked like he was gonna turn three shades of red he was so mad.

"Tell you what I'm gonna do then. I'm gonna hold you two on suspicion. Wake up the D.A. and when he says I can search your truck, I'm gonna search it."

"Do your worst." Jeff said un amused.

Jeff never took any shit from anyone. He knew we were going to jail. Me I just shut the hell up whenever cops are around me. Habit.

It took about twenty minutes before the District Attorney showed up in his bathrobe. Not good. Soon as he got out of his car he smiled.

"Search it. You have my authority." He said glaring at me and Jeff.

A whole bunch of folks from the town had gathered to watch what was happening. The first cop walked over and lifted the tarp separating the compost from the boxes of weed. He opened one box turned around pulled his gun out and faced us.

"Put your hands on your heads."

"Really?" Jeff was so bored with this whole thing.

"Yeah REALLY."

Since he knew we were going to jail for sure he just wanted to get inside, call his uncle and get out and get some dope. Your mind works real fast when you are a junkie, even if everything else is moving in slow motion.

31

I walked up to the Willits Jail and rang the bell. I took a last look around at freedom. It was surreal. Early morning birds chirping people going to work, and I am getting locked up.
The building looked pretty foreboding with the two rows of fences around it and razor wire on top. It was probably the cleanest looking building in town. For sure it was the newest one.
I pressed on the buzzer for an obnoxiously long time. A gruff voice came over the intercom.
"Who is it?"
"I think you have a room for me." I said.
"What's your name?"
"Labrava."
I waited for what seemed like an eternity. That two minutes waiting outside to be locked up inside seemed to last forever. I looked around not knowing what to expect. I took in the peacefulness of the outside world knowing I wouldn't see it for a long time if I ever did see it again. You never know what can happen. I was fully aware of this fact.
"Yes Sir. The Honeymoon suite is available. Come on in." The cop said over the intercom. Wiseass cop. You cannot prepare for something like this. You just have to let it happen.
The electric door popped open and I took a breath and went inside. Same drill as always. Strip. Bend. Nuts up. Cough. Dress. Get your bedding. Go to your cell. This was my new home.
This was the first time I really went inside for any length of time. I had never been to the joint, to the pen, to the big house, the PENITENTIARY. I've been to a bunch of state jails, juvenile hall, but not the pen. There is a difference you know.
After processing they put me in a room with six bunks inside with a table for the inmates to eat at. In each room were four bunk beds and the place was full.
So that's eight guys in each room, which makes twentyfour guys each side, fortyeight guys in the tank total. A lot of guys

were in for drunk in public, weed possession or misdemeanor violence. They were a bunch of rednecks and pot farmers just like me.
Most guys would sleep the day away and party all night, playing dominoes or cards or making pruno. These guys had cell-lab cookeries that were making Pruno by the quart. Late night parties making 'everything roll' which is exactly as it sounds, everything mashed up and cooked on a hot plate, then cooked into a log of deliciousness. A roll covered in mashed up crackers and soup and cheese all kinds of shit. Yeah man, now you talking.
 I had made a decision to come out of here better than when I went in. I had just turned eighteen and got caught in a major felony when I got locked up. I got convicted for having seventy seven pounds of weed in my pick up truck. Not bad for the first of fourteen trucks to come down. I got ten months and served about eight of them with good behavior. If you don't get in any trouble they will shave a little time off your sentence. Not much but every day counts. After I had to serve five years of informal probation.
I had it all planned out. I was going to Amsterdam as soon as I got out of jail. I would complete my probation in Holland. My girlfriend was Dutch and we both tattooed and worked in the oldest tattoo shop in San Francisco. Having a love interest in another country let me leave with no problem. After I served my time. I knew that was going to be a big hill to climb over.
I will never forget the first day of jail. One of the rednecks kept eyeing me.
"Where you from?" He asked me.
"San Francisco."
"You some big city slicker. Huh? A big shot.huh." He was full of attitude.
I just stared at the guy till he looked away. Then I knew. This is the guy my dad told me about. The one who needed to be knocked out so everyone knew to not mess with me. I waited till he went into his cell and I went in after him.
"Where you from?" I asked him. I think I startled him. He didn't hear me walk in his cell. Before he could answer me I hit him in the face with a right upper reverse punch. Then I

gave him an upper cut and dropped like a bag of chips. I walked out of the cell and one of the older guys looked at me.
"You handle that?" The old guy asked me.
"Yes Sir." I said.
"That's what I'm talking about." He said with a smile.
The old guy gave me a look and I knew everything was gonna be ok. His name was Bruce Hamilton or Hayvenhurst or something like that, some really American name. He grew weed by the acre and got caught with over a ton of it. He was gonna do a year in this place then they would ship him up state to the Pen. He turned out to be the Shotcaller in that tank, and also in the town outside apparently. He was always a pretty fair guy. Even the cops gave him respect.
That guy I rocked never bothered me again neither did anyone else.
I got into a routine, I would wake up, eat the breakfast, then when everyone went back to sleep, I would train karate working my way up and down the floor of the tank doing punches blocks and kicks till lunch, then do it again till dinner. I had already spent a lot of time training Karate in my life. I had a Miyamoto Musashi state of mind. I was determined to make this time inside make me a better person.
The first three months went by ok. I never got out of that tank. The air was kind of stagnant inside. I remember that.
The place was full of tweakers and dope heads. They made a scheme to get dope in the jail. I watched these guys pool their money together, put it on one guys books, then another guy would come pick it up. Then they all squeezed up to the window and watched him leave.
"Better get on it." A big redneck said to a skinny inmate. The redneck had set the whole thing up.
I watched the skinny guy go into convulsions until the guards came in. He was laying on the ground holding his sides and screaming like he was going to die. The cops took him out on a stretcher.
"Won't be long now." One guy said.
"I can't wait." Said another.

I watched these guys stare out the window the whole time that the guy was away. Saying how they were going to beat his ass if he doesn't come through. It's amazing they didn't give themselves away and blow the whole gig.

When the guy finally came back they sat like fiends waiting for him to take a dump in front of everyone, they put a sheet up for privacy but it wasn't very private. They couldn't give a damn if that dope just came out of his ass. They were going to put it right up their arm. Amazing.

While everyone was fiending on their dope, trying to be cool fixing it in different parts of the cell the guy who went and got the dope walked over to me.

"Was it worth it?" I asked him.

"Yeah. Only cause I didn't get caught. I like to get high. I don't shoot dope though. I had my buddy leave some tin foil."

The guy bent over and hit a little line of dope on his foil. You could smoke cigarettes and everyone did in abundance so the cops didn't notice.

"Want a hit?"

I looked around, everyone was either nodding out or trying to be cool as they wiped out their spoon and shot up again. I grabbed the little rolled up tin foil tune and took a big hit. I held it in till I was about to burst and let it out. Loaded. Instantly. I gave it back.

"Thanks."

"Its all good.

"You weren't scared about getting caught?" I asked.

"A little. Aint got much going on the outside anyway. My cousin sells that shit, he was the guy who came and grabbed the money off the books, and planted the dope. So we made a big sale besides getting high. Sounds like an all win to me and him."

"How'd you do it?" I was in shock at the risk he took.

The guy looked around the cell then peered out the door. In our cell everyone was loaded. In the other cells everyone was either playing dominoes cards or sleeping.

" You saw me go into convulsions?"

"Everyone did."

"Exactly. The cops aint allowed to ignore that. They gotta take me in to get checked out. Can't let a prisoner die on their watch. It's bad for business. The cops set an appointment for me for immediate pickup to the county hospital. My cousin waits there, just like one of the sick folks. When I come in, he goes in the bathroom and plants the dope and shit."
"Where?"
"Gotta be in a good spot for sure. Soon as I got out of the doctor I started getting cramps. I made a hell of a racket, saying how I will never make it back to the jail, I gotta take a shit, it's an emergency, whatever it takes to get in that bathroom. And of course the cop goes in and looks all around before I went in."
"Wow." Amazing.
"Lucky for me he left a little Vaseline or else I would have had to shove that rig and dope and foil up my ass dry."
"It doesn't sound too fun even with Vaseline." I said.
"Sometimes you gotta use that man pocket. These guys would not understand not pulling it off."
"You got bigger balls than me."
"I just got a bigger need."
I went over to my bunk and laid down to enjoy my high. Everyone in the cell was nodding out. It was kind of funny.
I stayed in that tank for about three months before they moved me to the other side. The other side was for people with less than half their time left. It was much better. You could walk around outside, lift weights and everyone got their own room. They were rooms, not cells. We got locked in every night, and there was a little window on the door for the guard to walk by and check on you every hour, but it was still better. I started counting the days.
Every night these kids would draw straws and the short straw had to sneak out of the jail through a hole in the fence run about one hundred fifty yards down a creek in the bushes where there was a liquor store. They would have their friends meet them and buy bottles of booze and then sneak back in the jail.
I was absolutely amazed at the risks people would take to get high. I never imagined getting high when I went inside. They

had weed and liquor, whatever they wanted. Except their freedom, which is they wanted the most and risked it further every night.

When I got to the other side I heard about my friend Jeff's time inside. He was my co defendant but he did his time right when I went on the run. He was out before I went in. Soon as people figured I was Jeff's co defendant the stories started flowing.

I guess when Jeff was here he got a job washing the cop's cars. He would put on his street clothes, take the city bus to Police station, wash all the cars then take the bus back. Jeff had it figured out real quick. He would have his girl meet him with dope in a hotel, bang her lights out then smuggle the dope back in and stay loaded. He sold just enough dope to some inmates, the right ones, the ones with power, so no one snitched on him.

If you keep busy inside the time goes by faster. I was drawing one envelope for an inmate for two items on his commissary. Being able to draw is big inside. Everyone is missing their family, and they like sending personalized envelopes back, which were my specialty. That helped me a lot staying busy because all of a sudden my time was up.

You can't sleep the night before you get out. The excitement is too great. I didn't even try to sleep. I sat on my bunk all packed up to go all night long. They always want to kick you out before breakfast. Better save that meal.

I was sitting on my bunk when the guard came over and unlocked my door. He looked down and saw my clothes and bedding all folded. He looked at his clip board, then at me and smiled.

"Labrava. Today seems like a good day to go home. Doesn't it?"

"YES SIR."

I jumped off my bunk, grabbed my stuff and walked out of there. I got to the door and looked back. Everyone was sleeping. There was all levels of snoring. It was kind of funny. Like a cartoon.

"SEE YA IN THE FUNNY PAPERS!" I screamed at the top of my lungs. About half the room sat up. The guard just shook his head. I don't know why I did that. I just didn't feel like slipping out without making a sound. Must be the Holden Caulfield in me.

They processed me out and I walked over to the next building, which was probation. I got my five years of forms to fill out. One form a month for five years. Sixty forms. Informal probation is no big deal. Just had to stay out of trouble. I wasn't worried, I was going to Amsterdam. Everything is legal there. What trouble could I get in I thought.

I took a bus from Willits back to San Francisco and went into the tattoo shop. My girl had left me a ticket to Holland and Sammy had left me a pound of weed from the Harvest. I took the pound and sold most of it in one deal, then took that money and went to where Jeff was staying and got loaded.

Jeff had graduated from smoking dope to shooting it. He held up a thousand pack of diabetic syringes.

"This is the only way to go."

"That aint for me. I'll just smoke it. " I sat there smoking dope on foil while Jeff was shooting up. It was kind of sad watching him try to find a vein. He wasn't the best at it.

That was the last time I ever saw Jeff. About three weeks later Zack called me.

"Jeff's dead." Zack said crying into the phone. They were real close.

I was stunned, even if I saw this coming a mile away. The first thing I thought was that didn't even take a year, from discovery to death.

"What happened?" I asked still in shock. I knew the answer.

"I don't now. Did too much I guess. He holed up in a hotel and paid for a week. Had a bunch of dope and coke on him when they found him. He must have been shooting speedballs. That's the new thing."

"Speedballs?"

"Yeah. He laid there for three days before they found him. He must have smelled up the place something fierce. It was in the paper and everything. The headline read 'Local man found dead' they didn't even release his name till they contacted his mom."

I hung up the phone and stood there for a minute. It was cold in the city all of a sudden. I felt the loss this one human being I knew so well which now left a void. Even if I hadn't spoken to Jeff in months I always knew he was there. Now he wasn't. That was my first big loss in life. Losing that friend. I didn't know a lot but I knew it was time for me to get out of there.

32

I landed at Schipol airport in Amsterdam wearing my best suit. Fresh from Jail in new country felt like a new beginning. I had no idea how true that was.
I used to always wear suits. I thought that looked classy. Suits that were a little big in the shoulders. Oversized. I came from the city so I dressed like a city thug. Just like the character OddJob in the James Bond movie. I always boxed and I thought it was cool after training to put on a suit. Classy. Snazzy. Serious. Probably cause that's how my Dad rolled. Even if we didn't get along too great, I revered him. He wore suits and he was a boxer and a giant. At least in my eyes.
I pushed a cart through baggage claim with basically ALL of the stuff I owned.
"What you got there?" The customs cop asked me looking at my pile of stuff.
"Everything I own."
"Proceed."
I would have thought they would at least want to give it a glance. Nope. There is an open customs policy in Amsterdam. Everyone can bring in anything they want. That's why there is so much drugs here. At least that's what I figured.
My girl was standing there with a friend of hers named Jeroen.
"Hallo."
"Hello."
"This is Jeroen."
He helped me with my bag and we went to the car. Little car. Everyone drives little cars in Europe.

"Let's get some weed." I said.
"We will." My girl was in no rush for me to get high. She new I like getting high. I got high a little too much in her mind.
"He's got to see it with his own eyes." Jeroen said.
Jeroen knew I couldn't even imagine buying weed over the counter. We drove into the city and went to a coffeeshop, which is where they sell weed and hash. Jeroen was as excited as I was, not to buy weed though, but to see me buy it. He pointed to another Coffeeshop a few doors down and explained how it worked.
"If the sign says coffeeshop with a C, then it sells weed, if it says Koffieshop with a K then it sells Koffie. Come on."
We went inside and they had a menu. I couldn't believe it. I bought myself some weed and hash and rolled a joint right there. It was so civilized. Everyone was smoking with tobacco rolled in it, which I wouldn't do. And not many people wanted to smoke a pure weed joint. I got known for smoking pure weed all the time.
 Me and Jeroen instantly became friends. He ran this really cool nightclub called the Man's Ruin. Just like the tattoo, with the girl in the Martini glass and the dice and the eight ball. I got a job being the doorman/ bouncer there the second day O was in Amsterdam.
It was a sunny day when I arrived in Amsterdam. A sunny day is a special thing in Amsterdam everyone is outside enjoying the weather.
We pulled up to the tattoo shop that my girl worked at and there was a bunch of guys with vests on having water pistol fights. They were grown men all running around like kids, all soaking wet, laughing and joking. They looked like cowboys on acid. I could see they were buck ass wild and way serious. They had a whole bunch of really nice motorcycles all lined up out front. This was the first time I had ever seen anything like this before. This was not in my realm. I was a city Thug. I wanted a muscle car. Not a bike.
"Who are these guys?" I asked my girl.
"They are Brothers." My girl said proudly. 'They are a really tight family of brothers. And they all ride bikes."

I looked around. There was about thirty of them having the time of their lives. One of the Brothers walked up to me.
"Is this him?" He asked my girl.
"Yes." She said.
He came in real close and stared in my eye, looked me up and down. I didn't back up or flinch at all. I knew he was trying me.
"Does everyone in your country have feet that big? Cause I don't know if we got shoes dat big in Holland."
"One of the other Brothers dumped a bucket of water on his head and he turned around and chased him down the block. I looked at my girl and said real serious.
"If he wants to see what I'm made of I can show him."
She looked at me like I was insane and rolled her eyes.
"Relax. Your gonna love these guys." She was right.
I am a creature of habit and I immediately got into a program in Holland. Idle hands are the devils workshop. I knew better that I needed to get busy. I joined a boxing team and started working in the tattoo shop in the day and working at the Man's Ruin at night.
The same thing every day works for me. I would wake up and go to the boxing gym and box with a coach and all these other guys around my age. Then smoke a joint while I walked all the way to the tattoo shop. When I got to the shop the owner would hand me about thirty needle bars. I would sit in the back and fill the needle bar orders for whoever was working in that shop, usually about four or five different artists. So four or five different artists could complain on the bars I made so I had to make them great. This is before factory made needles. Hell this is even before artists wore latex gloves.
After making needles for a few hours I would then draw or trace and if I did that long enough I got to do a small tattoo. This was a very good apprenticeship. I learned a real lot. My girl was the best and she helped me a ton. After dinner I would go to the Man's Ruin and be the Doorman.
The Man's Ruin was the local cool bar in town. Across the street was a bar called the Richter, like the Richter scale. The

whole name was, '36 op de schall van Richter'. 36 on the scale of Richter.

The Richter closed at three am and The Man's Ruin was open till six. People rang the buzzer, which said 'Members Only' underneath. Just like old school mob hangouts. I would open the slot and if I wanted to, I let you in. This was the in place. All the Brothers hung out here. And the Rockers and the dealers and whoever else was in the IN crowd. Herman Brood and his Wild Romance, the coolest band in town would come in after rehearsal every night.

I would be sitting at the door with one of the Brothers, me in my suit and him in his vest and let in who ever I wanted. The Brothers took a real shine to me, and me to them. I had gotten out of jail and moved to Holland. They sort of adopted me.

I had been in Holland for a few months when I went with my girl and the owner of the shop to the clubhouse to return a generator. The Brothers showed me all around the clubhouse. I was still into wearing suits. I had only ridden dirt bikes a little bit as a kid.

One of the Brothers looked at me.

"So, what do you think?" I looked at them all real serious.

"I now know what I am supposed to do on this earth. I'm gonna be in this family. I'm gonna be one of your Brothers."

My girl looked at me.

"Well that's not going to work for me because then I will become second in your life."

"Well then I guess it's not going to work for you." I said matter of factly.

They all started laughing, even her.

"That didn't take long." She said with a smile.

I slept like a baby that night. My ever changing plan was becoming clearer. I think what over whelmed me the most about the Brothers was how they treated each other. They greeted each other like they hadn't seen each other in five years, every time they saw each other. It was beautiful to see. That and how great they treated me made me want to be part of that family. I knew for sure that was what I was going to do.

33

"Wait your turn." Toni said to me as he stepped back into the fight and smashed one guy then another. I was out with the Brothers and we were in another bar fight. I stood anxious and at the ready to mop up any of Toni's leftovers.
Toni's motto is, 'When in doubt, knock em out.' Toni lived by that rule.
He taught me a whole bunch of things. All valuable lessons. Like showing class. You can show class by tipping big, or by knocking the right guy out at the right moment, or not knocking him out at all. It just depends on the situation. There are all kinds of ways to show class.
I bought a round of drinks for a few Brothers who were standing at the bar. Whenever a Brother walked in the bar I bought them a drink. They earned it in my eyes. I was starting to understand what it took to be a Brother. Which was A LOT.
"Prost." Prost means 'cheers' in Dutch. I was already getting a handle on the language. I held out my drink to toast Toni. Before I could down my drink Toni grabbed my face with his hand and looked me square in the eyes.
"You look me in the eyes when you toast me. Everyone gets a look."
"Got it." I said.
He let my face go. I looked at everyone one at a time and they each looked back, dead in my eye and we all took a drink.
I had been living in Amsterdam for over a year and I was evolving into the person I am now. I went from wanting a muscle car to a hot rod bike, and wearing a suit to jeans and a vest. I still had a thug mind set, just now more of a motor thug.
Amsterdam was as wild as a gold rush town back then. There were junkies everywhere. They would break into cars daily. Every morning there would be used syringes and burnt foil at the door step. At this time I was not in to dope yet. I had done it before but I wanted to stay away. I knew for certain the

Brothers and any one else I was near ESPECIALLY my girl would not be having it, so I stayed away.

In fact I started beating up junkies. They knew to keep off the block where the tattoo shop was. They avoided that block at all costs. They would get beat and come back with the cops.

"It was them." The junkie would be dragging some cop to the scene of where he was most recently beaten and robbed of his dope. He had a fat lip and a black eye. The cop was rolling his eyes.

"They smashed my works. Threw my dope in the canal. Arrest them." The junkie screamed.

"Lucky YOU didn't end up in the canal." I said.

All the Brothers laughed. The cop looked at the ten brothers sitting there and the beaten up Junkie.

"Now now theres no harm done. Run along." The cop told the junkie.

"WHAT? YOU'RE NOT GOING TO ARREST THEM?" The junkie was in shock.

Now the Brothers really had a laugh. The cop walked away, the junkie ran.

Days turned into weeks turned into months turned into years. I stayed clean and in my program for over two years. I evolved from what I was into what I am now.

I remember there was a sign painted in the shop. 'As you are I was, as I am, you will be.' I took that as if it was directed at me.

After about two years I was getting more than comfortable. My girl and me had broken up long ago. I spent most of my time with the Brothers partying like rock stars. Literally leaving bars that were closing at six am and walking to ones that just opened at seven.

On any given night we would cruise about eight bars, getting in at least two fights per bar. These guys walked everywhere like Vikings and the town treated them this way. Some cities really cater to the Brothers. Amsterdam is one of those towns. The Brothers are part of the mystery, the mystique of the town. I was in awe of them, I revered them, I emulated them.

"You get one chance to screw up with us, not two, so do good. Think about your actions." I was told.

The lessons were nonstop. I had changed completely without seeing it happen. That's evolution baby.

I no longer worked in the tattoo shop but I was still the doorman at the Man's Run. I had made a whole bunch of friends. Everyone wanted to be friends with the doorman. It was always up to me to let you in the door or not. If you didn't tip me good the last time you left you might not get in the next time. Whenever someone was leaving the bar my buddy Jeroen who was part owner and one of the bartenders, would yell out to the customer.

"DENK OP DE PORTIER!" Which means, Think about the Doorman. Then the customer would reach into his pocket and get me a tip.

On any given night I would make about three hundred Guilders. Gliders. This was before the Euro. 5's were Green. 10's were yellow. 25's were red. 5o's had a sunflower. 100's were Blue. 250's were Purple, The 1000 notes were also Green. Just like the 5's. Everyone tipped the doorman when they left. At the very least they would give a 5 note. One time this old drunk had made a real mess, knocked all the glasses over in a drunken rage. Pissed off my buddy real good. Whenever ANYONE got out of line my buddy would scream.

"LABRAVA......OUT!" and look at whoever the hell he wanted out. I walked over to the drunk and looked him dead in the eye.

"You can walk outta here like a man or I am going to drag you out like a drunk. Believe it. Your choice."

The guy looked at me and saw I was way serious, shrugged his shoulders and walked out. Then at the door he turns around and hands me a tip. I take the bill and toss him out shutting the door behind him. I looked down and the tip he gave me was not a five but a thousand note.

"He gave me a thousand note." I said. I held it up just as the buzzer was ringing.

"That's him. Swap it for a five." I stuffed the bill in my pocket and took out a five. I opened the door and the guy slurred something in very drunk Dutch. I knew what he was saying.

He wanted his thousand back. I handed him the five. He looked down through his drunk goggles and did a double take. He looked up at me and shook his head again and walked away mumbling something. I shut the door and did the right thing. I bought drinks for everyone.

One day my buddy walked in early.

"Come here. I need your help."

I followed him upstairs. He broke out some foil and a little packet.

"We have a long distance call from Persia." He broke out a gram of some unbelievable Persian Heroin. He had no idea that I had already had a small problem with this shit, the problem being was that I like it too much. And I didn't tell him. I got as loaded as can be that night. I still worked the door, you never think anyone can see if you are high, but they can.

I immediately knew it was getting time to get out. I had not learned the lesson yet that this is not a geographical problem. Dope is everywhere. And a real Junkie will find it. Anywhere.

I woke up the next day and I felt like I had been run over by a truck. I lived in a three room flat across the canal from the biker bar in town. My flat was one room each on top of another. With very steep stairs, like a ladder. Heat was from a kerosene heater which stunk.

I knew where to get dope. There was a part of town called the Nieuw market, it was about six blocks away. That block was like night of the living dead. The street would be PACKED with junkies, most of the clinging to life, all shriveled up and Zombie looking. They would be standing anywhere and everywhere smoking foil or shooting dope. Poor Dutch shopkeepers would be standing behind the glass scared to death. The junkies had absolutely taken over this part of town. I never went there, ever. But now I heard it calling, like with a megaphone.

There is a difference between someone who has been exposed and someone who hasn't. Once you have been exposed you always know dope is in the world. Even if I never did it for the first two years there, I always knew it was there. It's a voice in your head that says 'Dope is right over there, and you know how to get it.'

I spent my last months in Amsterdam by myself for the most part. I knew better than to get caught in that part of town. I was not under any rules, I was not part of anything so in reality I could do whatever I wanted to. I just knew it would be frowned upon. Imagine, I spent my first two years there beating up junkies, now I was starting to become one. I hadn't done enough dope in my life yet to see what was happening.

I drifted away from the people I knew who would not like me doing this and I started dabbling in dope. I think it was as much of a thrill to not get caught copping dope as it was doing it. I would wrap a big scarf around my face, put a jacket on with a wool hat and sunglasses. It was as cold as the North Pole so I didn't look out of place. Then I would ride my bicycle all the way around to the other side of town and enter the Nieuw Market from the other side, so there was not a chance of me running into anyone.

As you got close dealers from Surinam and Morrocco would approach in packs, all of them trying to make the sale first. They would come running up.

"Chinga dope Bro. Muja hebba. Brown. Vitte." Which means, 'I've got it. What you want. Brown. White.'

 And they are selling anything, everything, dirt, broken glass, so to avoid getting ripped off I had to have them burn some from the package I was buying. You could smell if it was real in an instant. They would turn around and ride back the way I came.

I started hitting that part of town more and more. Too much and I knew it. I would smoke for two days then go to the gym and lay in the sauna all day and sweat it out. I did this routine for about two months and I knew it was time to go. I had worn out my stay. I packed up and headed back to Schipol. It was a sad day leaving Amsterdam. I had changed on some many levels while I was there. I had a clear view of what I wanted to do with my life, and a small peek at the monster standing in my way. Myself.

34

I didn't have a lot of money when I left Amsterdam so I took a flight to New York City. It was cheaper than flying straight back to California. I had some friends in The City who played in Rock bands and I started working as a roadie for all kinds of local bands. Circus of Power, The Battalion of Saints, The U S Fury's, basically whoever was playing at any of the local clubs. The Cat Club, The Kitchen Club, Washington Square, The Wah Wah Hut, all over the city. Live music was big and there was a real scene going on. Heroin was the in drug. China White, Persian. Everyone did it. At least everyone in the crowd I was hanging in, but I didn't know that when I landed. I just knew I wasn't ready to go back to San Francisco. I still had my tattoo equipment but I wasn't doing that so much. It's kind of hard to tattoo when you are strung out all the time so I kind of backed away from the blood business for a while.

Everyone there shot dope. No one smoked it. I started living with this girl named Stacey. She weighed about ninety pounds soaking wet, with a monster size dope habit. She was as hot as can be in her heavy metal outfit, black hair with white skin like she hasn't seen the sun in a year. A snow white tan. We were in love with dope and each other which is a bad combination.

We lived just outside of Alphabet city. Our apartment was right above the daytime spot. Three short flights of stairs. Like four stairs each landing. I would jump down each level then kick the front door open. There were all kinds of Dominicans selling Heroin and Coke from about six a m till six p m. We lived in her Grandmas rent controlled apartment. It was a one bedroom, with a closet and the kitchen in the living room with a bear claw bathtub in the corner. The rent was next to nothing and we still could barely afford it. Everyone month her grandmother would be screaming that she was going to throw us out.

The night time spot opened up from about six till three am. This was a Heroin dealership that had been in business over thirty years in the same location. It was Mob run and it would take in over twenty grand every day of the week. They had lookouts on both corners. The building was in the middle of the block and the junkies waited across the street. There was a skinny black doorman named Clancy and he would call out three people at a time. If a beat cop came walking up the street the lookouts would scream out,

"YO MIKEY!" and all the junkies would walk in very direction. It was kind of funny. Those beat cops were paid off I'm sure, but they still would not be able to ignore thirty junkies waiting in a line for dope. In that line was every type of person, rockers, businessmen, homeless junkies, dealers, hookers, college kids, you name it. It just went to show you how Heroin transcended all classes, all denominations, all races. It didn't matter who you were or where you were from. Once you let it in your life, it became your master.

Soon as you walked in the building there were two mobsters, one standing one sitting. Nobody was really sure it was Mob run, but that was the rumor. That rumor made everyone behave. Can't mess with the Mob.

"NO ONES. NO FIVES. HAVE YOUR MONEY OUT AND READY." One of the Mobsters would call out as we walked down the hall. They both had big guns in their belts. And they had the best dope in the city.

There was an even later night spot that was open from three a.m. till six a.m. but there was always a great chance of getting ripped off there. Only the desperados and the predators are walking the streets from three till six.

Dope will make you find out what you are really about, or what you aint about. It made me find out.

 When you run out of money you will find some. Somehow someway you gotta fill that need. And the need is always growing. Always. And I had two habits to support. Mine and Stacey's We were always coming up with some scheme. I would stand near Washington square park with the rest of the street dealers. But I was looking for the big deal. And I

had NOTHING to sell. College kids always passed by looking for weed or pills and shit. Kiddie drugs I called them.
"What do you need?" I asked.
"Can you get a pound?" Said a guy about college age.
I looked at the guy up and down. Too young to be a cop. Just a college student.
"Two thousand. You got money." I said.
The kid flashed a wad of twenty crisp, hundred dollar bills.
"Let's go. Follow me." I took off towards my house and the kid was following me. I ran up the flight of steps and opened the door and there was Stacey sick as can be. She was always sick. She had a MONSTER habit. As soon as I walked in the door with the kid she got a look of horror on her face. She knew what I was doing.
"Give me the money. I'll be right back." I said.
"I don't know about that." The guy said. He was reluctant to give me the money.
"Wait here with my girlfriend. I'll be right back. Five minutes. It' the next building over."
He was still a little skeptical.
"Think I would take you to where I live if I was gonna rip you off. Quit trippin. Give me the money." I was impatient.
The kid took the two thousand dollars out of his pocket and gave it to me.
"Be right back."
I turned around and flew down the flights of stairs one whole flight t a time. I made a hell of a racket. I am certain the other tenants hated the junkies in 3-C.
I hit the block and made a left and within twenty feet I ran into Carlos who just happened to be the Kingpin of Dominican dope dealers.
"Carlos. What you got?" I asked him.
"Was it matter? Choo never got no money anyway."
I whipped out the wad and showed him. His eyes lit up light flashlights. He pulled out three bundles. That's thirty dime bags.
"Three hundy."
"Two fitty."
"Done."

I dropped the money he dropped the bindles, we both reached down fast to pick up our goods. I took off and shot a bindle on the next alley way I passed. Soon as I was done fixing I found a pay phone and called Stacey. She was expecting the call. She went right into freaked girlfriend mode.
"Hello."
"Is he still there?"
"Yeah."
"Kick him out."
"You gotta be kidding me." She was a natural.
"I'll meet you at the Hut." I said.
"Is he ok? Was he in handcuffs? How many cops?"
She was great. I heard her muffle the phone to tell the guy.
"My boyfriend just got busted trying to get you a pound. We're gonna need you to help us with some bail money. How much you got right now?"
She was good. I mean really good.
"Thanks for calling. Yeah. His friend is here. He's gonna loan us some bail money."
Boy was probably wishing he never got out of bed.
Once in awhile whoever got ripped off would go looking for me. And sometimes they would find me. Once in a while I had to punch it out. But not too often. Most people figured it wasn't worth the effort.

35

"Wake up baby. I'm sick"
I thought I was dreaming. You now that moment when all of a sudden you know it's no longer a dream. And you try to fall back into it. Control it. Try to grab back that sleep before another day comes crashing down on my junkie madness. Every day for a junkie is a quest. Every movement is a mission. Every time you put on your shoes you know what lies ahead is probably wilder than you could ever imaging. That's junkie life. And it aint fun.

I felt a slap on my cheek. I laid still. I felt another harder one. Then a good slap.
"What are you doing? What is wrong with you?" I said.
"I'm sick baby. Go cop."
"One it's freezing out there. Two aint no one out yet." I pilled the blanket around me tighter.
"Dimebag's out there. He's always out there early."
"Dimebag's a rip off."
She held on to the sheet and kicked me off the bed. She was pretty strong as skinny as she was. Or maybe that was the Monster that lived inside her. I started putting my clothes on. Stacey was sitting on the bed shaking and sweating. She would wake up sweating. She must have done a lot last night. Funny thing about dope, the more you do the more you need to do. And more and more and more until you crash and burn.
"There's some money in my jeans."
I reached down and picked up her jeans and I could see they were covered in little blood spots. I was getting more pissed off by the second. I counted the money.
"There's only eighty six dollars here. Are you gonna try and tell me you danced for eight hours and only made eighty six dollars? What you think, I'm stupid?"
"It's been dead. No one's been coming in. I love you baby"
"Sure you do. Wanna know what I think?"
"No."
'Well I'm gonna tell you anyway."
"Here it comes." He said. She looked real sick.
"I bet anything I can make a call or two and find out you were in the bathroom all night doing speedballs. That's where all the money went. And your wake up which is why you're sick. You did your wake up."
She doubled over in pain. She knew how to get me.
"Hurry baby I'm sick."
"I'm sick of the bullshit you're running on me."
"I'm not. That's all in your head. I love you.
"The only thing you love is getting high."
"That's not true. Don't say that."

"Truth hurts, don't it." I said as I walked out slamming the door behind me.

I hit the flights of stairs hard, it must have shook the whole building each time I landed. One of the tenants stuck his head out to see what was up.

"GO BACK IN YER HOUSE!" I said.

He shut the door quick. Most people don't want no part of nothing. Not a handout or helping people. Most people just don't want no part of anything. Not in the city. Not in the eighties.

First thing I needed was some chocolate. FIRST THING has gotta be sugar. I always thought about the junkies I saw in one of my early arrests fiending over sugar. I didn't understand it then. I did now. Gotta get that rush. I cut the line and grabbed a Snickers and some lawyer type got in my face.

"Didn't you see there's a line here buddy." He said with some attitude. I snapped.

"SO WHAT? You want problems? Cuz I got problems. You can have some of mine."

He stepped back. I don't think he was expecting this dirty smelly snot dripping junkie to jump in his face. And him in his suit, he didn't want to mess that up for sure. The shopkeeper intervened.

"DL... Why you always causing trouble? You need to get clean boy. You got your candy. Now get out of my shop. I'll climb over this counter and kick your ass my self."

The shopkeeper was named Tony and he had the patience of a saint. He watched me fall. At this point I was still on the way down.

I looked at the Lawyer guy once more, threw the dollar on the counter and left with out getting my change. That's Tony's tip for always putting up with me. He was way cool a family man with like six kids, he was always trying to talk sense to me.

I hit the dope hole, which was an area that all the junkies and dealers hung out at buying and selling dope. It was about three blocks from my house. This is the place to go before the Domincans came out around nine am. Six in the morning you came to the Dope hole. And Dimebag was always out early. He originally showed me the rope when I first hit the scene. Before my habit really took over.

Dimebag would preach his philosophy. "In and out. You gotta get in and out quick. That way you can sell small bags and by the time you get back six hours later all they can do is scratch for some more. If you stay there too long they might come back too quick and want a recount. Or even worse, a refund. Yeah. In and out quick." That's what he would always tell me. He was always preaching his street gospel.

Dimebag was certain he had it all figure out. Dimebag's real name is Byron. We used to be best friends before I got into dope hard. Now Byron couldn't stand me. His girl is named Sydney and she was always pretty cool to me. As long as I didn't get too close. She liked Stacey enough though.

I hit the Dopehole and my best friend Tommy was there just about to do his wake up. A real junkie doesn't run out of dope until he has some more in his pocket, or unless he absolutely has to do it cause he is sick. A real junkie wakes up thinking about firing dope first thing, his first breath if possible. Then he takes a piss.

In my body or in my pocket. I have it or I'm on my way to get it. That was how I rolled.

"Whats shaking Babaloo?" Tommy asked.

"Same shit. Been here long?"

"Seems like all day."

I set up a makeshift table and starting fixing my dope. My buddy Nature walked up and sat next to his girl Candy. Nature and Candy were into rocks not dope. Just coke in general but mostly they liked smoking rocks.

"Nature."

"What up D."

Nature got his name cause he always found a place in a local park and would build a badass homeless camp. No one could ever find it unless he took you there. Not even the cops. Or the park rangers.

There was a whole community living on the streets. I still had a place to stay in Staceys Grandma's rent control apartment, but not for long and I knew it. I just didn't know I was two steps from being homeless. Like I said you never see this shit coming, it just comes.

A hooker I know named Shelby walked up. Strung out hard.

"Hows it going DL?"

"Beat it."

"Can I get a little taste of yours. I'll let you hit it. Or the best blowjob of your life. How bout it baby?"

"She just offered me the same deal." Tommy said laughing.

"First of all I aint your baby. Second of all aint no one getting any of this but me. This is my wake up. I could barely sleep last night I was so excited about doing it."

"I've got money." Shelby whipped out a wad of cash.

"I've got money too. I'm gonna need my money to get some more shit right after I fire up this shit."

"But." She was desperate.

"BEAT IT."

Shelby got up and walked away cursing me in some other language. I don't know where she was from but it wasn't from here. A lot of people came to the big city and got CHEWED UP.

"Who's coming? You know?" I asked.

Candy leaned over. "Fatman for sure."

"We don't give a shit about Fatman. He only sells coke. We need DOPE."

"Yeah you know, dope, junk smack."

"Horse, Tar, Chiva, Brown sugar." Tommy fell right into it. It was like one of our many rituals before we shot up.

"H, Skag." Nature joined in.

"Brown tape, Black Eagle, China White."

"White Lady, White girl, White Boy, White stuff." Shelby only thought about white drugs.

"Bodhisattva, Original Formula."

"Mexican Brown, Scat, Number Eight."

"Black Tar, Brown Crystal, Sack."

"Andi if you wanna give it the respect it DESERVES."

"HEROIN." Everyone said 'Heroin' at the same time. Like I said, this was our ritual. We both looked at each other, then at our arms.

"It will be better in the next life." I used to always say that before I shot up. Another ritual.

We both sat back reeling from shooting our wake up. Nothing feels like the first shot of the day. One incredible rush that can't be beat. Then you spend the rest of the day shooting up over and over, while you are on a constant mission to generate money to get more. It's a vicious cycle.

A limousine pulled into the Dopehole kind of fast.

"That's my girl." Shelby said all excited. Shelby lived with a fine ass Blonde named Alexa. She was more of a high end hooker than Shelby was.

The limo stopped in front of us and the passenger door flew open. Alexa jumped out of the car spitting cum out of her mouth and holding a bloody switchblade. The limo driver stepped out of the other side freshly stabbed and bleeding on his white limo driver uniform.

"You cut me bitch." He said checking out his wound.

"What you think was gonna happen Huh? Punk ass bitch. What you think? You put your hands on me. You aint the trick dumbass. You're the Driver. You pay double."

"I'm gonna knock you out bitch." The Limo driver said.

"WHAT YOU SAY? YOU MESSING WITH MY GIRL PUNK?" Shelby went into ballistic mode beating the driver with her purse while he was trying to knock either one of them and not get too beaten. Candy looked at me.

"Help her D." Candy pleaded.

I looked at Tommy who shrugged his shoulders like, 'why not?' So I got up and flicked open this pocket knife I carried. It was nothing big, just enough.

"She cut you? Let me see." I said. I let him see I had a knife. It was too early in the morning for a knife fight I thought. I just wanted to get high.

The limo driver looked at me then the two girls and he got it, time to leave. I went at him with my blade and he did a football maneuver and I fell down. He took this moment to jump back in his car and back out of the dope hole as fast as he could. Shleby and Alexa stood there screaming as he left. I went right back to my dope.

Alexa sat down and had a complete breakdown until Candy gave her a hit of her crack stem. That calmed her down. The Fatman showed up and her and Shelby and Nature and Candy took off quick. Fatman only sold coke. Me and Tommy needed dope.

It was still early. Before seven am. We sat back to wait. Tommy was my road dog. If I was one step from homelessness Tommy he was three. I was living in my girls apartment. Tommy still had an apartment AND a car. A sick ass 69 Nova. I always though it's only a matter of time till he sells it, I would have. But Tommy hung onto it. He loved his car. I think it was the fact that he still had it made him feel less like a junkie.

" You having fun?" I asked him.

"What do you mean? Time of my life." Tommy said full of sarcasim.

"No I mean it man. Strange as it sounds. I'm have the best time I ever had."

"That's not how it looks."

"How's it look?"

"Like you fell from grace. You see Fatman over there?" Tommy pointed at Fatman.

Fatman was standing next to his car. The cokeheads were four deep all around him holding out money.

"That used to be you."

"Except skinny."

"No I mean it. You used to be on top, no habit, making money. Now you are just another one of the junkies."

"I'll be back on top. That's what I'm trying to tell you. This whole thing is like one big adventure for me. Life on the street is always one step in front of death on the street. Every day it's a challenge on ten different fronts. Copping dope, staying well, mugging fools, not getting ripped off, not getting busted, watching my chick, watching fools watch my chick. Even the getting sick part. It's all places I never been."

"You didn't like it better on top?" Tommy asked.

"Better?' I don't know. Different for sure. Everything happens on the street. Anything I can think of. I've made a serious

relationship with the monkey on my back. It's King Kong. And he's a comedian. Laughing at me all day long."
"You like it this way?"
"It's ok for now. Kind of exciting not knowing what's coming next." I said and I meant it.
Tommy pondered this for a moment.
"I'm not having as much fun as you. I must be in a transitional period."
"That's gotta be it." I liked Tommy a ton. He was my road dog, my partner. And living on the streets or damn near it's good to have at least one friend you can trust.
"Look who's here." Tommy said. Across the dopehole we could see Dimebag pull in with Sydney his girl riding shotgun.
"He's such a piece of shit." I said.
"Didn't you guys used to be friends?"
"Yeah but we aint really friends no more. Soon as he found out I was shooting dope he cut me loose."
Dimebag got out of his car.
"SHOPS OPEN. LINE IT UP." Junkies came out of every corner and lined up. Everyone wants their wake up. It's the most exciting part of a junkies day. Dimebag always makes everyone stand in a line. Makes him feel important.
"Lets go. I gotta hurry back. Stacey's probably shaking bad by now."
Me and Tommy got up and started walking over to Dimebag. There was about ten junkies waiting to get served. Fatman was just finishing up with his last customer. He was smoking a blunt leaning next to his car watching Dimebag. This street urchin local girl named Easy started walking towards the line which wouldn't have bothered me at all except she was about eight months pregnant. She looked like she had just crawled out from under a car. Normally I wouldn't try to stop anyone from getting high, but she had a kid inside her. It just aint right. Easy didn't care about that kid.
Me, Tommy and Easy all reached Dimebag at the same time. Dimebag motioned for Easy to step up.
"What you need?" Dimebag asked Easy.

"Nothing. She don't need shit." I said. I turned to Easy. "Beat it. Don't let me see you here again. Not till you pop out that kid."
"What? Who the hell you think you are? My dad? Well you AINT my dad. And if you were my dad you would be waiting for me to bring this home so you could get loaded and bang me." Easy was way hard from the street.
"BEAT IT!" I yelled.
"YOU BEAT IT!" She yelled back.
We were face to face. Brave little girl all eighty pounds of her. Dope will give you nerve you never thought you had. Dimebag stepped up.
"Woah woah woah. Wait a second honey hold up. Hey man who the hell you think you are? The Mayor or something? She wants to get high that's her business."
"She's pregnant." I said.
"I can see that man. If she don't care why should I? Come here Darling. How much you need?"
I had exactly as much of this sleaze bag that I could take. I blasted him with a right. I was amazed he was still standing. I grabbed him by his coat. Tommy stood up right next to me about to rifle Dimebag's pockets.
"Let him go." Fatman said with authority.
Fatman stood up off his car.
"Let him go why? Cause your Big?" I asked him while I held onto Dimebag.
"Nah cuz I got a neener. Let him go Holmes."
Fatman lifted up his jacket to reveal a nine millimeter Pistol.
Soon as I saw the gun I let him go. All the junkies took off running in every direction. No one wants to get shot.
"You're done man. I aint serving you." Dimebag said. He was very pissed off.
"Yeah you are. GIMME SIX FOR FIVE." I said.
"NOW, ME TOO." Tommy said.
Dimebag looked at Fatman who nodded yes, do it.
"Ok You want six for five? Give me the money." I handed my five twenties and took my six balloons. Tommy did the same. I turned to Tommy's car.
"Gimme a ride?"

"Yeah."
I turned back to Dimebag.
"Better not serve that girl."
"Hurry home to your little junkie girl scumbag. You're just another one of the junkies now."
If I wasn't in a rush I would have run back and blasted him again. That and the fact that Fatman would have shot me prevented me from doing that.
Tommy dropped me off right in front of my place.
I hit those stairs climbing them three at a time and making a hell of a racket. I am sure Stacey heard me coming up the stairs cause when I walked in she was putting cups of water on the table. That's how we started our day every day. Her putting the water on the table saying 'Good Morning' very sarcastically cause we were so screwed up and it was always anything but a good morning.
"Good morning."
"It's about to be." I said as I threw the balloons on the table. Stacey ripped into one and put it in the spoon. She added water and looked at the spoon a little perplexed. She then lit a lighter underneath it and got a look of complete horror on her face.
"Its Fake. David IT'S FAKE."
I stuck my finger in the spoon and tasted it. Sugar. Nothing but sugar.
"That piece of shit is DEAD."
Stacey immediately fell into a fetal position on the floor. I got up and grabbed a pistol I had. It really was a piece of shit. A beat up Saturday night special that I got for fifty bucks. I turned back and Stacey was holding her sides rocking back and forth.
"What are we gonna do? That was all our money. I'm sick. What are we gonna do?"
Stacey was going into panic mode. I had to calm her down. I put the gun on the table and sat on the floor next to her.
"It's gonna be ok."
"What are you gonna do?"
"I'm gonna fix it."
"How? How you gonna fix it? Lets just stop. We can stop."

That was bullshit. There is no way two junkies living together can stop.

"You now I can't let him get away with this." I said. I meant it. It was the principal of the thing. I'm not getting ripped of by anyone.

Stacey went into complete hysteria.

"What if some thing happens? What if you get busted? Or Killed."

"No ones getting killed."

"I've got a bad feeling."

"A bad feeling like what."

She didn't want to say it. I looked her in the eye.

"Like I might not see you again."

"That's not gonna happen."

"Remember what the Santeria lady said at the bodega?"

"The Santeria lady at the bodega is insane."

"No she's not. She can see shit."

"Tell me one thing that lady said was gonna happen, that really happened."

"What about Mario?" Stacey asked.

"What about Mario?"

"She said he was gonna die at that reading."

"Predicting some junkie is going to die is NOT predicting the future."

I held her in my arms and rocked her till she sort of relaxed.

"I gotta go." I said real quietly. She nodded yes and I grabbed her stuffed bear, Mr. Bugsy.

"Hold onto Mr. Bugsy till I get back." She took the bear and curled up on the floor. I grabbed the pistol and went out the door.

I hit the stairs hard banging down every flight, kicked the front door open and hit the street running. The anxiety and desperation had taken me over. I was running on pure adrenalin. I turned the corner and Dimebag was a few blocks over still selling dope. It took him a minute to see me then he took off running and jumped in his car and peeled out. I chased him but there was no way I was going to catch him on foot. I still kept running. There was nothing else to do.

I ran for about six blocks. I had an idea where he might be going. I stopped to catch my breath and I heard Tommys car. AWESOME.

"Get in." Tommy said as he opened the door for me.

I jumped in Tommys car and he peeled out.

"Son of a bitch sold me sugar."

"Me too." I was out of breath from running. "You know where he's going?"

"I got a good idea. Daytime spot just opened."

"Let's get this skizazz."

Tommy floored it. He was pissed. No one likes getting burned. Especially when you got a habit.

He pulled up to a spot that I had only been to a few times. I stopped going there because I had robbed a few junkies here in the past and I didn't want to keep going there.

"This is where he goes when the Dominicans are out. I called them and they wont serve him now so he will have to come here. You know he has to re up."

"Yes he does." I said.

"You been here before?" Tommy asked me.

"Yeah. A long time ago."

"Theres a hole in the wall over there. You go wait in that and I will wait here. He's got to come out one of these tow ways."

"Coo."

I got out of the car and Tommy slowly went around the block. About ten feet from the door way was hole in the wall that one man could fit in. I got in there and waited. I sat and thought about how far gone I was, how far my little girl was. Just two hoping to die dope fiends that have no hope of getting out of this situation together, not alive anyway. It's like ping pong. Whenever I wanted to quit Stacey wanted to get high, or the other way around.

Just when I was about to give up and go find Tommy, Dimebag pulled up. I watched him get out of his car and talk to the guy at the door who let him slip right inside, must be dealer courtesy.

In about six minutes Dimebag walked out of the door and slipped the doorman some bills and started walking my way. Soon as he reached me I jumped out of the hole in the wall

and blasted him hard as I could in the face. He went to the ground dazed and I jumped on him and started rifling his pockets. There were some junkies on the street but no one got involved. No one ever gets involved.
"What is wrong with you? You are so screwed up." Dimebag said.
"I'M SCREWED UP? YOU'RE SCREWED UP. YOU RIP ME OFF?"
"YOU SHOULDN'T HAVE HIT ME."
I kept rifling Dimebags pockets and grabbed his bindles and a wad of cash. He punched me in the face twice and I stared bleeding from my mouth and nose. Dimebag outweighed me by a hundred pounds but I was on top..
"YOU KNOW WHAT?"
I took out my gun and put it to his head. Dimebag froze.
"You sure you wanna do that?" He said.
I hesitated a moment then took the gun and put the muzzle against his thigh and shot it grazing him. He used to be my friend so I didn't want to kill him, I just didn't want him chasing me.
Tommy came screeching up to where we were. A crowd was starting to gather to watch the action.
"COME ON BROTHER. WE GOTTA GO. COPS WILL BE HERE."
"YOU'RE DONE. FINISHED. IF YOU THINK YOU ARE GETTING AWAY WITH THIS YOU'RE NOT."
Tommy revved the engine and opened my door.
I jumped off Dimebag and left him laying there. I had his dope and his money. Three bindles of ten packets each and five hundred dollars in twenties.
I could hear sirens approaching in the distance.
"TIME TO GO BROTHER." Tommy revved the engine again.
I stayed low and jumped into Tommy's car and he peeled off. I gave Tommy one of the bindles and kept two.
"That was close."
"Too close. Drop me off a few blocks from my house. I'll walk the rest. Come in the back way."
I figured the best thing was to get out of Tommys car and let him get home. I would go around the back of the building and

come up the fire escape. Tommy pulled over. We both looked all around.

"Careful with that shit D. Now it's straight from the source. Dimebag would have stepped on three times. I don't wanna go to your funeral."

I started to get out and stopped and looked back at Tommy.

"Thanks Brother. You saved the day." Tommy nodded and I jumped out of the car and hoofed it back to my house, looking all around the whole way, paranoid as hell. I got to the back of the building and climbed up the fires escape and crawled in the window.

Stacey was asleep on the floor exactly where I left her. I nudged her shoulder and she woke up.

"D? You're back?"

"Told you I'd be back."

"How'd it go?"

"Piece of cake." I helped her off the floor and put the bindles on the table. She ripped into one and started fixing. I put my gun back in the dresser and sat down to fix.

"I saw Dimebag." I said.

"Hows he doing."

"I don't know. Ok I guess. He's got a limp now." Stacey didn't need to know all the details. She put a filter in her spoon and drew up about sixty cc's into her syringe. I watched her fix in a rush like a little fiend and I felt so sad. We had become two monsters. I became a real junkie in that New York City apartment. Sometimes we wouldn't eat or shit for weeks. You don't have to when you are on a liquid diet. I didn't know it then, but that apartment was the last time I paid rent or lived in doors for a few years.

Stacey couldn't find a vein. She kept poking herself over and over in frustration.

"You're not getting it." I put my hands on hers to slow her down. She pulled the needle out and held it up.

"Help me."

I took the syringe and grabbed her arm. She was so skinny I could her whole bicep in my hand and squeeze it hard enough. I stuck the needle in and got a vein pretty quickly. I let her go and she backed up and gently took the needle from me.

"Go slow. Feel it first. It's probably stronger than usual." I said.

Stacey slowly pushed in the syringe full of dope. She leaned back in her chair and her eyes rolled up in her head and she fell off the chair hitting the ground with a thud.

"Stacey?"

I immediately starting to do what I thought was CPR, which was all out of synch and not how it's done I'm sure. I started blowing air in her, slapping her and she wouldn't move. I listened for a heart beat and I couldn't hear anything. I jumped up and got some ice from the fridge and put it in her pajamas. My brain started imagining how I was going to get out of this. A million thoughts a second are flying through my head all screaming that I have to save her. I started shaking her violently, stopping to blow air in her mouth, push on her chest, then shake her some more. Right when I thought I lost her, she opened her eyes and caught breath. I was overcome with joy and hugged her hard. She was way out of it from doing such a big hit.

"You're hurting me." She said in a daze.

I let her go and helped her into the chair.

"Why am I all wet?"

"You O D'd. I thought you were dead. I put ice on you to wake you up."

"What are we gonna do David? We're fucked up bad." She said as she started to cry.

"We're gonna kick this shit. You'll see. We can do it." I lied.

But we couldn't do it. Not together anyway. Shortly after that I came home one day from running around all day and there was a note from Stacey. As soon as I got inside I knew she had left. All her stuff was gone. I walked over and picked up the note and read it:

David

Listen I really really love you but I just can't do this anymore. My Aunt came to get me and she is taking me to a rehab up state. Don't try to contact me my family won't let you anyway.

There is a few days left on the rent for this month but then my cousins will show up to throw you out. So you got to leave by the first.
Don't be mad. I love you. We just can't get out of this together. You know I'm right.
Love Stacey

Stacey was right and I knew it.
I sat down like I had the wind kicked out of me. I looked around and saw that I didn't really have any possessions. Just some ratty clothes and my works, which I threw in a bag. I took one last look around and left. I didn't have a clue where I was going, I just knew I couldn't stay there. I headed to the Greyhound bus station and left New York that night. I called a girl in Miami I used to get high with named Jeannie. She was still getting high and had a place I could crash in. For forty eight dollars I took the next Greyhound South. I only thought about getting high. It was kind of scary.
I was at the beginning of a very long, very hard journey. I just didn't know how it was going to end.

36

I had been riding the bus for about eight hours and had been in the bathroom ten times to fix dope. I left NYC with a good bit of China White and I was going to try to make it last all the way to Florida. Lucky for me the bus was not crowded and most of the folks were sitting near the front. The bus driver kept looking in his rear view mirror and giving me stink eye every time I got out of the bathroom. I rubbed my stomach and made it look like I was sick, but I am sure he didn't believe that.
I was calling Jeannie from a pay phone at almost every stop. It was a local bus so it made a hell of a lot of stops. She was excited for me to come back and I was excited to be there. I had absolutely nothing except a habit, the clothes on my

back, what was in my bag and about $468 dollars. I figured I would get home, shack up with Jeannie and regroup.
The bus drove all night and in the morning we pulled into the station in Norfolk Virginia and the driver stood up and faced the passengers.
"Meal stop. Two hours. Be back or I'll leave with out you." He then stood at the door on the sidewalk helping every one out. I was the last one out. I looked like hell.
"You ok?"
"Yes Sir." Older guys always like being called Sir. Makes them feel important.
"You been in and out of the bathroom the whole ride. You sure you're ok." He eyed me suspiciously.
"Yes SIR." I said as I high tailed it out of there. I went over to the bathroom in the station, went in a stall and shot up in there. I came out feeling all right and I found a pay phone to call Jeannie. It rang a lot. She usually picked it up quick. Just as I was about to hang up I heard someone answer.
"Hello?"
It was Jeannie's mom. I INSTANTLY knew the jig is up.
"Hello Mrs. Walker. This is David, DL, remember me? Is Jeannie there?"
"Yes I remember you and no she is not here."
"Do you know where she is or when she is getting back?"
Yes I do. Jeannie went to rehab this morning."
"Why would she do that?" I played dumb.
"All the drug use DL. All the lying DL. I put her in there myself. And she won't be back too soon. I know you are on the way here and I am taking the time to tell you there is nowhere to come to. God Bless you DL and good luck." She hung up the phone and heard a dial tone. I
looked out into the station and there were people everywhere starting their day. The newspaper stand was opening, janitors were mopping the floors, business as usual.
I looked around and felt absolutely alone in the world. I was at a crossroads again in my life, one of many with nothing but a dope habit.
I walked over to the map on the wall and looked at exactly where I was. I was right near I-40 which cuts across the

middle of the country. I-10 runs through Texas which I had already done a few times already in my life. I didn't have enough dope to get to California, not with the habit I had. But now there was nowhere to go in Florida. A lot of my friends and family were there who had not seen my demise so I made a decision to get on a different bus and head West.
I had no idea what I would do when I got there. I figured I would take smaller hits and make the dope I had last for the journey. From where I was it was going to take another two days and nights to get to California.
One thing for sure, Heroin was very rare in Florida. I never saw it growing up. That was another reason I didn't continue on to Florida. Heroin was good and readily available on the West Coast so that's where I went. The pull of dope is that strong. Strong enough to change any plans as long as it has a hold on you. It had a hold on me.
I changed my ticket and two hours later I was on a different bus heading back to 'Points West'.

37

I was in the last three seats of the bus as it pulled into a station. It came to a jarring stop.
"Breakfast stop....two hours." The driver told everyone on the bus. I looked out the window at the town we had just pulled into and there wasn't a lot going on. I got up and walked off the bus, as usual I was the last one getting off. The driver was used to this.
"Where are we?" I asked the driver.
"Albuquerque New Mexico." I saw two taxis at a taxi stand and I took off towards them. The driver called out.
"We're only staying two hours here. Not two hours and two minutes. If you aint back, I'm leaving you."
"Yes Sir. Got it."
I took off running to the taxi in the front of the line and jumped in. He looked at me in his rear view mirror. I must

have looked pretty bad because he did a double take then he turned around.

"Where you wanna go?" He asked me in a thick Mexican accent.

"Take me to the worst part of town." I said.

"What?"

"Take me to where the poor people live. Take me to the projects, the mission. There has to be a place in this town where they are giving away free food and shit to the poor folks. Take me there"

He looked at me like I was crazy.

"You got money?"

I threw a twenty dollar bill on the front seat.

"This should cover the way there."

He grabbed the twenty and took off. The town was really quiet at six am, or maybe it was quiet all the time, I couldn't tell. All I knew was I had about one more hit of dope and then I would be out, with another day to travel to California. That's not good. Jonesing bad on the bus was not an exciting concept. I had to get some dope.

I had two hours to find some dope and I don't know anyone. That didn't matter. A junkie will always find his stuff. You know why? Cause It's EVERYWHERE.

As he drove through town I could see the streets getting poorer and poorer. He pulled over where there were a few street dealers standing in front of a dilapidated house that was all boarded up.

"This what you had in mind?"

"Exactly." The meter read Eighteen dollars. I held up a Fifty dollar bill and ripped it in half. I gave him half of the bill.

"Listen. I need you to wait right here. I won't be long. Then I gotta get back to the bus station. When we get back I will give you the other half of this bill. From the looks of the meter, that will be like a thirty dollar tip. Deal?"

He took the ripped half, not too happily though.

"Si mon. I wait right here."

I jumped out of the taxi and walked up to the first guy I saw.

"What you need ese?" He asked me.

"Dope. Chiva."

"You a cop?"
"No."
"You got tracks?"
I pulled up my sleeve and showed him some fresh tracks. He relaxed a little.
"How much you want?"
"How much is a gram?"
"Hundred."
"That's a little steep. How much for three grams?"
"You got money ese?"
I pulled out what was left of my wad of cash. I had about four hundred dollars left. Didn't matter though. I would buy dope over anything else, even food.
"You buy three grams I drop the price twenty each so that makes two forty. You got two forty Weddo?"
I counted it out and held the two forty up.
"Give it here."
"Not until the dope is in my hand and I know it's real. And we gotta hurry. I got a taxi waiting."
"My name is Carlito."
"Lets go." I said.
 We walked to a pay phone and he called his connection. They spoke in Spanish and he set up a meet. We walked about three blocks and there was a short Mexican dealer waiting on a corner. We walked up to him.
"Give me the money ese." I pulled it out.
"Let's see the dope."
 The spoke in Spanish and the short guy took three balloons out of his mouth.
"Open one."
They spoke in Spanish again and the dealer ripped one open and held it out to me. It smelled exactly like the Mexican tar Heroin I had done a few times in my life. I was over joyed. There is no relief like the relief of knowing you are about to get well. I grabbed the balloons and gave the dealer his money and he took off quickly. I took off in the direction I came. The dealer followed right behind me.
"Where you gonna go now ese?"
"Back to my taxi."

"Don't you wanna fix ese? I know you wanna fix. I got a spot you can fix in."

I stopped in my tracks. Yes I wanted to fix. Soon as that dope was in my hand I wanted to fix. However sick or well I was feeling before I got the dope went away and only anxiety is left. The only way that goes away is to shoot some dope.

I felt a calm reserve now because I had dope. I didn't want to miss the bus, but I figured I had enough time to fix before I got back, then I wouldn't have to try to shoot up in that moving bus bathroom, which was always a nightmare trying to hit a vein while the bus is moving. I figured I would take a chance.

"How much?" I already knew the answer.

"Not much. You just gotta give me a little bit. Like a twenty."

"Let's go." I said. I was on a mission. Carlito had trouble keeping up with me.

We got back to the dilapidated, boarded up house and he walked around the back. And I followed him. We slipped in the house through a broken window.

This was the first shooting gallery I had ever been in. There were about ten people inside, some sleeping, some fixing, some scraping crack stems.

"Better hurry. The cops come cruising around here after breakfast." Carlito said.

I took out the balloon the dealer ripped open and took off a little piece for Carlito. He immediately took out his works and started fixing. Everyone in the house was checking me out. Probably thinking if I was worth trying to rob. I guess they figured I would fight back because everyone stayed focused on the scraping or smoking or shooting they were already involved in.

I knew I had to get back or I would miss the bus so I worked fast. The dope was super strong and as soon as I shot it I could feel myself falling out. I held on till it passed knowing if I pass out inside this shooting gallery I might never get out alive. I came to with Carlito eyeing me closely.

"You ok ese? You almost fell out."

"Yeah I'm fine."

I grabbed my works and quickly exited the house. I ran over to the taxi who was still waiting.
"I almost left you Holmes." I held up the other half of the fifty dollar bill.
"Then you wouldn't have gotten this. Let's go."
The taxi driver took off and within minutes I was back at the station. Almost everyone was back on the bus. I ran up and got in line. The driver looked at me suspiciously.
"Almost left you. Didn't think you was gonna make it back."
"Thank you for waiting sir." I said as I jumped up the stairs. I know he didn't wait for me, but guys like that always like being called sir. And I needed to stay on his good side. Or at least not get on his bad side.
The rest of the ride wasn't so bad, besides the smell of the bathroom, which got worse and worse every mile. I stayed loaded until we pulled into the station on seventh and Market street in San Francisco.
I got out of the bus and looked around. The city has an exciting vibrant feeling. It's totally alive, even if I was half dead. I knew what I was doing. I knew where I was going. I started walking to the mission.

38

"I guess that's it." I said to myself. I was sitting in a doorway in an alley off Howard street in San Francisco fixing dope. I had been in the city for a few days and I was just bumming around the mission, using up the last of my dope. Trying to figure a scam, maybe something to steal.
Howard is in between Mission and South Van Ness. Valencia street is on the other side of mission boulevard. The dope dealers cruised up and down Mission and the hookers cruise up and down Howard street. This all went on between fifteenth street and twentieth street. Six blocks. Six by four. That's where all the action was.
They were selling dope in the tenderloin but that was way more populated, a lot more cops. I felt more at home in the

mission. Every now and then I went up to the Haight to see what was going on, mostly just to get out of the mission when it got too hot for me. The Haight was about Hippies, weed and Psychadelic drugs like acid and mushrooms. There were tons of runaways in the Haight so the competition was fierce to be a street dealer. It was way mellower in the mission.

I cleaned my spoon with my filter and drew up the last bit of dope I had and looked at the syringe. Forty cc's. Not much. And it wasn't too brown anymore meaning it was mostly water. Didn't matter though. I was getting as addicted to shooting up as I was to the dope I was shooting. It's bad when you are addicted to the needle. You find yourself shooting water.

I shot my last shot, cleaned my works and walked out of there. I walked over to the gas station on the corner of nineteenth and South Van Ness. It was about nine at night. People were coming in and out buying goods, getting gas. Normal people. I felt anything but normal. I reached in my pocket and pulled out what I had, Forty eight cents. At that moment I felt more alone on this earth than I had ever felt before. I just sat there bumming out. People would look at me as they went in and out of the store, but I didn't care. I was done. I had nowhere to go, no one to help me, just me and the clothes on my back. There was no one left to call. I had finally run my course. I was across the country with no dope no home and nothing but a big habit. I was just spacing out and I heard someone talk to me.

"Que onda ese we?" A young Mexican kid in his early twenties walked up to me. I was dirty homeless and I smelled. He was dressed real clean with some cowboy boots on and his hair slicked back.

"Wass a matter white boy? What you need?" I looked at him he seemed genuinely concerned.

"I just want a cigarette." I didn't even smoke cigarettes but it's what I felt like having. Smoke. And I couldn't imagine asking this guy for money. He hopped up and went in the store and came out with a pack of cigarettes and a lighter and gave them to me.

He sat down next to me and stuck out his hand.

"Mi amo Jose." I shook his hand.
"My name is David."
"You like chiva?" He must have been a mind reader. Although it was not too hard to see that I was just a down and out junkie.
"Yes." He gave me a piece of paper with his number on it and a quarter gram of dope.
" I don't have any money."
"I know that Weddo. You gonna work for me. You stand on mission and when a junkie comes by to get Chiva you call me and I meet you. Ok?"
"OK."
"You start tomorrow. Ten to ten. Call me in the morning for your wake up."
I couldn't believe it. I was in shock. I walked right back to the doorway and shot up again. Then I fell asleep in that doorway. There was other homeless people around so I didn't feel so bad. I was officially an outside dweller. Just another one of the homeless vagrants, but at least I had some dope, and a connection. Things were looking up.

39

San Francisco is probably the best place in the country to be homeless. They really cater to the Homeless community. If you had it really together you were getting two hundred and ten dollars twice a month in food stamps, about three hundred twenty five dollars in cash and a hotel to stay in for the first ten days of every month. I did not have it together. This was to help you get back on your feet.
To get that deal you had to wait in this huge line around this big building in between Market and Mission street under the highway. The building always had a huge line going all the way around it. I never waited in that line. I didn't have any patience. I had grown accustomed to sleeping ANYWHERE. Being homeless is an art, and I hadn't learned it yet. I was taking a crash course. More like a hands on approach. You

don't choose to become homeless, it sort of just happens. At least with me it did. I chose to not pay rent. I chose to keep getting high.

I would sleep on any sidewalk, in any doorway, where ever, sometimes in an abandoned car when I could find one. And that was when I finally laid my head down to really sleep which was about every three or four days. I would be walking the streets barely holding myself up. Kind of almost falling down over and over with each step, pushing your foot in front of you to catch yourself. When I finally did collapse on the sidewalk, or in a doorway and wake up with business people walking to work they would be stepping over me as if I wasn't even there. Or countless times I would seek refuge in a hallway of an apartment house, only to be woken up by the tenant's foot kicking me off their doorstep in the morning.

I started shooting speedballs shortly after I got back to the city.. That's what most people did. I didn't like coke so much but I got addicted to the rush the coke gave me, as long as it had Heroin in it. That took the rush away as fast as it came. There was something romantic about it. John Belushi died on Speedballs. I love John Belushi. It must be cool. Or so I thought. It's not.

It's really hard to see these things happening to you, they sort of just happen and you are a not so innocent by stander. I had become a stone cold, homeless in and out of jail junkie.

I'm from Miami, and drugs are in my culture, so I absolutely got it together quick. I would wake up, call Jose and get my quarter gram to start my day, shoot that then walk up and down Mission boulevard and middle dope deals. I never ripped anyone off so I had many return customers. I also sold decent size quarters, so people kept coming back, or would be waiting for me upon my return from the last meet. I was calling Jose forty to sixty times a day and shooting up every time. Every customer had to give me a little. I was like a pin cushion, shooting dope forty times day.

There was a shooting gallery on nineteenth and mission above a Mexican Restaurant. You walked through an alley on the street then up stairs. The place had three rooms and a kitchen. A guy named Al and a guy named Derek ran the place. There was a hooker named Blue that had a room there and shared it with her boyfriend Stewart. The entire apartment was virtually empty except for a bunch of mattresses on the floors. And Al had a desk.

The place always had junkies in it shooting or smoking dope, or smoking crack. If you had nowhere's to go, you paid a little tax and you could find refuge there and do your drugs.

Al was a violent loser who demanded dope the second you walked in the door, and if you didn't finish yours before he did he came out of his room and tried to tax you again.

Derek was a total scumbag ripping off anyone he came in contact with. These guys would sit with a pen and a piece of blotter paper from a desk, perforate it and patiently write on a hundred small designs so it looked like a sheet of acid. Then go to the Haight and sell it for four hundred dollars. That was like their best scam.

After about a month on the street I was not only jonesing every minute of every day for dope, I started jonesing to live inside. I had been living outside, getting kicked out of countless doorways and it was getting old. And it started turning from summer to fall and the rain came it made it worse. Life was just plain hard. I had to get inside. I made a deal to split the room with the hooker Blue and her boyfriend.

So the first place I paid rent in a very long time was a shooting gallery with a hooker and her boyfriend. And she was always making us wait outside the room when she was turning tricks.

"How do you let he do it?" I asked Stewart one time when we were waiting while she turned a trick.

"She pays the rent." He said very non chalant. He was kind of slow. She was definitely in charge of their situation. I looked out the window and the rain was really coming down hard and I felt nothing but relief that I had an indoor place to live in. Which was cool for three days. As soon as Al and Derek found out I was staying there and they weren't getting paid and I was back on the street.

40

"Where you staying?" Indio asked me. I started running around with a guy named Indio who was actually from Indio California. You can't run alone on the street for two long. You need someone to watch your back, to have dope when you don't have it and vice versa, someone to think up and do scams with. Too many predators, prison issue killers that only used jail as a revolving door to get rested up and then hit the streets harder than when they left. Indio was my road dog for my first year on the street.
"Aint got no place. I been moving from doorway to doorway."
"Come on." He took off and I followed behind him. He talked as he walked.
"You gotta get it together or your gonna die out here. You are doing all the dope you get. Never re-upping. How you think you gonna come up? You aint coming up that way. You gotta cut back your habit and try to get a little ahead. That way you buy a gram and sell your own quarters. Not Jose's. That way you can make eight quarters instead of four."
Indio was real good at living on the street. We walked to Potrero hill to a big furniture store.
"Come on we gotta go around back." Indio said.
"For what?"
Indio looked at me like an idiot that I hadn't figured out why we are here.
"So we can get you a box."
"For what?"
"So you can live in it holmes."
We went around back and there was a pile of cardboard boxes that sofas and love seats came in. Indio grabbed the biggest one and folded it flat so we could carry it easily.
"Come on."
We walked to an empty lot off of eighteenth and South Van Ness. It was a cardboard box neighborhood. I set up my box next to Indio and crawled inside. It was not much bigger than me. We had positioned it under a tree to protect it from the rain. That was my first out door dwelling. I shot some dope

and went to sleep in my cardboard box. It was in the shape of a triangle, which was good because the rain ran off it instead of being caught on top. I couldn't move around much though. I didn't want to damage my box.

I lived in that lot for about two months until one night I came back and the city had cleaned the entire lot throwing everyone's homeless homes away. Everybody who lived there was scavenging around to see if they could find their belongings. Night was coming and I was cold, I knew I had to find a place to stay. I walked to Al and Dereks shooting gallery and they weren't there. Only that Hooker Blue and her Boyfriend Stewart were there. I negotiated a deal with them to split their room for a quarter a day. That's like twenty bucks. When Al and Derek came back it was a big argument that Blue won and I got to stay. Al and Derek weren't too happy about it but they needed Blues money to help cover the rent and she had negotiated a deal with me which she was planning on keeping. So now I had a mattress on the floor in her room. Things were once again looking up.

The first time I overdosed was in that house. I was in the kitchen fixing with about seven other junkies and I fell out.

"Better save him." I heard one of the junkies say, then turned he back to his works.

"Yeah or else the cops will clean this place out." Said another.

Derek and Al picked me up and put cold water on my wrists and neck which revived me.

"Better not do that again." Al said.

"Yeah. Next time we won't save you."

Blue and Stewart helped me to our room.

"What happened?" I asked still kind of foggy.

"You fell out. You didn't go into convulsions, probably cause you didn't have too much coke in it. Derek and Al don't want no one dying here so they picked you up and put water on your hands and wrists."

"Why?"

"Cause for some reason that wakes you up. If it's real bad they would have put a bunch of ice on your balls."

"Thank God it wasn't real bad. At least you weren't doing the fish." Stewart said.

"The fish?"
"Yeah. Flopping like a fish. Convulsions. When you are done flopping like a fish you are usually dead. When you O D on a speedball it's intense. First of all, when you wake up, if you wake up, all you remember is shooting up but, the rush has passed. So you think you got ripped off. Then your lungs fill with water and your bladder fills with blood"
I sat back and took all this in. I was totally wasted.
"Thank you." I said.
"If you really want to thank us you can give us some of your dope." Nothing was for free. I broke off a little piece. Then passed out on my mattress.

41

There was a Chinese Restaurant on the corner of sixteenth and mission on the west side of the block. Next to that was a donut shop that all the junkies hung out in. Then a laundry, an apartment building, then a food counter where all the main dealers hung out at. They supplied the street dealers. This was the place in the city to find Heroin so there was always traffic. And you had to keep moving. If you stood in one spot too long the cops would arrest you for vagrancy. So I would walk up and down the block from sixteenth to nineteenth and back. Walking the streets all day and all night. For days on end until I finally collapsed wherever I landed. Some people tried to save me but I was beyond saving.
I was sleeping in a doorway and I felt a nudge and I looked up and there was my father.
"Get up."
I got up and he looked at me with disgust. He had moved up to Petaluma and lived with my sister. We were never close. My sister and my dad were close. My mom and me are close. That's just how it was.
"l've been walking the streets for days looking for you."
"Why?'

"Cause you need help. You're a mess. You're mother is worried sick."

We walked down mission boulevard and he kept looking back at me in disbelief. I looked the part, just a homeless junkie. He walked up to the pay phone on sixteenth and mission. Just above the BART entrance. That's Bay Area Rapid Transit, the underground subway to Oakland and Berkeley. He picked up the phone and dialed a number.

"Reverse the charges." He said.

"Hello. Yeah I found him." He looked at me up and down.

"I'm looking right at him. This isn't going to end pretty." He held out the receiver to me.

"Here. It's your mother." I took the receiver. I hadn't spoken to my mom in months. I started crying instantly.

" Hi mom."

" My son. I miss you. I love you."

" I love you mom."

"I had your chart read." My Mom believes in the stars for real. She goes to this old lady who reads the stars and makes a chart according to what they say. Like fortune telling.

"And?"

"And it says you are in it deep. Whatever it is you are in. It says you have been in it for six months and you have two and a half years to go. If you can just stay alive, which apparently is going to be hard. If you can just stay alive for that amount of time she says everything will work out after that. I would help you if I could. I love you so much. But the only person who can help you is you. Please remember I love you. Good luck." She hung up the phone.

"Well?"

"She says I'm in it deep."

"That's obvious. Why don't you come back with me?" I thought about it for a minute.

"I can't. I'm too screwed up. I won't stay there. I gotta play this out."

I wasn't in despair in my mind, even though it looked like I was in despair. It was all an adventure for real for me. Somehow in the back of my mind I knew I was going to come out of this one day. I was just getting high for now.

My dad walked with me and bought me a pair of sneakers. The ones I was wearing had the toes cut out so my feet could fit inside. I got them free from the Salvation army. My dad couldn't stand it me looking like this. Dirty, smelly, one set of clothes. After we got the shoes he gave me about a hundred dollars and got in his car and left. I watched him go and then went and copped dope with the money. I didn't seem him again for a very long time.

42

"SPEEDBALL EXPRESS TAKING OFF." I screamed as I walked down the block to fix. I was breaking a can in half to use a spoon as I said it. I was way out of control. Junkies are always looking for someone to fix with. It can be a very social drug. Indio linked up with me he had coke and I had dope. That's how we usually rolled, both splitting with each other.
A blonde hooker named Sarah decided to come with us. Her loser boyfriend Josh would wait on mission while she turned tricks on Howard street.
"Where's Josh?" I asked her.
"I don't know. He went up to nob hill to shoplift and I haven't heard from him all day. I hope he didin't get busted." I was sure he did.
Sarah was a normal girl, real good looking, just worn out. Dope will take control if you let it in your life. She was like a secretary or something before this. Now she was selling blowjobs for twenty bucks and a piece of ass for forty just to get high.
We crossed sixteenth and went into the alley between Mission and Valencia. This was one of our favorite fixing spots. There was also a parking structure that worked well across the street when this was too crowded.
We set up or works and Sarah held her syringe up looking at the color.
"Hit me in my neck."
"What? Are you crazy?" I had never even seen that before.

"Not at all. I don't have my hand mirror with me or I would do it myself. It's just like hitting another vein, except the rush is ten times faster."

"A hundred times faster." Indio said. "I'll do you and you do me." He said to Sarah as he took the syringe from her and plunged it into her neck. Soon as he pushed in the dope her eyes rolled back in her head and she would have fallen down if we hadn't have caught her.

"Wow. That was quick."

"Yep. She's out for a minute. Here." He held out his syringe. "Hit me."

I took Indio's syringe and hit him in his jugular vein and he almost puked. He stood there spitting for five minutes not able to talk. Sarah woke up from her rush.

"That was great. Want me to hit you in yours?"

"No thanks. Not that I don't trust you but I don't trust you. If anyone hits me in my neck it will be me."

"Suit yourself. You want a blowjob for another fix?"

"No thanks. I'm good." I knew Josh. Didn't seem right.

" I do." Indio said as he unzipped his fly. Sarah got on her knees and I split. Leave these two lovebirds alone.

About a month later Sarah made a bad mistake and got in a car with four guys. That is not what any hooker should do. One trick at a time is a general rule. She thought she was going to make some real cash but instead she got gang raped and stabbed and left for dead. She became another casualty of the street.

The four dudes got caught with the bloody knife in their car the next day. It was a stolen car and when they got stopped the bloody knife was found with some of Sarah's clothes and the jig was up. The beat cops that walked the mission knew everyone walking the streets and they took it personally. After arresting Sarah and Josh over and over they got to know them as they did everyone on the street, and felt a little protective of the neighborhood, even the vagrants. I never saw Sarah or Josh after she got out of the Hospital. I think they went back to the Midwest or somewhere. They were lucky to get out alive.

I started carrying my own hand mirror and shooting myself in my own jugular vein after that. The rush was amazing. I was walking around with four rows of track marks on my neck. I had lost about thirty pounds. I used to look at my reflection in storefronts and swing my arms and think 'I look like a scarecrow.' Didn't bother me though. Not much did.

43

I felt something wet on my face. I had found a hallway that was open and I slipped inside late that night and fell asleep. I wiped it off and I felt it again. I looked up and one of the tenants was dropping water on me from a cooking pot. Soon as I looked up at him he dumped the whole pot of cold water on me.
"GET OUT." He yelled as he ran back into his door and locked it behind him. Starting another beautiful day. I walked out of the hallway and headed towards sixteenth. First things first I gotta do my wake up, so I had to find a spot to do it. I walked over to the parking structure in between Valencia and Mission and went up to the second level. I broke out my works and started fixing. I looked over and there were some Mexican ladies who were watching me. The second level of the structure was at the same height as the first floor apartments and they were watching me in horror. I ignored them and kept fixing. I had saved some dope and coke from the night before for my wake up. Jose wasn't always so eager to give me my first quarter free anymore so I had learned to save some. Without that wake up shot you are sick all day.
As soon as I shot it I knew I was done. The rush was coming on to strong and too fast. I threw the syringe as far away from me as I could and I walked over to a puddle and leaned down to put water on my wrist. Only problem was I kept going down. I watched the ground come up at me fast. The next thing I knew I was strapped to a gurney in an ambulance on the way to the hospital. I reached for my dope in my sock to

make sure it's still there and the paramedic grabbed it and threw it out the window.
"What did you do that for?"
"That's what almost killed you. That's why."
I would cough twice and on the third cough nothing but water would come out. They had put a catheter in my dick and there was a bag on the side of the gurney filling up with blood.
"You're lucky we got there in time. You would have died otherwise."
"You shoulda let me."
"That's not my job. My job is saving you. Apparently your job is killing you."
Wiseass. I stayed at the hospital for two days and then snuck out on the third night. The street was calling. I had to get back.
When you hit the street after two days gone everyone thinks you got arrested. Everyone stays away because they are paranoid. Having the plastic bracelet from the hospital eased them up. Nobody trusts anybody on the street.
I had found an abandoned building on Divisadero street by the park. It had a big fence around it that I would climb over then it had this brick pattern on it. Some of the bricks would stick out about two inches and I could scale up the wall and into the building.
There were other homeless people in there. In fact every room in the building was full. There was no electric or heat. As I walked down the hall there would be people fixing in every room. I only used this place to sleep, and only when I needed to. Finding a place to stay was always a challenge. It was good to have a few places all over the city cause you never know where you might end up on any given day. I shared that place with a skinny girl named Tanya. It was really her spot and she just let me crash there when I needed to.
We woke up one morning all curled up in a blanket because I felt something squirming next to me. I thought I was dreaming till I felt it again. We jumped up and saw a little mouse had crawled into our blanket looking for warmth.

"Imagine how brave that mouse was. To crawl in the bed with us."

"Or cold." Tanya said.

I opened the shade so a little light could come in. I went over to the sink and started fixing. Tanya started setting up her works next to me. We both shot dope in our neck, and we would look at our selves in the mirror while we did it.

I held my breath so my vein would bulge out and tried pushing the needle in. The syringe I had was so dull it wouldn't go in. I finally got it to go in my neck and now I was going back and forth trying to get the vein. The veins in my neck were so calloused and the needle was so dull that it was not working. I looked at Tanya's reflection one time and she was staring at me. I looked back at myself and pushed the syringe and the needle broke.

"Uh oh." Tanya said. There was half of the needle sticking out of my neck. I reached up to pull it out and my skin moved swallowing it up.

"Oh no." Tanya said with a look of horror in her face. I felt my neck and I couldn't feel the needle. I picked up another syringe and shot my 90 cc's of a speedball into it and put it in the other side of my neck. I got the vein the first time and sat down to rush.

"You're gonna die."

"No I'm not."

"Yeah you are if you don't get that needle out. You should go to the hospital now. Like right now."

"It aint that bad. I met a girl on the street that the same thing happened to and she said the doctor said there was nothing they could do about it."

"Listen. I don't care who you met. I am amazed you aint dead already. It must be stuck in the callous of your vein. That needle could dislodge and go shooting to your heart at like a hundred miles an hour."

"Cut the dramatics."

"I'm serious. You better go get that out before you drop dead."

I left the house and didn't think about it again. I went about my business and middled deals all day. I must have shot up

forty times that day. Just a normal day. When it got dark I went back to Tanya's.
"Did you go to the hospital?"
"No."
"Well I thought about it. You can't come in here till you get that needle out."
"Come on. Don't be like that."
" Nope. You can die at any minute. We talked about it when you were gone."
"Who's we?"
"Everyone here. You can drop dead at any minute and just cause you don't get it, we do. If you drop dead here then they will close this place for sure. We don't want to have to dispose of your body. You gotta go."
I knew if she wanted to she could get some of the other people living there to help her throw me out. She wasn't really my girlfriend or anything. We just shacked up together sometimes.
The hospital was across town so I walked there stopping in every nook and cranny to shoot up along the way. I figured I would hear what the doctor had to say. I was sure there was nothing they could do about it.
I walked into the emergency room and it was jam packed. Standing room only. And it was three in the morning. I waited in line to speak to the head nurse. I was about ten people back. Everyone was getting a number and being told to find a seat. Every seat in the place had some one sitting in it. It took about twenty minutes until it was my turn.
"What's your problem?" The nurse asked me.
"I got a needle stuck in my neck." She looked at me like I was joking, then she realized I wasn't.
"How did you do that?"
"I mixed up Heroin and Cocaine in a spoon, heated it, put in a filter and drew it up to stick in my jugular vein. The only problem was that the syringe was so old and dull that it broke when I tried to get a vein." Her mouth was stuck open.
"The only problem? Honey, you got more problems than that. ORDERLY!" As soon as she screamed orderly two guys came out wearing hospital scrubs.

"Take him to x-ray immediately." The two orderlies sat me down in a wheel chair and wheeled me away. They backed me inside and the nurse looked at me.
"You got insurance?"
"Homeless." I said.
"I'll send the social worker. NEXT."
They took me to x-ray and took pictures of my neck. After that a nurse came over put me right on an I'V drip.
"You really do have a needle in your neck." She said. "But don't you worry. Doctors gonna fix you right up. We have the best surgeons in the state."
"I gotta have surgery?"
"How else you think they gonna get that needle out? Magic? You just relax."
They put me on something in the IV because I started to mellow out. There were three doctors all younger than me looking at my x-rays. They were kind of arguing.
"I'm gonna do it." One said.
"No I am." Said another.
"You aren't even on schedule today."
I waited till there was a break and I looked at one of the Doctors.
"Why does everyone want to do the operation?" I asked. The doctors looked at me like I was dirt.
"Because it's a really tough operation. You are probably going to die. But who ever pulls it off is a really great surgeon." He said.
He turned back to his colleagues. I felt about as bad and low and dirty and near death as I ever felt in my life. Within an hour I was on the operating table.
"Count backwards from ten." I don't think I made it to eight. The next thing I knew I woke in a nice clean hospital bed with a bunch of bandages wrapped around my neck. I could barely talk. That same young doctor walked in with a clip board.
"Good morning."
I nodded hello.
"The operation was a success." He put a little glass bottle on the desk next to the bed with the needle in it. It was so small I could barely see it. I picked it up to examine it closer.

"We took that out of your neck. It's amazing you made it here. If that had dislodged chances are more than likely it would have shot to your heart. You would have either died or had to have open heart surgery. Is that what you want?"
"No sir."
"Then I suggest you take a look around. The path you are on will only lead to death. Get off it. I don't know how. That's for you to figure out. Before it's too late. A social worker will be here to talk to you later today. We are going to keep you here for five days for observation, make sure you don't get an infection from that dirty needle. After five days we will take the stitches on the outside of your neck out. The ones inside will dissolve on their own. I'll be back this afternoon to check on you. Try to get some rest." He turned around and left.
I looked around at my clean bed and room. It had been over a year since I had slept in a clean bed like this. I thought about how far gone I was, how I hadn't spoken to friends or family in a long, long time. I started to cry my heart out. Absolutely alone with not a friend in the world. I started for the first time to think, how will I get out of this? Can I get out of this? I fell asleep and for the first time in a while I thought about taking my life back.

44

On the third day I couldn't take it anymore. The street was calling. I took my IV bag and slung it under my arm and put my street clothes over that and walked out of the hospital. Patients were always going downstairs to smoke so I didn't think anyone would miss me for an hour or two.
I had a few dollars left and I jumped in a cab to the mission. It was like a six dollar ride. People hadn't seen me in a while and when I opened my coat and showed them the IV bag everyone thought I was crazy. I stood on the corner until one of my regulars showed up.
"Where you been?"
"In the hospital."

"What happened?"
"It's a long story. Doesn't matter anyway. What you need?"
"Two grams of each. You still got the connection?"
"Yeah come on we gotta hurry."
I hoofed it to the payphone and called Jose. I knew his number by heart. He agreed to meet me and bring me a little taste. I bumped up the price and bought my own gram of each, so with the tax I had enough to last my stay in the hospital. If I had any sense I would have stayed away but some lessons take longer to learn.
After the deal I bought a new syringe and fixed in the alley. Then I waited at the bus stop. I took the city bus back to the hospital and snuck back in.
I got in my bed and closed my eyes. Mission accomplished.
"Better not do that again." I opened my eyes. It was the orderly who wheeled me in.
"Do what?"
"Leave this hospital."
"I went downstairs to smoke."
"Sure you did. Listen, no one here likes you. You are some street junkie that just wants to die getting high. We are in the business of saving people. The social worker was here when you were gone."
"Is she coming back?"
"You better hope so." He said as he walked out. I laid back and thought about what he said. I had a lot of time to think in the hospital. A lot of alone time.
Along this road there are all kinds of characters you meet. Some try to help you and some try to hurt you in the disguise of being your friend.
It was the first time I really realized how deep I was. I just had a needle removed from my neck. That's insane. I knew I wanted to get out, I just didn't have a clue how.
"Good Afternoon." I opened my eyes and there was a middle aged white woman sitting in front of me with a clipboard.
"Mr. Labrava?"
"Yes."
"I'm Mrs. Stanton. I will be your social worker. Am I to understand you are indigent?"

"What's that?"
"Homeless. No money, no where to go."
"Yep. That's me."
"It's my job to help you get back on your feet. Please fill these out as best you can. Please be truthfull." She sat back patiently as I filled the paperwork out. I handed it back and she looked it over.
"This seems to be in order. When you get out of this hospital you come see me at the welfare office. Do you know where that is?"
"The big brick building with the line around it?"
"Yes that's it. You won't have to wait in the line. You get released tomorrow in the morning. I will give you an appointment at two p.m. which will give you plenty of time to make it. You qualify for assistance so we will be giving you two hundred and ten dollars in food stamps twice a month, three hundred twenty five dollars at the beginning of each month and a hotel room for a week at the beginning of each month. This will last for four months then you will have to apply again."
I was trying to contain my happiness but I don't think I did that well.
"This program is to help you got off the street and get on your feet. Not to help you be a better street drug addict. We will help you find a job. Do you understand Mr. Labrava?"
"Yes maam. and Thank You."
"You are welcome. I will see you tomorrow at two. Don't be late." And with that she walked out. I laid there and I thought how lucky I was. Not because I lived through the operation, or that I had a chance to start again, but because I was getting more money to get high. I still couldn't see past getting high.
I got discharged form the hospital and walked to the welfare office. It was about twenty blocks. I still had bandages wrapped on my neck so people were staring at me where ever I went.
I got to the office and found the social worker and she gave me my food stamps and my three hundred twenty five dollar check which I immediately cashed and bought dope. The hotel room was two blocks east of South Van Ness on

sixteenth. So that was about four blocks from where I normally was selling dope.

I used that room as my headquarters and the money they gave me to come up. I split up and ballooned up a few grams of heroin and made quarters and became my own boss. I gave decent sized quarters, making six to a gram so I had a lot of return customers. Most dealers would cut a gram into eight or ten quarters and sell them as twenties.

After a week in the hotel I was back on the sidewalk. I had a bunch of customers that would only buy from me. They would wait till I got back and not buy from other dealers which pissed a lot of them off. There were these two guys from the Midwest, Michael and Marcus, Marcus had a girl friend named Heather. They were straight out of the trailer park. Real rednecks, country folks that came all the way to the west coast because they like to get high. Michael could steal cars like no one else. He would roll up in a new Mercedes or BMW every single day. Marcus could open any trunk with this little flat screwdriver. He could open a trunk faster than the owner could open it with the key. Heather just did dope and looked good. Real good. She was usually the decoy.

These three would clean out entire parking lots at night. Open every trunk n the lot. They hit some really good licks. Some of the trunks were loaded with computers, cameras, once they even found a suitcase with like twenty grand in it. They would go downtown and stay at one of the most expensive hotels in town and shoot dope for days.

I was standing on sixteenth and mission about a week after the hospital when they rolled up in a new Mercedes.

"Hop in." Michael said. The front seat was empty. Marcus and Heather were in the back. I jumped in. It was a really nice Mercedes.

"Where you'd get this?"

Got it last night around Market street. He pulled onto the highway.

"Where we going?"

"Martinez. The city is a little hot. With the four of us we can do some shoplifting there. Heather will be the decoy. I have a guy that will but all the camera film we can get. It'll be easy." Famous last words.

I shot my last bit of dope on the way out there and as soon as I did I knew this was a bad idea. I was getting further and further away from my world, which is where the action is.

"We should hurry." I said already feeling the anxiety of running out of dope.

"It wont take that long. Two or three stores and we will have enough for all of us to get high."

The first store we hit was a supermarket and everything went pretty smooth. I stayed in the car and they went in and did their thing. I sat there wondering why I even went. I had enough money to re up, I sat and thought about just leaving them but I was so far away from the city.

The second store was a drug store.

"You sure you don't wanna go?" Marcus asked.

"Naah I aint no good at that anyway. I just wanna get back to the city."

"One more stop after this and the we should be good." He grabbed the keys and they all jumped out of the car and walked inside. It seemed like they were in that store forever. They all came walking out then they started running, with the store manager behind them.

"STOP! THIEVES! STOP THEM!" The Manager yelled. They jumped in the car, Marcus put the key in and peeled out.

"That didn't look like it went too well." I said.

"We just gotta get back to the city and we will be fine. We should ditch this car."

As soon as he said that there were red lights flashing behind us.

"Too late."

They all started eating whatever drugs and pills they had. The siren on the car was blaring and the cop was about an inch off our tail. Marcus pulled over. The cops jumped out of their cars with their guns drawn. We all got out and laid on the ground. I was in handcuffs on my belly with Marcus on one side and Michael on the other. I felt like crying but I didn't. I knew I was going back to jail, again. Everything started moving in slow motion, again.

45

I got six months for the Martinez escapade and ended up doing three. I lost my benefits from welfare for not keeping up with it so I was back on the street when I got out. I didn't have as big a habit when I got out so I could work myself back up. I middled enough deals and saved enough money to sell quarters again with out tapping into my own supply.
Spring turned into summer and it got warmer on the street, which is good if you live outside. I didn't always have to find a hallway to sleep in. The nights were warm. I got used to sleeping right on the sidewalk. I would wake up with business people stepping over me on their way to work as if I wasn't even there.
I started hanging out with these two hookers Patty and Debby. Patty was way more together than Debby, and cuter. Not that that mattered to me. The ONLY thing I spent money on was dope. I barely even bought food.
 Patty had a one room flat in between Howard and South Van Ness in the twenties that she split with Debby. They would let me sleep in their closet when it rained, which was a trip because when they turned tricks and I had to be quiet. And they turned tricks ALL the time.
One night late I was standing on seventeenth and mission selling dope. Patty got out of a car right in front of me. The car pulled away fast.
"Whats shaking Patty."
"You got any quarters."
"Nice ones."
"Coke too?"
"Dimes."
"Cool give me two quarters and two dimes." Patty never tried to work me down the price she just paid it.
"Wanna go fix?' She asked me. The street was quiet, not a lot of business.
"Sure."

We walked to nineteenth and South Van Ness. On the corner was a gas station and next to that was a real estate management company. Behind that building was a lot full of the stuff they would clean out of peoples apartment when people moved, or got kicked out. Normal people would scavenge through the stuff there every day. It was also a cool place for junkies like myself to shoot up at, especially at night.

"Me first." Patty said. "Hit me in my neck." That girl couldn't have weighed more than ninety pounds but she could take a huge speedball and stay standing. She had a MONSTER habit. She stood there rushing out for a minute while I fixed my speedball. When her eyes stopped rolling in her head she looked at me totally relieved.

"Your turn. You want me to do it?"

"No thanks I have a hand mirror." I never let anyone shoot me up, ever. Especially in my neck. It takes a whole lot of trust on both sides to shoot someone up in their jugular vein. A LOT.

I held my hand mirror in the light so I could see my neck and held my breath. I put the syringe in and saw the blood flow into it.

The next thing I knew I was laying in a puddle of water with Patty jumping up and down on my chest, screaming and crying at the same time.

"HELP! SOMEONE HELP! PLEEEEASE!" She was frantic. I looked up at her.

"What are you doing? Get off me. Where's my dope?"

She immediately bent down and started helping me up.

"We have to go. We have to go. I've been yelling. You were out. Dead. Come on hurry."

I got up and my whole back was wet. My chest hurt from Patty jumping up and down on it. We got out of there fast and walked up the block. A few people had gathered at the driveway of the building and were looking at us.

"You see? I was yelling so loud. I thought you were dead. Come on."

We hurried out of there as fast as we could and walked back to the Mission.

"I gotta go turn a trick." Patty said. "You sure you're ok?"
"Yeah. My chest hurts a little. But hey, Thanks for not leaving me."
"You're welcome." She turned and walked back to Howard street to turn a trick. I went and found a doorway up in the twenties off Valencia to sleep in. The apartments were a little nicer up there. I would walk along and try every door knob till one was open. This led to a hallway that had four or six apartment doors. I would curl up and sleep in there till someone kicked me out which was usually on their way to work in the morning.
I didn't see Patty for about a month. I was doing way better. I had come up a little and was buying quarter ounces of Heroin and coke and splitting it up and selling it. I was still was living outside with only one set of clothes, but I didn't care. I was moving around the city from dwelling to dwelling surviving anyway I could figure it out. Every day was an absolute fight for survival.
There was a small building behind that real estate place on nineteenth where I overdosed. I lived there for a few months. I would hang my stuff from a string in a slot between the two buildings so no ne could find it. There was a little over hang I would crawl under to sleep. Finally someone in the building next door saw me and started screaming that they would call the cops unless I split. Some stupid citizen with nothing better to do. I wasn't bothering him. I wasn't even on his property. But I definitely knew it was time to find a new spot.
The next time I saw Patty was a sunny day on the mission. Warm and sunny with a lot of people on the street. The donut shop was filled with dealers hanging out waiting for customers. Most of the dealers were Mexican, from way down in Mexico. They dressed like cowboys, with cowboy boots and hats. And NONE of them did drugs. They were all about money. And they ALL had workers like me. They needed them so they could sit back and not get arrested. All the action was at the donut shop.
I was standing with Indio just hanging out enjoying the sunshine when Patty walked up. She looked real bad. She was shaking and sweating all over.

"What's wrong?"
"Debby took my wake up and split this morning. I'm so sick I can't even turn a trick."
I immediately went in the donut shop and spit out all the balloons I had in my mouth. I picked a big quarter gram of dope and twenty of coke and came back outside and handed it to Patty.
"I don't have any money."
"You can have this free Patty. If you had left me that night I would be dead right now. Everyone is saying that if I had went with Debby instead of you I would be dead now cause she would have left me. You get it free."
"Thank you. Thank you so much."
"Thank YOU Patty. Go."
She turned around and took off to go fix. I only saw her once or twice after that. People would disappear and reappear on the street all the time. Most of the people on the street were from somewhere else in America, or the world. Patty must have decided to go back t whereever she came from. Or maybe she just died. A lot of people died.

46

I started getting picked up for vagrancy a lot. That was the cops trip. They would arrest you for being on the street then make you piss in a cup and document your track marks. They can only keep you over night on a vagrancy charge but after three or four of them they can give you a little time. Not much, but any time inside a locked box is the worst time you can spend on this earth. Better off to be strung out junkie standing on a corner in the rain at three am waiting for a dealer that is not coming than to be locked up. Or dead. At least you still have a chance to come out of the first scenario.
I was starting to want to come out of this life but I didn't know how. I had been living on the street out doors using the jail as a revolving door for over a year and a half. It was getting old but the grip of Heroin is stronger than anything

else. I had never really tried to stop before. I was just a hoping to die dope fiend, running scams to feed my habit.

There was a guy named Mason that had real long hair. I think he was from Kansas or Montana or somewhere in the Midwest. His trip was stealing bicycles. Nice ones. Then sell them for dope. He rode up on a new Cannondale.

"Nice bike." I said.

"Four hundred."

"I aint buying it. I'll trade you some dope for it."

"Nope. I'm gonna get four hundred for it." For some reason I wanted that bike. And I knew how to get it. I waited all day till he was out of dope. He couldn't sell the bike and he came back to me.

"Wanna do that trade?"

"What trade?'

"You know. For the grams of dope."

"Don't have anymore, not enough to trade anyway." I lied. "But if you give me the bike, I'll fix with you."

He thought about it for a minute.

"OK."

"Get off the bike." He got off the bike.

"Let's go."

We walked to an alley and fixed. Soon as he was done he jumped up.

"Where you going?"

"To get another bike."

I fixed some dope then rode the bike all around the city. The adrenalin rush was amazing flying down the streets in San Francisco. I was having a blast like a little kid. I rode back to the mission and was cruising around on the bike when two beat cops rode by slow. They see me every day walking up and down the block so they knew damn sure that wasn't my bike. They slowed down and cruised next to me.

"Better get rid of it." The cop said before they took off. They must have got a call or something, either way I knew next time he saw me he would arrest me for this stolen bike. I rode across town to a real big bicycle store. I walked the bike inside. There were a bunch of kids working and one old man.

"What can I do for you?" The old man asked me.
"How much is this bike worth?" He looked over the counter at the bike for a moment, then at me.
"About two grand new. Why? You looking to sell it?'
"Yeah. I'll take four hundred for it. ok?"
"No problem, as soon as you can show proof of ownership. Like the receipt from where you bought it, or the bill of sale from who you bought it from."
"I'll go get it. I'll be right back."
"Sure you will." He said sarcastically. I wheeled the bike out of the store. He knew it was stolen. I got on the bike and one of the kids from behind the counter was outside waving me around back. I rode over to him and he held out four crisp hundred dollar bills. Neither of us said a word. He handed me the money and I got off the bike and walked away. I was so happy my feet could barely hit the ground. On the one hand I was glad I had come up so hard. On the other hand I knew I was just digging a bigger hole for myself to get out of.
I got back to the mission and Indio was waiting on the corner.
"How'd it go?"
I flashed the four crisp hundred dollar bills. Indio's eyes lit up.
"Lets go carnan." We took off and met Jose on Seventeenth and Howard and got some dope and coke.
"We just got this." Jose said. " My brother just got back from Mexico. Try to sell a lot."
Me and Indio took the dope and took off running.
"Lets go to the bart station." Indio said. We used the bathroom at the bart station a lot. You didn't have to have a ticket. You just ask the girl in the glass box at the gate if you could use the bathroom and she would buzz you in.
"You first."
The girl buzzed me in and I went into the bathroom. I set up my works on my porcelain desk. That's what I called the tank on the toilet. I bet at this point I had shot up in every bathroom in the city. Some more than a few times. I looked at myself in the mirror. I was a mess.
"It will be better in the next life." I said to myself. I wasn't trying to die or anything like that. It's just what I said when I

shot up. I guess I was hoping out loud that it would be. I plunged that syringe into my jugular vein and saw the blood run into it and mix with the water. Once again I woke up on my back. I heard a mans voice.

"Boy. I didn't think I was getting you back. You were as blue as my jeans." A paramedic was looking at me. I was laying on my back with my shirt cut open. I looked out the open door way and there was Indio and about twenty people looking at me.

I stood up real quick and was breathing hard. Really hard long deep breaths.

"You might not be so lucky next time." The paramedic said. There were two paramedics with all their life saving stuff all spread out on the floor all around me. They started cleaning up.

"Can I go?"

"You probably should before the cops get here." He said. "You know somebody probably called them."

I walked out of the bathroom quick and up the stairs out of the bart station. Indio was following me.

"What happened?" I asked him.

"About a minute after you went in some lady got off the train and wanted to use the bathroom. I didn't even know you fell out. She started screaming 'Man down" and that she could see your feet through the vent in the door. The girl in the booth called the paramedics. I took them about ten minutes to get here. When they got the door open you were blue homeboy. I mean it. They worked real fast and blasted a shot of something through your chest and in like one second your eyes opened."

"No shit."

"That was real shit homeboy. I never seen anything like it." We got away from there and went a few blocks away so Indio could fix. I was kind of dazed from overdosing and still breathing hard from whatever shot they gave me. That was the third or fourth time I almost bit the big one. The only thing I thought was sooner or later I probably won't be so lucky. Part of me didn't care. Part of me wanted out. It was an internal battle and I was losing.

47

Indio got busted for the third time and they sent him upstate. To the big house. The penitentiary. There was a revolving door from the street to the pen. Big prison issue killers would get out go right back to the street. They would head straight to the mission and hit the street hard all rested up. Been doing pushups for years.

There was a six foot seven inch black guy with real light skin named Albino. He wasn't albino, that's just what everyone called him on account of him being so white. Albino was ruthless. I've seen him hold dealers up by their throat with one hand till they gave up all their stash and money. I was standing on nineteenth and mission the first time we met.

"What you got Homeboy?" he asked me. He was standing there with some young girl.

"Quarters and dimes. Dope and coke."

"I got sixteen bucks. You give me a dime of each?" I thought about it.

"Sure." I figured he might come back, become a return customer. I spit out two balloons and gave them to him. I stood there waiting for another customer. That's what I did. I stood on a corner and sold dope.

"HEY HOMEBOY! I WANT MY MONEY BACK!" Albino was screaming at the top of his lungs as he walked back up the block. I stood where I was. Maybe he wasn't talking to me. He walked right up to me and kept screaming. He towered over me and he out weighed me by about two hundred pounds.

"I WANT MY MONEY BACK HOMEBOY."

"Why's that?" I stood my ground.

"Cause those dimes were too little."

"No they weren't. They were fine. Nobody else complained."

"CHECK IT OUT HOMEBOY. YER GONNA GIVE ME MY MONEY BACK." He was making a commotion towering over me screaming. People started looking. This aint good I thought.

"IF I DON'T GET MY MONEY."

Then I heard a loud CRACK and Albino fell to the floor. A skinny white guy named Pete was standing behind him with a ball peen hammer. He had cracked Albino with that hammer on the top of his head. It didn't knock him out though. Albino was too big. He got up on one knee dazed. Pete wailed him again this time knocking him out cold. A pool of blood stared to form around his head. I was sure Pete broke his skull.

"Come on. Let's go. Before the cops show up." Pete said and we took off. Pete was a prison issue dope fiend in its purest form.

"I been waiting to get that piece of shit for a year." He said as we ran down the block. I heard he got cut loose. He robbed me last year when he was on the street. I been waiting. I knew he would show up. I was eating a burrito and I heard him yelling. I walked in the back of the restaurant and the first thing I saw was that hammer. The cooks were yelling at me to get out so I grabbed it and ran."

"Thanks." I was truly grateful.

"He's lucky that hammer was the first thing I saw. If I saw a knife he'd be dead right now."

We found an alley and fixed dope and then hit the street. Albino got taken to the hospital with a busted skull. Everyone on the street was talking about how Pete was gonna be dead when Albino got out of the hospital. Pete wasn't tripping though.

"I can't wait to see him again." He would always say. I stared running with Pete for a few weeks. I would stand on a corner and Pete would be a few blocks away looking for a customer. When he found one he would walk the guy over to where I was standing.

"What you got Homeboy?" Pete would ask me. Like he barely knew me.

"Quarters and dimes. Dope and coke."

"You got the money?" Pete would ask the guy, and as soon as the guy looked down at his pocket, BAM! Pete would hit him with a knockout punch. Usually the guy would be out on his feet sucking air in as he fell to the ground out cold. We would rifle his pockets and take off. Pete would knock out six or seven guys a day, every day. He broke his hand one time and that slowed him down for about an hour. He wrapped it up and continued his assault on the neighborhood.

The days started running one into another fast. I didn't even know what month it was let alone what day it was. My life had become a constant pursuit of getting high and not getting arrested.

I had a new place to stay. I would go down the escalator to the bart on the south east corner of sixteenth and mission. Halfway down I would hop up and crawl into this real small space where no one could see me. It was just big enough for me to lay down in. I lived there for a few weeks. It was getting cold and I would stuff my clothes with newspapers and cover myself with whatever I could find for warmth. I was totally sick of this life but I had no idea how to stop it.

There were these bible crusaders that would walk around trying to save junkies. Twice a week they would walk down the mission and take anyone back to their house who wanted to go with them. They had a big house on Cesar Chavez avenue, and it was communal living. This was my first attempt at getting clean. I walked down to the house and knocked on the door. The guy who answered had seen me on the block a few times. He knew my story probably better than me.

"What do you want?"

"I don't know."

"Yes you do. Or else you wouldn't be here." He opened the door. "No drugs in this house."

"I know." I stepped inside. We walked over to the kitchen table and sat down. There were kids all over the house. Everyone was cleaning. Everyone was looking at me.

"Here's how this works. My name is Rick Anderson. I'm a counselor here. This is a state run facility to help people like you. People on drugs. This is communal living, do you know what that means?"

"Everyone works together."

"Exactly. Everyone works together. We do a bible study twice a day."

"What if I'm not a big believer?"

"It doesn't matter. It's all about finding a higher power than drugs. You can call that higher power whatever you want. We also do missionary work in the streets three times a week."

"I know. I've seen you out there."

"How strung out are you?"

"How strung out you think? Strung out bad."

"How bad?"

"I shoot about forty speedballs a day. From the minute I wake up then basically whenever I can."

"Expensive habit."

"You're telling me."

"You are gonna get sick. Have you got any drugs on you now?"

"No." I lied. He probably knew it.

"It's almost dinner time. Why don't you get cleaned up and I will introduce you to some of the guys. After dinner we have a meeting."

"What kind of meeting?"

"Nothing formal. We just talk about what we're feeling. How grateful we are to have found the lord and to not be on drugs."

"Oh."

I got up and went to the bathroom. I had two dimes of dope and a dime of coke. I mixed it all up and shot it. I looked at myself in the mirror as my eyes were rolling and I had to grab the sink so I didn't fall down. That was my last shot I said to myself. I threw the syringe and works out the window and they landed in the alley. I came out of the bathroom and everyone was just sitting down. I sat down next to a kid named Robbie that I knew from the street.

"I thought you got arrested." I said.

"I did. They gave me three months in Bryant street. When I got out I hit the street, copped some dope from a guy from the tenderloin. He came back ten minutes later with his buddy and robbed me. They beat me senseless. I guess I had enough. I remember these guys walking up and down mission so I thought I would give it a try. Been here ever since."

"How long is that?'

"Almost three months."
"Wow. Long time."
"Seems like three days. Time seems to stand still here. On the street time is flying by. Probably cause we are wasting so much of it. Flying by so fast we can't even notice it. "
I thought about that while I ate, how much time I had wasted. I had been living outside for almost two years. Hadn't spoken to anyone that I knew before. A couple of my friends had come out from the East coast to try and save me once. They heard how bad I was doing. You now you are doing bad when the news travels across the country. I started drifting thinking about the past. It seemed a million years ago.
About six months earlier I was walking out of an alley and I looked up and saw a friend of mine named Big John walking with Albino. Now John was 3500 miles from home and Albino is not any friend of mine so I stopped walking. Albino pointed me out.
"THERE HE IS!" I started to take off.
"Where you gonna run?" John said.
"What are you doing here?"
"Looking for you."
Me and Big John had gotten high plenty of times together. John is like six foot six and used to sling dope called Original Formula on the Lower East Side. I met him in Miami years earlier when me and a few other people, A.J. and Joey Vomit lived in a night club called the Junkyard. This was the poor peoples night club. It wasn't all glam like the other clubs above fifth street. Doing dope was how we passed our day.
John handed Albino twenty dollars and he took off. We went to a restaurant in the height and had lunch. I went into the bathroom three times during that lunch to shoot up. There was no helping me.
"You ok?" Rick said to me. I looked up and everyone was looking at me. I had nodded off thinking about the past.
"Yeah. I'm ok." I ate my food in silence. After dinner everyone cleaned up together. This was the first time in a long time that I didn't have dope in my pocket. The anxiety was growing every second. It's in my body or in my pocket. I got it

or I'm on the way to get it, or I just got back from getting it. That's the drill.

We all gathered in a big room and it was exactly like an NA meeting. I never been to an NA or AA meeting, but that's what they said. Everyone was sharing their past experiences, and talking about how grateful they were to have not done dope today.

Hearing their stories just made me want to get more dope. One thing I knew for sure was I had to get off dope myself. I couldn't do it with help. Then I figured I would always need that help. I wanted to be in control of myself by myself.

I waited till everyone was asleep and I snuck out of my bunk. I tip toed to the front door and opened it quietly.

"If you go out that door you can't come back." I almost jumped out of my skin. It was Rick. He was standing in the darkness. He stepped into the light.

"Those are the rules. It's not a revolving door. Once you go out there's no coming back. This is a big decision for you. You can go crawl back into your bunk if you want. No one will know."

I thought about it for a moment.

"Thanks." I said as I opened the door.

"Good luck." Rick said.

I hit the street and ran back to the mission. I literally ran like it was a race. The whole way back all I could think about was getting high. Getting well as fast as I can. And how difficult this is going to be to take my life back. I had just failed my first real attempt.

48

Hitting the street with nothing was like starting again from the beginning. I had to middle deals and come up again. I did all the dope I had before I went to the rehab. It was getting harder and harder to be a street dweller. It was taking it's toll on me. I was just getting sicker and weaker on my liquid diet. I was hungry. I needed food, a place to stay.

I would get a to-go container and stand outside a nice restaurant and wait till some people left the table with some food on their plate. Then I would run in and take the food before the bus boy would grab it. Nine out of ten times I would get chased out by the staff but I ALWAYS got the food. I knew which stores threw out the food with a one day expiration date on it. One day old isn't bad I thought. So between stealing to go plates and dumpster diving I would manage to eat.

Life was getting harder and harder on the street. There was always a new influx of people moving in and out of the neighborhood. It never took long for the street to chew people up. I saw these two French kids show up. They made music, like they had a CD of their own music. They thought it was cool to get high. It took about three months before she was giving blow jobs on Howard street while he waited on mission for her to finish. There are literally hundreds of stories like that. THOUSANDS. The street is a monster that is chewing people up.

I knew I had to get out. I used to walk around looking down at the ground. Always looking down searching for something, anything, money, dope, whatever. I know what I was really looking for. Dope. It's a real drug addict thing to do. I was in the mission on a mission.

I was walking on the mission looking on the ground like I always did and I saw a crack in the sidewalk. In the crack I saw a brown paper bag. I reached down and picked it up and kept walking. I looked in the bag and couldn't believe it. It was full of balloons of dope. I put it in my pocket and walked down the block. I crossed the street and walked back up the other side and went in the burrito shop across the street from where I found the bag. I bought a burrito and I sat there and waited. In about ten minutes a bunch of dealers walked over to the spot where the crack was. One of them reached down and freaked. They all started looking around. I sat back and ate my burrito with a smile. I knew the dope I had found was real.

I walked over to a friend of mine named Jay who lived a few blocks up on Mission boulevard. Jay was an older degenerate junkie, about sixty years old, living on the mission for years. We rebagged all of the balloons. In each balloon was a gram of dope or coke in a piece of plastic, then it is burned shut, then it goes into the balloon and gets tied with a knot. So it is about the size of a green pea. That way you can hold a bunch in your mouth and swallow them if the cops show up.. I had to change the color of the plastic and the balloons on all of them. There was about twenty grams of each. It was almost an ounce. This was a BIG come up.

Jay called one of his friends who bought ten grams of each off me. This gave me enough money to get a hotel room for a few days. I went a holed up in the hotel room for a few days just shooting speedballs. I would wake up and hold my first breath, look in my hand mirror and plunge the needle in my neck, then sit there rushing out. Then do it again. Over and over and over. My whole world was the needle.

After a few days my money ran out again. I got kicked out of the hotel. I was once again homeless on the street. Staying in the hotel made me remember what it was like to live indoors. A few days after that I was shooting dope in a parking structure with a few other junkies. We had all filled up our syringes and were just about to fire up, when six cops came running into the parking lot. Everyone went running in every direction but the cops caught us. As the cop grabbed me I sprayed my Speedball out in the air, so all they got me for was drug paraphernalia. There was not enough dope in the syringe to charge me with possession. It didn't matter though. I had been busted enough that the judge gave me six months. It was probably the best thing to happen to me in a long time.

I knew I was going to do at least four of the six months. I got sent to a way bigger state jail than what I was used to. It wasn't the pen, just one step under.

There's no big story to tell about being locked up. Basically time stands still for you while it goes on for everyone else. Jail is like gladiator school. If you came off the street you weren't too freaked out by jail, at least I wasn't. Don't get it wrong jail is not the place anyone wants to be. But if you came off the street, which is a monster, jail is a place to rest

up, sleep and eat. Imaging how bad life has to be for jail to be a relief. Real bad.
I had zero money when I got caught so I was put on an indigent program. I got two pencils, two pieces of paper two stamps and two bags of skittles.
The first thing I did was draw on the two envelopes and start my hustle. I would sell one envelope fully drawn for two items on the commissary. Same hustle different jail. The drawing gave me something to do to pass the time. Everybody wanted something drawn on they're envelopes. There were other guys that did the same hustle and we all sat at the same table drawing all day long.
Nights were harder. I couldn't sleep. I don't think I slept for a year. The speed freaks, crankster gangsters would come in and sleep for days, miss every meal. The dope heads couldn't sleep at all. The usually stayed up all night partying. I mostly couldn't sleep cause I was thinking about dope. I would lay there and dream about it all night. It was torture. I was torturing myself and I knew it. But I lived for it. I couldn't wait to hit the street again.
They gave everyone an intelligence test in the jail. I guess that was to help you see what you were capable of, what you could accomplish on the outside, when you got out. In all the times I had been locked up, I had never had any kind of rehabilitation done. This was the first time. Usually the only thing you do inside is TIME.
 There was another guy there with the same birthday as me named Danny. Same age and everything. We became friends.
Everybody was getting called in to have an interview after the test. Some guys were all about getting help, being rehabilitated, not coming back. Some guys had more lessons to learn. I got called into the interview room. There was a young black man sitting behind a desk. Younger than me.
"Sit down. Relax." I sat down in the chair in front of his desk. It felt like the principals office.
"How are you doing here? You like it?"
"Is that a joke?"

"Not at all. I am wondering why you are here. You see, you scored higher on the intelligence test than anyone ever did in the history of this institution."

"You're putting me on. For real?"

"Yes for real. You only missed one question. So I ask you, why are you here?" I thought about that.

"I like getting high."

"A little too much. I see you have gotten arrested quite a few times in the last year and a half. If you keep going the way you are going, you are going to be spending a good portion of your life incarcerated. Is that what you want?"

"No sir."

"Then I suggest you use your brain, because you have a good one, and figure something else out. It would be a shame to waste what you have. I can't change things for you. Only you can. This test was designed to help you figure out what you are capable of doing and what you would like to do. You on the other hand can do anything you want. I would think you have gotten high enough by now. There is nothing left to learn doing drugs. Time to learn something else."

I sat there thinking for a moment. For some reason his words had some impact. I got up to go and I turned back.

"How did Danny Williams do? He has the same birthday as me."

He flipped through the files, read a page and looked up.

"Not as good as you." I turned and left. For some reason I thought since were born on the same day we would score close. Guess not.

The days passed quicker than I thought and before long I was walking back down the mission. That is some shaky ground to be walking on. Fresh out of jail, old stomping grounds. First day back. Old habits do die hard. I had a friend put a hundred dollars on my books for food which I never spent. I saved it for this day to buy dope.

I was walking up and down the mission deciding if I was going to dive back into that pool. I knew I wanted to get high, I just didn't want to go back to what I was. I was done being a junkie. I didn't want to be that anymore.

The street was changing. Crack had now been invented and the street had got more ruthless with crackheads all over it. They are a different breed.

When I got inside I wrote down all the dealers numbers I could remember. It was about ten guys. I saved that piece of paper till now. I walked over to the pay phone on seventeenth. I used to walk up to this same phone and use the chrome as a reflection to shoot dope in my neck. Soon as I would start cleaning it off every junkie on the street would run.

"You're gonna bring the COPS." They would scream at me. I didn't care. But now I did care.

As I looked at the phone I knew I didn't want to go there again. I had to make a calculated plan. I knew this wasn't going to be in any way easy. In fact this was going to be the hardest thing I had ever done. Taking my life back. I decided then I would not use the needle anymore. I was dying to get high so I decided I would back track one step at a time. I would smoke dope like when I first started. On tin foil, chasing the dragon. And no more coke, no speedballs. Just dope. Heroin. I would retrace my steps and regress back into what I was before this all started. That was my plan. It seemed like the only way to become what I once was. If I lost my keys I would have retraced my steps till I found them. I figured I would go in reverse and retrace my steps till I found my life again.

I picked up the receiver and three of the seven numbers I had answered. I ordered three grams, one from each dealer. And I made the appointments fifteen minutes and a few blocks apart.

I met the first guy on Seventeenth and South Van Ness. Mario. I used to knock people out who owed him money for a quarter gram of dope. He owed me a few quarters that he never paid me, from before I went inside. He would get me to knock them out then not pay me.

"Weddo. Long time."

"You got it?"

"Yeah. You got the money."

I showed him the money. He took out the gram and I grabbed it from him.
"What you doing ese. You gonna get killed like that." I put the gram in my pocket and knocked him out cold.
"Who's gonna get killed? Not me. I owed you that." I met the other two guys separately and did the same thing. The second guy took off running as soon as I took the gram. I used Pete's tactic on the third guy, as soon as he looked down to his pocket I knocked him out cold. People always look down at their pocket when they reach into them, it must be physics or something.
I took off running out of the mission as fast as I could and ran all the way to the Greyhound bus station. I bought a Nestles crunch bar because it hand tin foil wrapped around the chocolate. It was the only candy bar that did that. All the junkies liked crunch bars. I went in the bathroom and smoked some dope. It was as sweet as I remember. I got loaded and I felt that I was on my way to recovery. I had a plan.
I figured I wouldn't come back there after I robbed those guys. In reality there was a revolving door of guys coming up and down from Mexico. They never stayed long. It only took a few months till they either got caught, deported or split on their own. I probably would have never seen those guys again, but I wasn't coming back.
I had to get out of the city but I didn't know where to go. I had been living out doors on the street for long enough. I couldn't go home. I didn't want to go anywhere that I had done dope already. I thought it was a geographical problem. It's not. I was the problem.
I had a friend from Miami, Joey Vomit who lived in Tacoma and was painting houses. I called him up and he said his boss would hire me. I figured I would try it up there. I just didn't want to be where I was, doing what I was doing, so I split. I got on that bus with three grams of heroin, the clothes on my back and a habit.
I was sad as I left the city. It was night and I was watching the people walk around living their lives. They all looked so normal. I felt anything but normal. I was sad but excited. I

guess I like a challenge. The previous challenge was to get high. Now the challenge was to not. Challenge accepted. As we pulled on the highway and headed north I was more excited than I had been in a long time.

49

"Come on get up. We're gonna be late." Joey said as he ran into the kitchen to grab some coffee. I had another sleepless night. I don't think I slept through the night for over a year. I would lay there, night after night and think about dope. I would fantasize about getting high tossing and turning all night long.
The first year was the hardest. I was off the needle and hadn't done dope in a long time. I relapsed once in the first year. Anyone who says they put dope down and never picked it up again is either a liar or as strong as the rock of gibralter, or stronger than me
It didn't take me long to find dope in Tacoma. There was a block downtown where people were slinging dope and coke. There is a street in EVERY town where people are slinging dope and coke. And a junkie will find it. I found it. I would take my check and buy enough dope on Friday and get loaded all weekend, then be worthless all week. I would beat myself up for letting myself down.
I did this all in secret, never letting Joey or his wife know. They had just had their first kid and she was pregnant with the second. We were painting two houses a day. We did two interiors or two exteriors or one of each every day. I was a functioning junkie. I had taken part of my life back. I was working and paying rent, living indoors. I was off the needle but still smoking it. This was a big step. I still wasn't off dope yet. My body had taken on a new chemistry.
Like I said you can only become a junkie once. I still couldn't see past getting high. I couldn't see the aftermath, which was that I had to lay down for days afterward and recover. Hibernate. I couldn't even crawl to the bathroom. It felt like I

was run over by a truck. It takes a while to see the whole picture and the whole picture aint pretty, in fact it is more like a horror movie, and I was the monster.

I looked out the window and it was pitch black outside. That's how it always is at four in the morning. Dope is a great motivator. It got me up every day at four am to go work, then work my heart out all week so I could buy more dope. I was still screwed up and I knew it. I was working to get high. Not good.

I painted houses and lived with Joey for a few months. Once again I knew I had to get out of there or sooner than later or I would be back where I was.

Me getting high near Joey and his pregnant wife and kid was not the best place for me and I knew it. I had to make a new plan. As soon as I found dope in that town I knew I was done. I was still running. Running as far and as fast as I could from myself.

I used to skateboard all over. I had a Z deck that I shaped myself with a jig saw with independent trucks and Kryptonic wheels. Real old school. I have been surfing and skating since I'm nine, and I was still addicted to the adrenalin rush of bombing hills. There were plenty of hills to bomb in Seattle. I had never been up there so me and Joey took the bus up there to skate around. We spent the whole day bombing hills, smoking joints and just being normal. There were all kinds of kids skating in the city, there was a little city made skate park we found.

"Cool board." A guy walked up and was checking out my skateboard.

"Made it my self." I held it out. I had designed the deck with magic markers.

"Nice. Where you guys from?"

"Tacoma."

The guy's name was Kenny and he worked for a moving company. He offered me a job and I took it. It was time to leave Tacoma for me and keep running. I was copping dope every week, spending my entire paycheck on it, then portioning it out for the whole week and Friday doing it again. It was a vicious cycle that I wanted out of. I tapered my habit down to almost nothing and made a plan to move to Seattle. I didn't know anyone there, I didn't know how to find dope there and I decided I wasn't going to look.

I went back to Tacoma, got my stuff, smoked the last of my dope, threw out the remnants, swore to myself I would never do it again, AGAIN, said goodbye and took the bus to Seattle.

I took a room in a hotel on hotel street. Hotel street is like skid row in Seattle. It was where all the cheap hotels were. A lot of Alaskan fisherman were staying in the hotel I was in when they would be in between voyages.

Kenny picked me up in his truck the next and took me to work. His boss hired me on the spot and sent us out to move a house. I can tell you that moving houses aint no easy work. Try moving a piano down a flight of stairs. Then up another one. This was hard work. Harder than I had ever done. And neither Kenny or me was any type of muscle man.

The moving companies would take the customers to the cleaners. They were charging about two hundred dollars an hour and they would estimate how long it would take to move the house, which was usually about eight hours. I wasn't getting paid enough to get out of the hotel so I started making deals with the house owners. I would get them to pay me and Kenny each a hundred dollars in cash and we would shave an hour off the estimated time. It was the same price either way for the customer, only the moving company got pinched. Me and Kenny had to work extra hard to make up the hour but we did it. It took the moving company about two weeks to figure it out and fire me.

I had enough money to stay in the hotel for a week then I was back on the street. One of the fisherman talked me into going on an Alaskan fishing voyage. He had just come back with a huge check and was telling me how easy it is. I went to downtown Seattle and went to three interviews over the next week . I had no idea what I was about to get into. I got hired and I came back with my orders. I showed it to the guy who got me the interview.

"You don't want to go on this boat."

"Why not?" I asked him. I was already a little freaked out about going into the open sea. The Bering strait. Crab fishing.

"This is this ships maiden voyage. It's first time out. You never go on a ships maiden voyage. Bad luck." He showed me some pictures of what I was about to do. It didn't look fun. On the deck in rain gear, cold as can be.
"Last maiden voyage I was on, the lead got loose and came flying across the deck. Hit my buddy right between the eyes. Split his head wide open. He died instantly."
Scratch the Alaskan fishing voyage. I probably would have died out there anyway I thought.
My money ran out and Kenny let me live in the moving van. He would park it at night in the yard and I would climb in before he locked the fence. He was the first one there and the last one out each day so no one knew.
The door of the truck swung open. The light was blinding.
"Good morning." Kenny said.
"For you maybe."
"Listen. I don't know how long we can keep doing this. I think one of the workers saw you leave the other morning and I can't lose my job." I was devastated.
"Give me another day or two."
"All I'm gonna do is leave it unlocked so you can get in. If you get caught, you haven't seen me since you stopped working here. Ok?"
"Yeah. Ok."
I got up and hurried out of the yard. I had to try and make this spot last as long as I could. Kenny had been real nice to me and I didn't want him to have to pay for that kindness. I was in a bad way and I knew it. The voice in my head was SCREAMING to go get dope. Screaming into a megaphone blasting in my ear drums.
I walked over to a phone booth and went inside. It was a glass booth, one of the old style and it blocked me form the cold and wind. I stood there and just thought about my life. I decided to call my father. He tried to help me once he might try to help me again. I put my coins in the slot and dialed the number. It rang six times before he picked it up.
"Hello."
"Dad?"

Click. He hung right up. I stood there and listened to the dial tone for a moment then hung up the phone. I stood in that booth for a few minutes and looked out at the city. There was no one to call. I was in the great Northwest about as far as I could get away from home and still be in this country. I had nowhere else to go. Time sort of stood still for me. I knew I was at the biggest cross roads of my life. Absolutely alone and deathly afraid of myself, it was at this moment I would say I had an epiphany, a defining moment in my life. A moment of clarity I think it's called.

I decided right there I had to figure a way out of this mess now or I was going to go back to San Francisco and be the best junkie could be till I die. It had been almost a year since I left the city, I wasn't worried about the dealers I robbed. I was more worried about myself.

I made a command decision. I realized I was different from normal people because they had never been exposed. They had no voice in their head screaming to go get dope because they didn't know dope was even in the world. I decided I would pretend I had never been exposed, that all this had never happened to me. That I had no idea at all that dope was in the world or that I new how easy it is to find. I decided I would back track further and trade addictions. Anytime I even thought about dope I would smoke weed. This was my new plan. I had lost my way in the world. I was now going to retrace my footsteps to the point when I lost my way and find it back. I had to start again, and to do that I had to go backwards. Back to when this started and take a different road. And this wasn't going to be easy. No more smoking dope on foil. No more dope period. If I even thought about dope I would smoke weed. I made another big decision to back track even further. I had to reverse this lifestyle completely and become what I once was before it was too late.

I stepped out of the phone booth and the cold hit me hard but I was still excited. I was excited about taking my life back.

50

"Hey. Wait. STOP." I turned back and there was a guy about forty dressed real nice chasing me down. He had my application in his hand. I stopped and he caught up with me. He was out of breath. He looked down at my application.
"David?"
"Yes sir."
"You're hired."
I had been pounding the pavement applying at ever restaurant in Seattle. I wanted to work somewhere that was indoors and I could eat at. I knew restaurant work so well because my dad owned a few growing up and I had done ever facet of restaurant work. He held out my application.
"This is the best application I ever saw.'
"I grew up in the restaurant business. It was my family business."
"I see that. It's very impressive. You are going to have to start in the dish pit but you can work your way up. Deal?"
"Deal."
He owned an upscale Mexican restaurant on first street way above Pike Place Market. He took me inside introduced me around
"Have at it." There was a mountain of dishes that needed to be done.
"We just lost both our dish washers in one day. They both quit so you have your work cut out for you." He handed me an apron.
"No problem." I attacked those dishes with a fury. I was as happy as a kid. I had a job indoors. Things were looking up. At the end of the day the boss came over. The mountain of dishes was gone. Everything was clean.
"So. How was your first day?"
"Perfect. Can I get an advance?" he had to laugh.
"You coming back?"
"Absolutely."

He gave me a two hundred dollar advance, which was enough to get a hotel for a few days and some weed. I was eating every meal at the restaurant, so I didn't worry about food. The only thing I did worry about was staying clean. Getting off dope is not the easiest thing in the world to do, but a lot of people do it. It's STAYING off of dope that is the hard part. Not many people get that job done.

I worked my way out of the dish pit and got to be a prep cook within one week. They got two new guys to replace me. Being a prep was cooler than washing dishes. I got to eat as I worked. I came in later and left earlier and made more money. I started doing two shifts a day, prepping food all day, then working the line or salad bar at night. Whenever I even thought about dope I had to run upstairs and hit my one hitter filled with green weed until it passed.

It's kind of like being startled in the dark thinking about doing dope when you don't want to do any. You jump out of your skin and your heart starts pounding. Weed was my new old addiction and I didn't mind at all. If I even thought about dope I smoked some weed till it stopped. Yes weed helped save me. I wasn't living outside to smoke weed. I wasn't robbing people to smoke weed. I wasn't using myself as a human pin cushion to smoke weed. I still couldn't sleep, but I was on the way to myself and I knew it. One day at a time. One hour at a time. One minute at a time.

I split an apartment on Capital hill with another guy that worked at the restaurant named Johnny.

Johnny had the best weed in town so I was never out. I would work all day then skateboard at night through the city with a bunch of other kids that skated. The only thing I was doing was living. I had no big aspirations except staying clean and letting time go by. That's what I was doing, accumulating time off dope.

I worked in the restaurant for over a year. Then I also started doing jobs around the city. I sold flowers on Pike Place market, bounced in some night clubs I roadied for some bands, whatever was out there to make money. Just not sell drugs.

After a couple of years I started to get my sense of self back. I still had the voice in my head telling me to get dope, except the voice wasn't yelling anymore. It would just calmly say, 'Dope is in the world and you know it.'

This was a crucial time in my life. I was just accumulating time clean. I was just letting time go by. On the one hand there was this giant foreboding presence that I constantly ivied with which was the monster in myself that I had created. On the other hand I was slowly reverting back into who I was before I was exposed. I was working two shifts in the restaurant, getting there early and leaving late. I would skate for a few hours every night with a bunch of guys who tripped on acid and bombed hills. We listened to a lot of White Zombie. I smoked tons of weed did art like I was a kid again, drawing and tagging on every thing. Whatever I could do to keep busy. I knew if I stopped motion bad things could happen. I knew how far away I was. I knew in the back of my mind I was going to win. And the only way to win was one day at a time. Sometimes one minute at a time.

It's pretty amazing that Seattle is the place I really took a hold of my life again. Especially because dope is huge in that town, or at least it was when I was there. The mind is a powerful thing, in fact the most powerful tool we have. It works like a super computer and I set mine to a default program. Going start all over again. And it was working.

There was a goal in the back of my mind but I knew the only way to reach it was patience. I wanted to be one of the Brothers. I wanted to be a member of the family I met in Holland. I wanted to own bikes and understand them. I had a clear goal and the only way I would even start that journey was to finish this one. And that was going to take more time. I knew I had to be clean way longer than I had been loaded. I had to comfortably feel that my dope habit had really left me, that t would and could never happen again. And I had to do that alone.

Once I had a few years clean I felt safe to venture back out into the world. Not to chase my dreams yet, just be a person. NOT a person chasing something he can never catch. NOT a junkie. Just a man.

I went through countless triggers. Thousands of times something would trigger a thought about dope. A movie or TV show, or a conversation, or seeing someone with his eyes pinned back. His pupils dilated. Any of those things or a hundred different ones or just plain boredom..... ANYTHIING can be used to be a trigger to set my brain in motion to get dope. I made that go away. I willed it out of me. I used to want dope so bad that I could find it anywhere. Now I wanted it as far away from me as possible. At the same token I wanted to be able to have it near me, sell it even and not do it. I was absolutely not into selling dope, just to stress a point a real gangster doesn't get high on his own supply. That's rule number two.

It is so important to be a ware of your surroundings at all times. Know how much change is in your pocket and which side of the umbrella your shoes sit. I was well aware of the road in front of me. And I was excited to be on it.

My dad had now moved to Eugene Oregon and the place he lived at needed a painter, so I packed up my stuff and took the Greyhound bus to to Oregon.

51

"Here's your place." I looked inside and thought 'not too bad for someone who used to live in a cardboard box'. The manager of the complex was showing me my apartment. This was an apartment complex with about six hundred apartments. Eugene is a college town. People were always coming and going at this place.

"You don't have to pay rent. That will come out of your pay. As fast as you can paint apartments is as much as you get paid. The faster you do it the more you make. You understand?"

"Got it."

My dad had a place an apartment at the complex a few buildings over. They gave me one in the back. My Dad didn't do much except smoke weed and read books since he retired and had a triple by pass. He was the only person I knew in the town so we spent some time together which was cool. We hadn't done too much of that in thos life so far.

Eugene is a college town so it was always cracking. Local kids would walk up and down 13th street and sling weed and psychedelic drugs to the college kids. Mostly mushrooms and acid. Once in a awhile a guy would show up with Peyote buttons but that was very rare. I always loved Psychadelics, especially acid. I liked making my whole brain work. I started tripping on acid fairly often which made me look at my previous life as pin cushion in horror. I couldn't believe I had done that to myself.

I spent the next few years painting. I saved up for a bike and flew to Miami to get one. I got a good deal on a rigid frame evo, and I shipped it back to Eugene. I was slowly putting my life back in order, piece by piece. I made some friends, I met a girl, I spent my time being normal. Working a job. Painting houses and living life just riding my bike around. I was never into drinking alcohol and I always smoked tons of weed. I was learning to appreciate life again without the constant struggle of life on a mission. It was slowly disappearing from my mind. The voice that used to scream was now only talking. It was no longer telling me to get dope, it would just whisper, 'Dope is in the world and you know how to get it.' I was beginning to realize that awareness would never completely go away.

I was feeling more and more comfortable in my own skin. I bought a 1962 Volkswagen Van and going everywhere in it. The inside was like a ship. It was totally redone inside in teak wood. I got it from this college kid that lived at the same complex I did. It was all green with rainbows and had NAMASTE painted across the top. Life was good. I was going to shows again. Dead shows. I started to feel in control of myself and it felt good. I was becoming who I was. I could talk about dope or my past, even joke about it. If I saw someone with his eyes pinned I got away from them.

In my job I spent a lot of time alone in empty apartments painting them. I had lots of time to think. I started to formulate a plan. It wasn't going to happen overnight. I wanted to be one of the brothers. I wanted to be in that family. And I wanted to do it an ocean away. I had a lot of work to do.

A great deal of life is relationships. I don't care who it is someone helped them get to where they are. There may be some kids born to millionaires, but they don't count. For the rest of us, it is a ladder to the top and we have to climb it.

There were Saturday markets in Eugene. Every Saturday in the middle of town was a craft fair. Like hippies selling their crafted goods. Like tie dyes and shit. Everyone was selling weed. And pipes. Glass pipes. Hand blown glass pipes.

"What you got there?"

I asked the dready walking by with three glass pipes in his hand.

"Chicken bones. Just took them outta the kiln, Twenty bucks each. Want one?" He held them out. I had never seen anything like this.

"How'd you make this?"

"You wanna buy it or not?" Impatient hippie.

I bought the pipe for twenty dollars and he took off. Other kids were opening up gun cases full of pipes they made. I was amazed. I thought these pipes were the coolest things ever.

"It changes color."

"What do you mean."

"It changes color as you smoke it. Watch it will become every color in the rainbow."

I was amazed. I started buying cases of glass for five hundred dollars and selling them for a thousand. Doubling my money. I could swing the cases to my friends in Miami through the mail and up in Washington. I went to the country fair and I saw some live glass blowing and I immediately said to myself, 'I can do that.'

I was infatuated with learning how to be a glass artist. But no one would teach me. I started studying everything I could find about it. I found out it's actually called lamp working and I was living in some kind of lamp working capital.

It really was a secret society, and all the glass artists wanted to keep it that way. I started learning and studying about glass. I went to that Saturday Market every week for a year buying and selling glass cases. All the heavies at the time were in Eugene Bob Snodgrass had a new school, Bob Badtram was doing ocean to mountain to space to alien scenes on pieces blowing everyone's minds.

I didn't have money or time to go to Bob's school, or any school for that matter, I had to work. I would have loved to go to a glass blowing school, that just wasn't going to be possible. I had to find a teacher.

I met one cool dude at the Saturday market who was really killing the glass game named Arik. Everyone was talking about this Arik Krunk glass. That he was the Mac Daddy. Super thick color changing inside out glass pieces. All kinds.

Arik Krunk was living in the forest outside of Eugene in a motorhome with his wife Sarah and soon to be daughter. They had a cool set up by a stream with a few kids living in their cars right near him. So this is like, here is Merlin the Magician and these are the apprentices trying to learn the tricks. Arik was just absolutely focused on blowing glass pipes all day long. The best ones. Better than anyone else. I met up with him at the Saturday market to buy some glass.

"I'd like to buy an assorted case."

"Not a problem."

"Can I watch?"

"You can watch, but I'm not answering of your questions."

"Why not?"

"Homeboy you don't even have a torch."

"Fair enough." I said. "I gotta get a torch."

I made an appointment to drive my Volkswagen van out to the forest the next day and watch my case be made. I was so excited, I knew I had to get the trick. This was my one time glass blowing seminar and I was not allowed to ask questions. I knew I had to get the trick the first time.

As I pulled into the forest I pulled over and took about four hundreds micro grams of LSD. Acid. Trips. LSD used to be legal and made by the Sandoz corporation and given to schizophrenics. It makes your whole brain work. It is definitely not for everyone. I was already good at tripping. When I first got acid I was fifteen years old and working in the second oldest head shop in the country. I was the kid

behind the counter selling you papers. It was paper trips. Little pieces of paper with Snoopy on each one wearing a T shirt that said Joe Cool. One Joe Cool was a ten hour trip.
My buddy Tony walked in and he had a book of one thousand Joe Cools. Tony's dad owned the head shop and Tony managed it. He gave me the book.
"You can't give these to anyone."
"Why not?"
"Because you don't know them like we know you. We know you are good in your head so it's ok. Acid will intensify whatever someone really feels inside. So whoever you give this to might be wrong in their head it might bring that out. And it might not be a good result. You understand?"
"Yes."
He gave me the whole book. I went to school the next day and gave out at least a third of it. No one freaked out. Needless to say I have been a Psychadelic believer ever since.
Psychadelic drugs and pot were now my drugs of choice. Dope had left me, and thankfully so. I still knew it was out in the world, and I was aware of this fact. But I am great at pretending. And I pretended this horrible drama with dope had never happened to me, and it was working. I was reverting back to the hippie I was before that all started.
One thing about acid is I can really handle it. No one even knew I was high. I pulled my Volkswagen van into the clearing Arik had set up. There were three other kids in their cars just living in the forest to watch Arik blow glass. Everyone wanted to learn this trick.
The motorhome he had was small with a glass blowing bench built into the back. I sat there for fourteen hours the first day while Arik made stems for an assorted case. Bubblers, hammers sherlocks chubs sidecars and a couple of jars. Arik works, his wife Sarah hung around and I took notes. Great notes. I wrote down everything Arik did complete with illustration. At the end of a silent fourteen hour day, these kids pulled a rope from the river and pulled a bunch of cool beers out of the creek, made a campfire and had a party. Hippe life at it's realest.

"I need cigarettes." Arik said as he walked out of his motorhome.

The next day was a recap of the first. Not a word spoken as Arik made and pushed bowls, then attached them. I took extensive notes once again, writing every single detail of what I saw complete with illustration. I knew this was it and whatever I learned here was what I took away from this encounter.

After the last piece was put together and inside the kiln, Sarah looked at my book. It had some crazy drawing of Arik applying a picee of gold for fuming on it. He used almost NO color. All fuming meaning he used gold and silver which he fumed from the flame to the glass in layers to get every color of the rainbow.

"Read me something you wrote." She asked me.

I looked up as high as anyone one man could be and read off a page of what I wrote showing them both the illustrations I had made. They both looked at each other and smiled. Arik looked at me.

"If you get a torch I will teach you how to do glass art."

"Really?"

"Yeah really. No one ever sat here for fourteen hours a day, not moving not talking."

"Or took notes like that." Sarah added.

52

I bought a motorhome for two thousand dollars and built a glass shop in the back of it. A lot of glass artists had motorhomes with glass shops built inside them. Arik had one and he helped me build mine.

I lived in that motorhome for the next year in and around Eugene, staying in parks and driving weed up and down the coast from Bellingham to Eugene. I had friends that would front me forty packs, which is forty pounds at a time. I would drive the pounds down in the right lane doing the speed limit. I never got pulled over once. Even if I did I had a hidden compartment where I stashed the weed. This was after a five hour packaging session. We would use a seal a meal and triple seal the pounds, wiping them down with alcohol in between each seal.

I would hit Eugene and stop at someone's house and hand out the pounds and they would get sold by a network of kids on skateboards. I would do glass art in my motorhome in the back of the house while I waited for them to return with the money.

Wherever I stopped I hooked you up. You always have to hook people up all along the way. You have to pay it forward at all times, that's how it works. I would spend the money like its going out of style. I figured it was that or it would stop coming to me. That's how I was taught.

I was like a money generator. That's one of the benefits or results of being a junkie. You can be a homeless hopeless human with nothing but a habit, but you will find a way to generate four hundred dollars a day to support that habit. Realistically there are NO benefits of being a junkie. None. But surviving it is another story. I got stronger and stronger every day that I stayed clean off dope. Stronger in my own will each and every day.

"Whats Up?" I said.

"You my man. Come on in." Patrick's eye's lit up when he saw me with my duffle bag at his front door. He knew he was going to get paid. Patrick had a big house off thirteenth street with five or six other kids. There where these big houses all over Eugene with kids living in them. This house was filled with dreadie kids. Kids with dreadlocks, white kids that listen the Grateful Dead and are into Psychadelics.

"I got the super dank. Forty pounds. MTF crossed with some purple. It's dank."

"Matamuskan Thunderfuck? Really?'

"Yeah. Crossed with purple. Can I bag it up here?"

"Absolutely." Patrick said as he walked down the hall. The Dead was playing in three different rooms. We went to the back and I poured out a few pounds and started bagging it up in to quarter pounds. That's what I mostly worked with. I figured if anything happens, like someone comes back with a story, like how he lost it, at least it would only be a quarter pound that got lost and I could cover it. That way I was comfortable fronting out as many quarter pounds as possible. It's all about turnaround. Getting the product out there and getting it back. Quick.

"How much you got?"

"Twenty pounds. I woulda had forty, but the other twenty wasn't al the way cured."

"Wanna sell it in one shot?"

"Depends."

"On what?"

"On how much profit I can make. I'm certain who ever wants it in one shot wants to pay me way less than I would make working it on the street."

"Considerably. But maybe he can make it worth you while. He traveled here from Chicago. They pay four a pound out there. He is looking to pay three."

"And what are you gonna tack on?"

"Nothing. He will take care of me."

"And all the weed is going back to Chicago right? He's not gonna sell it here in town?"

"No."

I thought about it. I was getting pounds on the front for two grand. On the street I was making at least four thousand but it took a week to get that done. Selling that all at once I make a quick twenty grand.

"Done."

Patrick went and got his friend from Chicago who was sitting in the other hitting the bong listening to the Dead. He had all hundreds so after the money and weed changed hands I was back on my way to grab the other twenty pounds. I really wanted to just sit down and do glass art but I had to make a living.

When you are a beginning glass artist you have to sit down day after day and keep practicing. If you only sit down every now and then you will only get frustrated. I was happy to be making money, but I really wanted to get back to Eugene and practice my glass art.

By the time I got back up north the other twenty pounds was dry and I bagged it up and headed back. I was in between Salem and Eugene cruising down the highway when all of a sudden my rear axle made a loud crack. It felt like I hit a bump or ran something over. My motorhome came to a screeching halt. I pulled onto the shoulder in the last twenty feet.

I got out and looked at the smoking rear end and the fifty foot skid mark I made. My brain shifted into high gear. I knew I had to get out of there fast. I also knew I couldn't leave twenty pounds in the motorhome when I go to get help because a state trooper could roll up on my motorhome and then I would be screwed. I had to work fast. I looked all around at my surroundings. I was in the middle of two exits on the Oregon highway. Not a lot around there. There was a big industrial yard on the other side of the fence about a mile up the highway.

I went into the motorhome and pulled out the pounds. It was four triple sealed bags together they were as big as a duffle bag. I stuffed them into a green army duffle bag clipped the top shut, locked up the motorhome and went running up the highway with my twenty pound package. It was bouncing around as I ran. It must have looked like it was full of feathers. Or cotton.

At the exit was the entrance to the industrial park and all the workers were just getting done working. There was a line of cars leaving the plant. I walked up to the first truck I saw hoping I could jump in the back. I had to get to a pay phone and call a tow truck before the highway patrol showed up.

"How far is it to the next gas station?" I asked the guy driving the truck.

"About a mile up the highway." I held up forty dollars.

"Can you give me a lift." He grabbed the forty.

"Hop in."

He opened the door and I hesitated for a second. I was going to jump in the back. I didn't want him to smell the weed. I jumped in his truck with my duffle bag and he took me to the gas station up the road. I called a tow truck and hitched a ride back to the motorhome. The guy in the car kept looking at my duffle bag but he didn't say anything.

When I got to the motorhome the tow truck was already there.

"Axle's broke. I gotta put it in a dolly."

"Whatever it takes."

He called another tow truck that brought a dolly and they towed my motorhome to their salvage yard outside Salem. They had a repair shop there and they called around to get me a new axle.

"It's gonna take about a week." The guy who owned the yard said as he walked up.

"What is?"

"Getting an axle for this motorhome. We found one, same year make and model, but it's in Texas. Gonna take a week to get here."

"I live in this motorhome."

"Not a problem. You can live in it in this yard till the axle gets here. We lock it up at night, so you will be locked inside the yard."

"Cool." I knew I had no choice. Plus I had to move the new twenty pounds within a week. I called Patrick and explained the situation and he started coming back and forth moving pounds. I sat in the motorhome for a week and practiced my glass art while I waited for the axle to be shipped. It took about five days to move the entire twenty pounds so when the motorhome was fixed I headed back up north to pay off the weed.

I knew I had to let more time go by. The voice in my head never went away and I knew it never would. I knew I didn't have to listen to that voice and it would one day quiet down to barely a whisper. The real voice, the one you hear when you close your eyes is your voice. That voice knew I was done with my past. That David died and a new one was here. Now I just had to live. And let time go by.

I rented a house in Graham Washington and my glass teacher Arik came up there to live with me with his family. We built a two torch glass shop in the backyard. We lived outside a trailer park. Across the street were horses running on the neighbors farm. Next door was a small forest that we grew some outdoor weed in. Life was good. I was driving back and forth about once a month with a motorhome full of weed making good money and melting glass in my shop the rest of the time.

It was the best possible scenario to live with Arik who was also my pal and have the shop in the back yard. We got liquid oxygen delivered to the house and really got into it. I melted so much glass it's what I dreamed about at night. Instead of dreaming about getting high.

I was past the point where if dope was near me I would do it. I knew I wouldn't do it, but I might go running out of the room. Couldn't be near it, or talk about it let alone joke about it in the past tense. I wanted to be able to stand right next to it and not want it.

I was regressing back from the junkie I had become to the hippie I originally was. Psychedelics will make you think. Dope will make you hurt. As time went on it was easier to remember that. I knew I was on the way to taking my life back. I new it was not an overnight process. I knew that it was going to take years to feel whole again. Didn't matter. I knew I was going to own my life again. Then squeeze every bit of life out of it.

53

I heard a loud knock at six am and I thought 'Who the hell would be here this early?'

Hoping it wasn't the cops I looked out the peephole and saw Marcus the old hippie who lived in the park community. I opened the door. Marcus lived in the back of the park with his wife and like six dogs and nine cats. They both had hair down to their ass, transplants from Woodstock and Haight Ashbury, They were just enjoying life quietly. We had become friends over the past couple of years smoking joints and watching sunsets, or on a clear day sitting on the porch looking at the mountain. It was a tight knit little community that lived by the park.

"You got a hack saw?" Marcus said as he walked in.

"Somewhere around here. Let me look." I turned around to get a hacksaw. Marcus was covered in mud. He was holding a PVC pipe sealed on both ends, which was also covered in mud.

"Got any coffee.?" Marcus always made himself at home.

"You know where it is. Help yourself."

It took me a minute to find a hacksaw. Long enough for Marcus to make a pot of coffee. I put it on the floor next to the PVC pipe.

"What's in there?"

"Open it and find out." Marcus was smoking a big joint. He sat back to watch. You can bet he wasn't gonna cut it. He had to be at least sixty five. I think he had retired a few years earlier. Manual labor and Marcus parted ways long ago.

"Cut it right here." Marcus pointed to an exact spot on the tube below the cap.

I took the hacksaw and cut into the pipe. It didn't take long till I had cut through and A bunch of plastic bags spilled onto the floor. Each bag was filled with really small pills, each one about as big as a grain of rice.

"What are they?"

"Hard to say. I buried it in sixty seven."

Marcus reached down and picked up a folded piece of paper that was also in the PVC pipe. He unfolded it and read it.

"Summer of Sixty Seven by the looks of it. Big Brother and Rejoice with the Youngbloods were playing. One dollar per head." He handed the flyer over. I looked at it closely. It was totally psychedelic, with faded day glow colors. It was brittle but intact. You could see where it had been ripped off of a wall.

"I bet this is even worth something."

"Not as much as that. That is either the cleanest LSD or the finest Mescaline I ever saw. That's why I buried it for a rainy day. Me and my old lady been thinking about doing some traveling. I figure now is as good a time as any."

"And you figure I know where to get rid of it."

"That and I trust you. Which is big."
"How much?"
Marcus sat back and smiled and relit the joint.
"Twenty five cents. Those barrels are made of tigers milk or some other hippie shit. Either way you can see it lasts. Each bag has a thousand in it. Ten bags is a gram. Hundred mics a barrel, ten thousand barrels a gram, twenty five grams. Comes to sixty two thousand five hundred for all of it. And that's a deal, yes sir."
He passed me the joint. I took out a pencil and paper and did the math. He was right.
"One thing though. You gotta give me the money now. No fronts. I got other people, I'm just giving you the first crack at it."
I sat back and thought about how I could get that much cash fast. Marcus pulled out this little black light flashlight. He turned it on and held it over the barrels. They all shined day glow bright.
"Give me a few hours."
"You can have all day, till sundown. Then I'm gonna call my friend Hank. Give him a shot. I'll leave you one bag as a sample." He got up and walked to the front door, before he opened it he turned around and looked at me and put his finger up to his lips.
"Shhhhhhhhh." Marcus smiled and walked out.
I knew I had to work fast so I picked up the bag of barrels and took off in my pickup truck. I knew what a big come up this was. There was only one person I knew who could pull this off, my friend Joe who lived about five minutes away.
"Did you try it yet?"
"Of course not. I came right here. I believe him. I don't want to get all twisted up until we figure this out."
"The smartest thing to do would be to cover the whole thing in one deal and see what we got left."
"Yeah but who's got dough like that?" Joe thought for a minute looking at the bag of barrels on the table.
"I got it. One dollar a piece is a steal. We call my cousin Rob and sell him seven grams. At one dollar a piece that's seventy

grand. We split the difference with the rest of that cash and the barrels. Deal?"
"How do you know he's got that much cash on hand?"
"He just harvested his house and two others. He's got it."
"You think he will do it?"
"If it's as good as you say it is he will."
We jumped in my truck and took off for Rob's place. It was like twenty minutes away in the next town over.
"You tried it?"
"Not yet." Rob had about six barrels in the palm of his hand. Maybe ten.
"How you know it works?" Rob took all six. Or ten.
"What are you doing?"
"You said it was a sample. I'm sampling. Seventy Thousand is a lot of cash. I'd have to dig it up. Literally. I never buy any fruits or vegetables without sampling them first."
"Not a problem." Joe said. We sat back and smoked a joint. Didn't take long before Rob was as high as a kite. We spent the next eight hours digging holes in his backyard looking for his buried cash. Rob laughing and giggling like a little kid with his eyes as big and bright as flashlights.
" I think I hit something." I could feel my shovel had hit something hard. It didn't take us long to dig out a steel strong box. By now Rob was as high as could be, but incredibly clear.
"Open it up." He tossed me the key. I opened it and we all got quiet.
"How much is that?"
"Hee hee that's a cool million. Yes siree bob cat tail yes sir. Been lookin fer that fer awhile now knew I'd find it soon yessir gotta peel off seventy K fer ya then get my barrels you said they come in all colors I want all colors Ok? All colors them some clean barrels yessir gonna peel off that seventy and go get my barrels. Yessir."
We passed the box up and walked back up to Robs house. He counted the seventy grand quickly and amazingly accurately. We split to go get the rest of the barrels from Marcus.
"I told you it would work out." Joe said. I was figuring this out on a pad with a pencil.

"By my calculations we get fifteen grand and nine grams each. Ninety thousand barrels each."
"That's correct. Not too bad for one days work."
"Not too bad at all."
We went back to Joe's house and split up the barrels and the money. As I pulled off all I could think was I'm gonna get a bike. Seven thousand dollars in cash was more than I had at one time in along time. Plus Ninety Thousand Barrels. My mind boggled at the possibilities. Even if I lost a bunch or gave some away I was for sure going to have enough for a bike. Maybe two.
There was no way I was going to nickel and dime the barrels out I had to find a one time sale so I made some calls and put myself on the next plane to Miami.

54

"Fifteen Grand?"
"Fifteen grand." The bike was real nice but not worth fifteen grand. Mostly because I didn't have that much. Truthfully I wanted another bike so bad I would have paid whatever price. I had only been in Miami for a few days and I still had about Seventy five thousand Barrels left. I handed out a bunch of samples and then offed one gram in two pieces for five thousand each and with the change from the first deal I went off to buy the first bike I liked. I found a beauty. The bike was clean. Rigid frame, Evolution motor, five speed, custom paint. The paint wasn't my style but I knew I would change that quick. It looked real good and I knew I wanted it, but for my price.
"I'll give you twelve five." I held up the Twelve thousand five hundred dollars. I made sure it was all in twenties so it looked like a really big stack. I saw the guys eyes bug out. Money speaks all languages and all dialects. Money closes the deal.
"It's all I got. Take it or leave it." That's the take away clause. Always works.

This was a big deal for me. I had flown to Miami to buy a motorcycle. I hadn't done dope in a few years and I was on the way back to what I considered being a man is again. Owning a Harley Davidson was a big part of that. Junkies don't own things like Harley Davidsons. Owning a bike again was another symbol to me that I had a grip on my life and nothing else did.

I was going back and forth from the East Coast to the West Coast. I was spending time in Miami moving weed in all amounts. I was working on my glass art whenever I was on the West Coast and working on making dollars on the East Coast.

The first thing I did with the Rigid Frame bike I had bought was to take it apart and repaint it. I figured I would learn the bike better and that's what a custom bike is all about. Customizing it to your specifications. My friends owned a bike shop so I would spend my days there wrenching as best I could on the bike. They would be in conversations about motors and I wanted to be able to take part in those conversations but I didn't know enough so I didn't say anything. I had help but I didn't understand the bike like I wanted so I made a decision to go to school to learn all about it. I started looking into that. I had in the back of my mind what I wanted to do but I was still a few years a way from feeling completely whole enough to do it and I knew it.

I got a U haul Truck and put the bike in the back and drove back out West. I made some real money on the ninety thousand barrels and I bought a second bike and left it there for whenever I went back. All my friends had two bikes. That way you had one to ride in case one was broken, which was fairly often.

I didn't have anyone to ride with when I got back out west. My glass teacher didn't have a bike and neither did any of my friends. I would ride up and down the Redwood highway. It would take four hours to get to Eugene Oregon from Graham Washington and I would ride that all the time. Or ride an hour up to Seattle from my house. I would sleep on the ground all night in my bedroll next to my bike at the rest stops. I had already slept on the ground plenty in my life, but not like this, with the excitement of being alive. Sleeping on the ground next to my Harley Davidson didn't bother me at all. This is how I thought a man should operate. His bike first above all else. Every dime I had went into riding and maintaining my motorcycles. I was logging in time, putting in the motions of what I thought it took to overcome any obstacle.

I started formulating a plan. I rode my bike everywhere. I was making good money on glass art and I decided to pack up and go to school to learn motorcycle mechanics. I figured I could support myself doing glass art while I went to school.

The waiting list to get in the school was a few months away so I used that time to ride my bike up and down the coast just logging time and miles.

Hollywood reached out to me three times in my life. Which is amazing in itself. I can easily describe the first time Hollywood reached out to me and the outcome as, 'the worst mistake of my life.' Definitely the biggest missed opportunity.

I think every American dreams about being in the movies. It's an American thing. I don't think I dreamed about it any more or less than any normal person. I wasn't chasing that dream or anything. Kind of like a dream you know will never happen. Like fantasizing about how you would spend your lottery winnings if you won.

The first time Hollywood called me I was way too young and reckless to understand what an incredible opportunity was being bestowed upon me. Unfortunately you can't always see opportunity coming, even when it makes a home invasion on your life.

I had ridden my bike from Washington to Eugene to visit some friends. I was riding the bike everywhere. Sleeping on the ground was no problem in the summer. I was accepted and planning to go to Motorcycle school. I had already been approved for a student loan for The MotorCycle Mechanics Institute in Phoenix Arizona. I had a clear plan. First I was going to learn everything about the bike then get back to Holland and ride with the Brothers that I had met. This was like my goal in life. I kind of felt that if I can complete this task then I will have for sure taken my life back. It's good to

have a plan. It makes you feel solid. Like you have some direction. Like you have something going. You do have something going, you got a plan man.
I pulled in to Eugene early and everyone was asleep. I rode over to the bike shop and was checking out the bikes in the storefront. I figured I would smoke a joint and call my friend Judd in Miami.
"Whats up?'
"Same shit. What's up with you."
"Just rode my bike to Eugene. Everyone's asleep here so I figured I would call you."
"You should call P.J. He's got a job for you."
"Doing what?"
"In his next movie. Just call him. And don't screw it up. I gotta get back to work. Call him now."
"O.K."
"And don't screw it up."
"I won't."
Something about those words, 'Don't screw it up". Whenever anyone told me not to screw it up. I did. I hung up and dialed my Buddy P.J. We all grew up down the block from each other. P.J. always had it together. He graduated from New York Film Institute and was making movies ever since. One of those really talented focused people you meet at an early age. Some of us take a little longer to get the clue.
I dialed P.J.'s number and he picked it up right away.
"I got a job for you."
"Collecting?"
"No you knucklehead. I'm going to put you in my next movie."
"For real?"
"For real. And it's in South Africa. Do you have a passport?"
"Of course."
"We leave in two weeks. You gotta work while you are there."
"Doing what?"
"Drawing stuff in the art department. Loading gear. Basically doing movie shit until we film. It will take a bout three months of prep until we can start filming. We have to cast the film, scout locations, all kinds of stuff. You are going to learn a lot."

"Thank you."
"You're welcome. My assistant will help you get your paperwork in order. You gotta get some shots."
"For what."
"Malaria and stuff. It's pretty volatile over there."
"Malaria?"
"Don't worry about it. It's all an adventure. And David, don't screw it up."
P.J. hung up and I started to feel the familiar feeling of the excitement of the unknown.
Two weeks later I was on a trans continental jet flying from San Francisco to South Africa to work on and star in 'From Dusk Till Dawn 3'.

55

I had already been planning on going to motorcycle school in Arizona, and the school started a new class every nine weeks so I just pushed off my enrollment a few months to do the movie.
South Africa wasn't exactly as I imagined it to be. That Apartheid vibration was still in the air. Here I am skateboarding around with my Hi Tops, baggy pants and wallet chain, and everywhere I went I would be getting stared down with hate. There were a lot of people sleeping on the ground everywhere and a lot of poverty. There was a very visible separation of the classes.
I had a cool little apartment about ten blocks away from the movie studio and I would skateboard there to and from work. From living in Holland I could speak Dutch pretty good, which is a little like Africaans which is the language they speak in South Africa it being a Dutch colony.
The first day there P.J. introduced me to everyone. They had a little introduction and pep talk. I had never been on a movie set before, so I had no idea how cool this whole thing was. I met a guy named Marcos who worked in the South African side of the film company and he also surfed. He showed me

where I could buy some weed, which I did straight away. The weed wasn't any good but then I found another street dealer who had hash for sale and I got some Lebanese hash that was really good for cheap. I bought almost an ounce the first buy which I figured would pretty much last the rest of the trip.

I got the malaria shots before I left and they gave me some pills to take while I was there. The pills made me depressed. I didn't want to stop taking them because I kept hearing all these horror stories about people getting bitten and contracting malaria and almost dying.

They put me to work in the art department drawing all kinds of spooky shit, then they had a team of people that would build whatever got drawn up. I was in the art department drawing one day when P.J. walked up and handed me a few pages from the script.

"Learn these lines. You are Johnny Madrid."

"Yes Sir."

"And get a haircut."

"What?"

P.J. didn't hear me. He was leading an entourage of producers about to go another location scout. I looked at Marcos.

'Did he say, 'Get a haircut?"

"That's what it sounded like to me."

"Aint no way I'm getting a haircut." I said as I went back to drawing.

"If you want the part you will." Marcos said as he walked out.

I thought about that for a minute as I looked at the lines. I was missing my girl and my friends in Eugene. I was depressed from the Malaria pills and I damn sure didn't know how good I had it. It wasn't until I saw the film a year or so later did I realize P.J. was having me read for the lead. Maybe if I knew that I might have took it more seriously. At least I had made a deal with P.J. that I would only cut my hair if I got the part. I had no idea that me reading was only a formality. I had the part. My buddy was the Director. Can you believe it? I still screwed it up.

I didn't really learn the lines, I just kind of glanced at them so when the day came to read for P.J., and the producers and investors, I was totally not prepared.

I had to skate across town to an office for the casting. I got real stoned before I left my apartment. I had to smoke a ton of hash to counter act the malaria pills. That was my rationale.

I walked into the casting office and P.J. was here with the Producers and some guy who was filming the casting. As soon as I walked in they had me stand on this X and P.J. said 'ACTION" and I was supposed to start reading the lines. Instead of knowing the lines I would start laughing. Maybe because I was stoned or maybe because I was looking at my childhood friend and I found it funny that we were in South Africa. Every time I started laughing P.J. would jump out of his chair and run up to me and grab me.

"This is serious."

"I know."

" So don't screw it up."

"I'm trying not to."

We did the lines a few more times and then I was excused. I knew I didn't get the part. At least I really thought I screwed it up.

I skated the whole way back to my apartment only thinking about leaving South Africa. I think after time the malaria pills got stronger and stronger. It probably accumulated. Either way I was feeling worse and worse. I didn't have the Hollywood bug yet. I was more into being home doing glass art and riding my bike. I wanted to go to motorcycle school then go ride with my friends.

I tried to get into it but I couldn't. I couple of people told me to just wait till they start filming but that was a month away and I felt that I was just wasting time there because this was not my real goal.

I walked into P.J.'s office.

"I wanna go home."

"You're kidding me."

"No really. I aint having fun here. I need to go home. I'll pay you back. I just gotta go."

"Brother. This is a mistake. I know not a lot has happened yet."

"Did I get the part?"

"No you didn't. They are going to go with a more seasoned actor. But I'll put you in the movie somewhere."

"I know you would. I just really, really wanna go home. I'm on a different path."

P.J. looked at me with a sad smile. Not sad for him but sad for me as he was watching me make another bad mistake. Sometime you just got to let people learn the hard way.

"OK. Find a flight. You are going to pay me back this year."

I turned around and left his office. I felt like a weight was lifted off of me. The weight of responsibility was gone. I was no longer responsible to the job at hand. I was back on my path. I had no idea the weight of regret is much heavier and rests on your shoulders for much longer.

I was walking out of the office and I ran I to Marcos carrying storyboards.

"Howzit mate."

"I'm leaving."

"Why's that?"

"I'm not having fun.'

"Fun's just about to start. Stick around mate. You won't regret it." He turned and kept moving into the office. I looked in and saw all the people moving around, looking at white boards with writing on them, moving paper around, basically being busy. They had the bug of making a film. They were bubbling with excitement. I just wasn't feeling it. I turned and went to pack.

Within two days I was boarding a plane back to San Francisco. From there I would catch a plane to Seattle and get a ride to my place in Graham Washington.

I sat in my seat and a young couple sat next to me from Los Angeles. They talked about how great South Africa was and how they hated to leave Their beloved South Africa. Beloved. I couldn't believe they even used that word. I sat there counting the hours until I got home. Something like twenty hours. I was dreading it. But not like the feeling I was about to feel.

As the wheels of the plane left the earth I suddenly knew it was the worst mistake I had ever made. It hit me all at once. I walked away from a great job. I missed a golden opportunity.

Worst of all, I let down a friend. And I couldn't turn the plane back either. Massive regret. Nightmare. It was a very long flight.

56

The twenty hour plane flight was brutal. I had plenty of time to think. I figured I better make this work. Better get back to chasing my dream. Aint no one else going to make it happen but me.
Soon as I landed in the U.S. it was like the race had started. I had felt I wasted enough time and I had to get back into my program.
I got back to Graham and immediately went back into motion. I packed up my life in my motorhome, which was also my mobile glass blowing shop as quick as I could. I let my glass teacher know I was leaving and he could take over the house.
I rented a U haul to haul my motorcycle in, said my goodbyes and headed for Arizona to go to the Motorcycle Mechanics Institute. This was the first part of my plan.
I was totally excited. There is no feeling like embarking on a big journey that you don't know the outcome, except that you know one way or another, come hell or high water you are going to realize your dreams, and make them you're reality.
I pulled into Phoenix at night and found a trailer park near the school. Phoenix was brutally hot, even at night. Living in the motorhome was not going to be easy. I planned on getting settled and renting an apartment. I always grew weed and I had a complete indoor growing set up. Lights, hoods, ballast, everything I needed to have an indoor grow operation. I figured this is how I could sustain myself while I studied. Seemed like a good plan at the time.
I checked in and took a tour of the school the next day. It was so hot the motorcycles would be falling over in slow motion because the kick stands would be sinking into the asphalt. Most guys had a flattened beer can for their kick stand to stand on.

I spent a week in Phoenix looking for an apartment. I finally found one that would work and put a deposit down. There was still about two weeks until the end of the month when I could move into my new apartment, then another week until school would start. So I had about three weeks to kill. I spent most of my time trying to stay cool in the daytime and riding my bike around at night. The girl I had been seeing in Eugene and Washington, Milly had moved in with her family in Tuscon, which was about one hundred and ten miles away give or take. It was a nice ride on the bike. It would take about an hour and it would clear my mind. I had a lot going on. Math was never my best subject when I did go to school So I was a little concerned about all the calculations and motor work I had coming. I still smoked a ton of weed, took an occasional pain killer. The voice in my head telling me to get dope, HEROIN was a lot quieter, but still there.

There was a lot of alone time in Arizona. Milly's family didn't like me and we had a few raging battles before I wasn't allowed over there anymore. Alone time aint good for a recovering addict. The saying, 'Idle hands are the Devil's workshop' is true. Gotta keep busy. Aint no down time. Down time gets you in trouble.

After our last big raging fight her family forbid me to come back so I rode back to Phoenix. Riding the bike in the daytime out there was like having a hair blow dryer blowing hot air on you. Which is not the best thing for an air cooled motor. There was nothing for me to do but kill time until school starts. It was about two weeks away. In a week I would get my new place. Everything seemed to be going according to plan. It's funny how when everything is going smoothest a big monkey wrench shows up. That's life.

I was sitting in my motorhome trying to melt some glass, which was brutally hard in the heat. The trailer park was filled with either students of the school or trailer park people that were trying to survive in the heat of Arizona. I should have just kept my head down and kept melting glass and I might have gotten out of there ok. But I was always looking for that fast buck. That quick scheme to make fast cash.

Sometimes you don't have to look very far. Sometimes it finds you.

I called my friend Carl in Washington just say what's up. Carl always had something going on.

"What up?'

"Same shit. How you like Arizona?"

"Hot. Hot like Hadies. I got a few things figured out. Just waiting for school to start, get my new place and I'm putting things in motion."

"You got some time to kill?"

"Almost two weeks."

"Wanna make some fast cash?" Those are some words I was waiting to hear.

"What's the catch?"

"No catch."

"There's always a catch." I was skeptical to say the least.

"No catch. Just fly out here and rent a car and drive around for a few days. I'll give you a percentage. I got thirty P's here. Beautiful shit. Come on. You could use the dough."

"How much?"

"Hundred per. We move all thirty and you get three grand. I got them gone. You just gotta accompany me around town making deliveries."

"How long you think this will take? I don't know if I can be gone for a week."

"Three days, four the most. Come on. You can do it. I'll pay for the ticket now. Waddya say?"

It's strange how you know some things are a bad decision but you still make that decision, thinking you can out smart the forces of nature and make it come out your way. You can't.

"All right. Buy the ticket. But either way I gotta be back in three days."

"You got it."

The next day I stashed my bike at the school and told them I had to go see my mom in Florida for a few days. I didn't think it was a good idea to leave my bike in the trailer park, even if I locked it up. I got on a plane that night and was in Los Angeles by ten P.M. I knew something wasn't right. There was an ominous feeling in my bones. Looking back that was because I was once again deterring from my plan. You always have to stick to the plan.

Carl picked me up and we went to the hotel. He was a party animal, rocking twenty to forty pounds every couple of weeks. Snowboarding, girls, parties, Carl was definitely living the rock star life.

We got in the hotel room and I couldn't believe my eyes. He had thirty pounds all piled up in a corner and there were two friends and three girls with him. They were sitting at the table snorting lines and drinking beer. I looked at the pounds. "How'd you get those across the California border without anyone seeing?"

"Nate helped me with that." Carl flew down and his friend Nate drove the pounds in a camper.

 Wanna snort?"

Carl handed me the straw.

"No thanks I gotta keep my head together. I suggest you do the same."

"You do what you want or not. Me, I'm gonna party." Carl sat down with Nate and the girls and drank and snorted lines of coke. I curled up on the couch in the next room and tried to sleep. It took awhile, I had to clear my mind of the bad feeling I had. I knew it was useless to try and talk Carl and his friends out of partying. Better off for me to get some shut eye.

I woke up the next day before anyone else did. I took a walk to find a cup of coffee and thought about just leaving. I had a few things set up, my glass shop, the indoor weed grow, not to mention motorcycle school. I knew it was a bad decision to stay. Carl's biggest problem was he was young. That's why he needed someone to rock this with. People tend to try and rob a young snowboarder from Bellingham Washington. Kids were getting ripped off left and right back then. For twenty and forty packs at a time. Dudes tougher than them would look right at these kids and say "We lost it. Sorry. It was only twenty pounds. We'll pay it back next time."

What was Carl going to do? Call the cops? I don't think so. Most of the time Carl and his friends were rolling so hard they just looked at it as an incidental expense. On the other hand the guys ripping these kids off were looking at it as insuring themselves more work. Now Carl would have to front them more weed just to get his money back. It was a vicious cycle.

That's where I came in. That's how me and Carl became friends, collecting. I had no problem collecting debts. Collecting gets half. Not a bad gig. Or like in this case, making sure he didn't get ripped off. I had my coffee and thought about what to do. I decided I would at least rent him the car like I said I would. I wanted to see how easy the first day went. Then I would make my decision on how long I stayed.

When I got back to the hotel everyone was awake. The girls were gone and there was a tall Mexican dude leaving. We almost bumped into each other as he left. He was carrying a little back pack probably with a pound or two in it.

"Who's that?"

"Friend of mine. He took a pound to show around as a sample."

"Where's the girls? Where's Nate?"

"I kicked them out. Nate went to get breakfast. We got work to do. I'm gonna get ready."

Carl took out a little straw and a piece of foil and opened a bindle with some Mexican Brown Heroin in it.

"What's that? What are you doing? You said we had work to do." I snapped.

"I've been up all night snorting lines. I need to level out."

"Level out? What the fuck does that mean?"

"What's your problem?"

"My problem is I am an ex junkie and I don't need that shit near me."

"So go wait in the other room." I started hating Carl with a passion.

Carl lit a match and held it under the foil. The little brown spot started moving and he took a big hit of dope and sat back feeling it. I could smell the acrid sweet smell of dope. It was making my mouth water and my skin crawl. I stood there watching him.

I hadn't even been near heroin in a few years so this was heavy for me. Carl handed the straw over.

"You sure you don't want a hit?"

"I'm sure I don't."
"You're not going to become a junkie from one hit."
"You can only become a junkie one time. Not twice. I already am a junkie."
Sometimes you can't stop yourself. I had no idea I would find dope in front of me when I left Arizona. I would have never gone. I was still in the keep it away from me period. But it's all a learning experience.
Carl took a big hit of dope and held it in. I watched him and my mind and body wanted a hit. Carl let out his hit sat back and held out the little straw again.
"You sure?"
"Shut up. Fuck you. Go get ready."
Carl looked at me and understood real quick that I had turned into someone else. Fortunately for him I turned right back into the ruthless junkie he had heard about. Which is exactly what he needed. Just being near dope turned me back into the psycho I once was. Dope scared the shit out of me now. I was not ready to give up my life again or all the clean time I had accumulated.
Things move fast in slow motion when you are living the mistake first hand. We grabbed a pound to go show some of Carl's friends near San Diego. As we left the hotel I was looking around to see if anyone was taking any notice of us. Everywhere I looked it was business as usual. The cleaning ladies were cleaning rooms, people were checking in and out.
"What about the pounds?" I asked. I didn't think we should leave them alone for the cleaning lady to find.
"Nate is gonna stay and watch them. He gets paid for that."
"Don't you wanna wait till he gets back?"
Carl looked at his watch.
"Can't wait. We gotta go. Gonna be late otherwise. I put a do not disturb sign on the door. Nate will be back in ten minutes."
"Ten minutes aint nothing. We can wait."
"But."
"Shut the fuck up." Carl shut up. He had no choice. He wasn't the muscle of the operation. I was pissed dope showed up in our mix. I didn't expect that and it pissed me off big time.

Nate showed up in ten minutes exactly and we left to go rent a car. Then drive around and show the sample to potential customers.
Renting the car was no problem. We got in the car and Carl took another hit of dope.
"How much of that shit do you have?"
"I only got two grams. It's almost gone.?"
"We sat in the car and Carl got loaded further, then we took off to go drive pounds around L.A.
The first two spots we went to didn't work out. It was the same story everywhere we went, everyone wanted to buy some pounds but no one had any money. Everyone wanted Carl to front them the weed and let them go work it on the street.
"You aint doing that." I told him after we left the second spot.
"Why not?"
"Cause you wont ever get it back. I aint staying here to collect all this dough. You said you had the whole thing set up. You are doing what they want to do………except you don't know anyone here."
" I know a guy in Escondido. Let's go see him."
"Down by San Diego?"
"Yeah. I know him from last years harvest, he told me to come see him when I got here. He is good for twenty pounds for sure."
"Nothing's for sure."
"At least he will know where to get rid of them."
I was already feeling the jones come on just being near dope. It was too soon for me to be this close. Dope was not in my picture anymore and I liked it that way. It doesn't matter how long you been away from dope, two months or twenty years. When you pick it back up again, you are right where you left off. And when I stopped I had a Monster habit. I didn't want to have any habit anymore and I knew it.
We went cruising down I-5 toward San Diego and on the left we passed a big check point or something.
"What was that?"
"What was what?" Carl said.

"That." I pointed in the rear view and you could see the cars backing up to a toll plaza.
"It looks like a toll plaza."
"Why would there be a toll plaza out here?" I knew something was wrong. It just felt wrong. We pulled over on the next exit and pulled into a rest stop on the side of the highway. There were a few cars there with people hanging out, eating their lunch or resting. I parked the car and next to us was a car with two young couples in it. Carl got out and walked to the pay phone to call his friend. We were so unorganized. I walked over to one of the guys parked next to us.
"What is that back there? That big toll plaza?"
"Federal checkpoint." The guy said. The way he said it was like everyone around here knew that.
"Federal checkpoint for what?" I asked him.
"For whatever Holmes. Drugs. Illegals. Even fruits and vegetables. Whatever the man can bust you for."
"Is there any other way around?"
"Nope."
I stood there thinking about this for a moment.
 The two couples walked in the opposite direction. The guy looked at me with a smile.
"Good luck Holmes."
I turned to walk to where Carl was sitting over looking the ocean.
"My friend says he just re upped and he won't need any weed till next week. Then he can take ten." Carl said kind of disappointed.
"So we drove out here for nothing."
"Seems that way."
"This is bad."
"What is?"
"This deal. It's all bad. That's a federal checkpoint we passed. And there is no other way back."
"We gotta dump that weed."
"No we don't." Carl didn't want to just throw they weed away.
"You can lose one."

"No I can't. We'll be fine. It's in a turkey bag. They won't smell it at all."
"You willing to take that risk?"
"Yes. We'll be fine. Let's go clean out the car."
Carl got up and went to the car. I got up reluctantly and followed him. I had to play out the cards I had dealt myself.
"We gotta go back to the hotel." Carl said
"Yes we do. Without the pound. You can take the loss."
"No I can't. Everything is going to be fine. They just wave the cars through. Lets go. The car is rented in your name so you gotta drive it. I'll give you and extra grand."
"And what happens if we get busted?"
"I'll bail you out and pay for your attorney. But that's not going to happen."
Famous last words. We wrapped the pound in a bunch of dirty clothes and re-stashed it underneath the backseat.
I started the car and got back on the highway heading back towards Los Angeles. As we approached the checkpoint the cars were lining up about forty cars deep. The cops were mostly waving cars through. I knew it was all bad. I had an ominous feeling. I could see myself getting busted in a matter of minutes. I wanted to get out of the car and start walking but I was close enough to be seen by the cops and I figured they would jump in their cars and pick me right up. Besides there was no where to go.
"This is bad. This is bad. I should get out right now." I said.
"Stop saying that. We're going to be fine. Just act normal."
We pulled up to the guard and he looked at us and shook his head. We must have looked pretty banged up. Carl had been up most of the night, and I had the attitude and feeling of defeat. I was already down in the dumps for making a bad decision by leaving school and coming here to make a fast buck. Regret is a powerful thing.
The cop leaned in the window and took a good look at us. It was a lady cop with a huge rack.
"Where you boys coming from?" She asked us. We had no clue.
"Disneyland. We were looking for Disneyland but I think we took the wrong exit."

"That's for sure." She waved to some other officers to come over.
"Pull your car over there." She pointed up ahead to the side of the road where some other cars had been pulled over and were being inspected. I started making the drive for the last forty feet of this journey and I knew it.
"We're going to jail." I said. Carl was finally silent. The silence of recognition. He knew I was right.
Three cops came over with a dog.
"You two gentlemen stand right over there." The cop pointed to the guard rail we were parked next to. They let the dog go and he went pretty crazy looking inside and outside of the car.
"Well. According to this dog you have weed in this car. Want to tell us where it is? Or do we have to rip the car apart?"
Carl stood up.
"I have an eighth in my pocket in the back. Can I get it out?"
"Yes."
Carl grabbed a pair of pants from the back pulled out a small bag of weed and and handed it to the officer. The dog seemed to be satisfied and he relaxed.
"This is all there is?"
"Yes sir." Carl said. It was a little too late for 'Sir'.
"We wouldn't arrest you for this anyway." The cop said. For a minute I thought we might just get out of there unscathed.
"You gentlemen go with this officer and wait in that building. We have to search the car. If this all there is, then we are going to let you go."
We walked into the building and they drove our car into the back where they do the real search. I knew we were done. I turned off like a switch and got silent. There was nothing to do except play it out. I sat on that bench and started running through my mind the ramifications of this bad decision I had made. I was clean, about to go to school, on my path. Now I was sitting on a bench in a police station about to embark once again on an all too familiar journey. Jail, bail, attorney. Not too mention all my stuff was in Arizona. I was falling deeper into depression as the seconds ticked by.
All of a sudden three cops walked in.

"Gentlemen. Stand up and put your hands on your heads. You are under arrest."

That old familiar feeling was back. That slow motion feeling when all of a sudden everything is out of your control. Everything was now going to be controlled by the system. However long or short this was going to take was no longer up to me.

"I am so sorry bro. I should have listened." Carl said.

"Shut up." I was furious.

"Soon as we get inside I will have my buddy bail us out."

"Sure you will. Like I mean it. I'm SURE you will."

We waited there for a few hours until some plain clothes cops came and picked us up. One of them was this biker looking guy. Beard, boots, Harley Davidson T shirt. I thought to myself, can't trust anyone, anywhere, anymore. They are either cops or just too careless and stupid to survive on the streets. I knew this was my mistake. I didn't have to go Arizona. I could have said no. Sometimes saying no is harder than just uttering one syllable. Sometimes it takes internal fortitude that only grows through time. I knew I had dealt myself some bad cards, I had been locked up in my life enough to know aint nothing to do but play those cards out.

They took us to a big federal holding building near San Diego and put us in separate rooms for questioning.

"I got nothing to say." Was all I would tell them.

"Your buddy had more to say than that."

"Good for him. But I have nothing to say."

I didn't think for even one minute the cop was dong anything but lying. I knew Carl wouldn't give me up. There was nothing to give up on me. It was his gig.

Jail is always the same. I got my bunk, my bedroll and started thinking about what I was going to do. Mostly I needed to learn form the mistakes I had just made. That is always the biggest lesson, learning from your own mistakes.

Carl got bailed out by the next day. I guess the people who owned the weed needed him back on the street to control the other twenty eight pounds that were still in the hotel.

"I'll get you right out." Carl said to me through the bars as he was leaving with the other inmates that made bail that day.

"You better." I said. I knew he wouldn't. I knew I was on my own. I had no money on my books so I started drawing on envelopes and post cards right away to get items off the commissary. After a few days of not hearing from Carl and watching other guys make bail I called some friends in Florida who helped me make bail.
I got out and got back to Arizona on the next flight.
On the plane I tried to see the good in this situation. It was hard but I realized once again it's all a test in this life. I was offered dope and I refused. That was the test. I smiled thinking I had passed the first big test in a very long time.

57

I made it back to Arizona and told them a story how one of my family members in Florida was sick and I had to postpone my enrollment. The school was very cool. They had enough going on with students coming and going and dropping in and out. They had no idea I had gotten arrested and offered to switch my campus enrollment to their other facility in Orlando Florida if I needed to. This was now an option I had not thought of.
I had to stay in Arizona and keep flying back and forth to San Diego while I went through the motions of going to court. I would meet Carl there and we would stay in a hotel right near the court. Carl had a high dollar attorney and I had a court appointed one. The first parts of the case went quick, arraignments, hearings, discovery, pre trial, the whole bit. It took about two months to get to the pre trial.
As the case started Carl's attorney stood up and addressed the court.
"Your Honor, before we begin, and in the interest of saving the court time and money my client would like to make a statement."
"Go ahead." The Judge said. Carl stood up.
"Sir. I want to say I grew that weed up in Washington and drove it down here myself to sell it. My co defendant here had

nothing to do with it all. He was just giving me a ride. He didn't even know the weed was in the car."
"Is that it?" The Judge asked.
"Yes Sir."
"Sit down."
The Judge called the attorneys up to his bench and they had a little conference. They came back and the Judge called my name. I stood up next to my attorney.
"Yes your Honor." I had been in court enough times to know how to address the Judge.
"I'm looking at your rap sheet and it seems like you get in trouble every two or three years." He looked at me but I didn't say anything. He looked back at the paperwork.
"In light of what your co defendant said, and the fact that your attorney has stated you are about to start school, which is true, is that correct?"
"Yes your honor."
"This court shall impose three years of supervised probation. Report to the court clerk."
"Thank you your Honor."
"Try to stay out of trouble son."
I looked at Carl and shook his hand. We didn't say anything. Nothing needed to be said. I never saw Carl again after that. Not in my life.
I couldn't wait to leave the west. I had already done all the paperwork to show I had family in Florida, which is the only way I could transfer my probation.
Once again I was on a mission. This was a wake up call from HELL. I now knew I could never ever let my guard down again.
I had learned enough to not let it stop me though. I wasn't going to beat myself up over the past. I couldn't change it and I knew it. Got to just keep moving forward.
I got another u haul trailer and packed up my stuff and headed for Orlando Florida.

My dream was very far away in distance and also in time but I never lost focus. I wanted to understand the motorcycle front to back. I wanted to own my own bikes and live over seas in Holland and ride with the friends I had made earlier in life. I could say I wanted to go back in time before many of my big mistakes and start again. Go back to a better time in life. But you can never go back. Only forward. Three steps forward and two steps back.

It took three days to get to Florida. I would drive without the radio only stopping only for gas. Just driving in the silence with only the thoughts in my head to keep me company. I had a lot on my mind. I wasn't in any more of a rush than what the state had given me to report to probation. I had seven days to get to Florida. I wanted to find a place and get situated. I was going to school in Orlando and working in Melbourne at Choppers Inc. Which was the premiere Chopper building shops on the East Coast. I grew up in Miami with the guy who owned it named Billy and he agreed to give me a job. I wanted to find a place to live in between the two.

I knew I had to be careful up in Northern Florida. Laws are different up there. It is redneck city. I never had formal probation before. I had informal probation a couple of times but that's like nothing at all. Basically just stay out of trouble. I knew this was going to be different. Reporting in, pissing in a cup, not being able to smoke weed. I knew this was going to be tough. I knew I had to get my living and working situation together right away. My money was running out fast like always. I always worked and had a scheme going. Always hustling. All my friends were hustlers. But now I had no real hustle. I had to find one.

Albie was my friend and a hustler just like me. He was one of the first people I met when I got to Orlando for school. We had met almost a year previously, but only on the phone. We met in a strange way. I couldn't cross the border to get up north into Canada but I was the one that had the connections. Albie wanted those connections. He was up North and I wasn't. I was in Bellingham Washington, which was as far North as I was able to go. I got no business in Canada. Too cold up there for me anyway. My friend Davey set the whole thing up. He was also from Florida. That's how shit worked. This guy wants to meet that guy and if you set that meeting up and they work and make out good, you get paid. And you

might be getting paid for years, if you were lucky, and if you established your mark which I did.
Davey handed me the phone.
"Albie wants to talk to you." I took the phone.
"Whats up. We gonna make this happen or what?"
"That depends on you." I said.
"How's that?"
"Pretty simple. You send the coin right now. The coin is for the connection. You get it? You send it like immediately and you get to meet the guy. You don't send it, I come up there, you do not meet the guy, I do the deal, it's a one time deal and that's it. Take it or leave it." Albie had no idea I couldn't come up there if I wanted to.
"Call you in an hour." He said.
"Good choice." I said before I hung up. The money was there in fifteen minutes and everything went smooth as silk. I met Albie after I had been in Melbourne about two months. He met me at a gas station to but some of my glass pipes. He walked up with a huge smile.
"What's so funny?"
"You are man. I been dying to meet you since the border." We became best friends immediately.
I rented a house in St. Cloud Florida which is was about forty five miles from Melbourne Florida, and about twenty miles to the Motorcycle Mechanics Institute, 'M.M.I.' in Orlando which was in the other direction just to give you an idea. School was from 5:30 P.M. to 11:30 P.M. That gave me enough time to work all day in Melbourne, then get back to go to school at night.
The probation officer I got, Mr. Wallace was a serious man. A church going, dare to keep kids off drugs type of man. In other words he found his calling being a probation officer. He let me know this fact as he stood behind me while I pissed into a cup the first time. He let me know if I give a dirty test he would do everything in his power to see that I serve the remainder of my sentence incarcerated.
I already had a problem with authority, so having to report and having him call me and having to take piss tests didn't sit well with me. Most people back then described me as a

problem case, a guy with an attitude. It was the first time I had been absolutely straight since I started smoking at ten years old. My motivation was to stay out of jail, to stay my course and get back to Holland.

I wanted to understand motorcycles. I didn't necessarily want to make my living turning wrenches, which I did for a few years, as much as I wanted to be able to fix my own motorcycle. I grew up with friends that were total motor heads, and I could never engage in those conversations about motor work and I wanted to.

Making it through school for eighteen months was no easy trick either. The drop out rate was more than fifty percent. And not necessarily for the math or mechanics but keeping life together in a foreign place proved difficult for many of the students. Most of the students came from somewhere other than Orlando, and holding a job and not falling into the temptations that are on every corner in Florida proved too difficult for many.

I was getting the best of both worlds. At the school I was getting a Harley Davidson accredited education. At Choppers Inc. I was getting a first hand education in Choppin' Wackin' and Zappin' . The guy who ran the shop and owned it, Billy was an absolute Wizard at building bikes. He didn't just order parts and assemble a bike as much as he he MADE his own parts. Or went to the junk yard to find old parts and make them work. A bike from Choppers Inc. was an absolute piece of custom made art that you could tear it up and down the street on.

I started building my own chopper on the weekends and after work. I could already tig weld pretty good from doing glass work. All my friends had custom Choppers. The real big rear end tire's were just coming out. The bike I built had the second 230 series tire ever put on a bike.

I rented a small house with a big yard and parked my motorhome/glass shop in it. I found a head shop in Orlando that agreed to buy sixty five two piece production pipes from me and five head pieces each month. This is how I survived. I would study my ass off and the last week of each month I would sit down and make the pieces for the shop. All the production pieces had to look the same, the head pieces could be as big and gaudy as I could make them. Glass art has been saving me since I started. It became my get away from everything and my way to make money. It was less hazardous than my previous occupation which was being a junkie and a scammer.

My life got real busy which is exactly what I needed. The first six months of school was Motorcycle Theory. We lost about half the class in that period. Then each class after that was two months and we would lose at least forty percent of the class. It just kept getting smaller and smaller. That alone is motivation to graduate. I would study like hell, then lay down to try to go to sleep, and turn the light back on and study more. I absolutely realized how important this was for me. I had to finish what I started. I had accomplished things in my life before, none of them good, and none that took any time or dedication like this, so graduating from school was of major importance to me.

MMI had all kinds of rules that had to be followed. If you miss one day you might not make it through that course. Mostly because there was so much information given on any given day that if you missed it you couldn't catch up. Miss two day and you are kicked out. You also could not get in any fights there. If you put a bunch of knuckleheads together you are bound to have an occasional problem. I saw guys wait till the last day to smash a dude in the face at the lunch truck then never get their diploma.

After about ten months of school I started hanging out with a kid who most teachers considered to be the best mechanic in the class. His name was Monroe and he was from somewhere in the mid west. He couldn't read or write. He would take his exams orally. Meaning they would ask him the questions and he would answer them. Some kids thought this was unfair. He would take apart and put his motor back together hours before anyone in the class then sit there with his arms folded. But when it came time for the exam he would fail ever question. He would leave them all blank. He was real quiet. But he knew motors.

"Why didn't you answer any questions?" The instructor asked him.

"Ask me one." Monroe talked with a real slow southern drawl. The teacher was a way cool cat. He smiled.

"OK. Question one. Describe the assembly and dis assembly of a four barrel carburetor. Monroe smiled as he got off his stool.

"Well Sir, first things first gotta lay out the work mat. Can't be scratching the customers chrome."

Then as quickly, efficiently and calmly as can be Monroe took apart an S&S four barrel carburetor describing it as he did it. A lot of kids already were motorheads, they knew every year and every model built. I just wanted to know bikes. Harley Davidsons exclusively.

Me and my friends always rode hard tail bikes. Rigid frame, that is. No shocks. No stock bikes. Choppers. At Daytona and Bikertoberfest, which are the big bike rallys in Florida we always had the coolest bikes on the strip. That's why Choppers Inc. got so big. The bikes that came out of this shop were so cool. Real innovative shit. The first hubless rim came out of Choppers Inc., also trimmed up velocity stacks, six gun risers, all custom made billet parts. And we ran around with a real wild crew. I didn't drink but everyone else did.

A week before Daytona my phone rang in the middle of the night.

"Hello."

"I'm right outside your house. He hit me in the face. Gave me the boots. For no reason. At a party. In front of everyone" It was Monroe. He was very upset.

"Come inside."

"No. I got a crow bar. I'm gonna make his head meet it. I need you to go with me."

I took a deep breath. Here was my buddy and he was upset.

"I'll be right out." It took me less than a minute to get in his car. When I got in Monroe looked like he had been in a fight. Or two of them. As soon as I got in the car Monroe peeled out. He had this old GTO he had been restoring. The outside was a little beat up but the motor purred.

"You know that asshole John Williams?"

"Big John Williams? That redneck from Tennesee?"
"Yeah that's him. There was a party tonight. The whole class was there. They got a kegger. Everything was smooth."
Monroe had to catch his breath. He was upset. He was driving like a maniac.
"Relax. Go on."
"I want to get to the party before he leaves."
"We will. Go on with the story."
"Like I said, everything was smooth. Then this asshole redneck shows up with his brother and they are drunk drunk. They were bothering everyone. Calling us all kids and punks. I had to take a piss real bad from drinking beers and it looked like there might be a fight. I didn't wanto to piss in my pants and I was next to the bathroom. I went inside and pissed like a racehorse. Wasn't inside longer than two minutes. When I opened the door, Big John cracked me in the face with a right. Then him and his brother gave me the boots. For no reason."
"No one helped you? No one from the class?"
"Some girls that were there started screaming for the cops and they took stopped beating me."
I was not surprised no one stood strong with this kid. He was real quiet. The two brothers were bullies from up north in Tennessee somewhere. Most of these kids were kids just trying to get a diploma. Have a cool party on a Saturday night. We pulled up to the party and the cops were already there breaking it up. One of the students walked over to the car when he saw us.
"What happened?"
"They ended up punching some girl in the face." The kid said who was leaning in the car. I think his name was Sam or something.
"She got knocked out cold. Someone called the cops and they took off."
"Lets get out of here. Nothing we can do now." I told Monroe. He reluctantly drove away slow.
"We can't let them get away with this."
"We won't."
"You promise?"

"Yes. I promise."

Monroe dropped me off and I didn't get much sleep that night. This kid was my friend. I had to make this right. And not get thrown out of school doing it.

Monday was quiet at work. We took off and drove the sixty five miles to school in silence. When we got to school the two brothers were in the parking lot. I walked up to them. Some other kids gathered around. I had a friend or two at school who also stepped up.

"Lets go punk." I said to Big John.

"I aint getting thrown out of school. " He said.

"Me neither. Lets just walk right over there." I pointed across the street. "There's an open lot. I don't think anyone is going to mind me bashing your teeth in."

"I aint fighting round here."

"That's cause you're a punk. And a bully. Gonna sneak up on this kid with your brother." I looked at Big John's brother who was bigger than him.

"Let's go across the street and handle it." Me and John were face to face and the five minute bell rang. That's the bell that says we got five minutes to get to class.

"I gotta get to class." John took off.

"How about you? You don't go to school here. Lets have at it." Big John's brother looked at me and a couple of my friends.

"Another time, another place." He said.

"That's for certain." I said.

That was a tense week at school. We weren't allowed to fight and every time I ran into this asshole I invited him across the street to handle it. It got brought to the attention to one of the instructors and they made an announcement that every one better lay off.

The following weekend was the start of Biketoberfest. The big motorcycle rally in Daytona about an hour away. Everyone was going, the whole school. All my friends rode their choppers up from Miami and we all rode into Main street together. Like I said I ran around with a wild bunch. They would get loaded and drink and fight and do burn outs on their choppers everywhere we went. And we had the coolest looking choppers on the block. Any block.

We parked in front of a big bar called 'The Bank'. The streets were lined with bikes on both sides. Whereever we parked there would be a crowd of people around our bikes taking pictures and posing in front of them. My boss Billy wasn't as famous as he was about to be in the coming years, he was still on the way up, which was cool to watch. Choppers Inc. always had the most innovative shit, and people knew it.

I walked outside to have a look at the bikes and I saw Monroe with two other younger kids from school.

"What are you doing here? You're not even old enough to get inside."

"Big John is at Froggy's. With his brother. You said you were gonna make this right."

I looked at Monroe with his sad eyes. He hadn't been the same since this happened. He was sort of broken after the beating he took. He wasn't ripping down the motors in class as fast as he used to. And he was my friend. I got him a job at Choppers inc. so we spent a lot of time commuting together. When your friend calls you answer.

"Hang on. Wait right here."

I turned around and went into the bank and walked up to my crew. They were drinking with a bunch of hot chicks and having a good old time. Daytona can be REALLY wild. I looked at my friends.

"Remember that guy I told you about? The one that jumped my friend Monroe? He's over at Froggy's. I'm gonna go handle it." I turned around and headed through the crowd to the front door. It was a packed house just like every other bar in Daytona is during Biketoberfest. As I got to the front door I looked back to see all my buddies were behind me, all putting on gloves. My Pals. That's what pals are for, backup when you need it. I didn't need it though. We walked down the block and across the street. Behind all my buddies was Monroe and the other two kids. We got to the front door and the bouncer waved us in.

"Wait over there." I told Monroe. He knew he couldn't get in the bar. He was too young and he looked it.

As I walked through the door at Froggy's and made my way through the crowd I zipped up my hoodie and slipped my leather gloves on. I knew I had to see Big John before he saw me. That was very important. The bar was as packed as a rock concert. Froggys was indoors and outdoors and probably held about a thousand people. We made our way to the back in a single file line with me in front. As we passed different people they would see us and say 'Don't fight'. You could tell we were on a mission.

We got to the back of the bar and I saw Big John. He was standing with his back to me talking to a girl and drinking a beer. I looked to the right and saw my entire school class standing together. There was about twenty guys left in the class at this point. I looked at my buddies.

"Just keep the Brother off me." I said.

Then I walked over to Big John. The girl saw me coming and her eyes lit up and John saw that and turned around.

"Back for more?"

I had momentum on my side and blasted him in the teeth with a right cross. He was standing on the edge of the patio and hit the ground hard knocking the wind out of him. My friends made a semi circle around the fight keeping everyone away. I jumped on Big John's chest before he could get up and beat him till he was unconscious. He took a real beating. Then we stood up and left just as quick and quiet as we walked in. We took our hoods off and our gloves off as we walked out. Big John laid on the ground bleeding and unconscious. Bouncers were running to the back.

"There's a fight in the back." My buddy said to one as we walked past.

On the way back to the Bank I decided to make a conscious effort to use everything I see and feel and experience as a lesson applied to my personal goal. Which was to graduate and get my chopper and the new one I was building back to Holland plain and simple.

Monroe waited outside and I came back out of the bar. We walked back over by Froggy's and in the alley we could see the ambulance with the red lights flashing and Big John all bandaged up.

"Thank You." Monroe said real quiet.

"That's what the whole thing's about. Sticking up for your friends. Your friends come hell or high water."

I had been building my second bike after work. Every dime I made went into the bike. My boss Billy was getting in different motorcycle magazines more often and one of them was called the Horse Mag and it was run by a guy named Geno. He drove out to the shop one day for a photo shoot and I told him the story of what happened in Biketoberfest.

"You should be a writer in the magazine. We need a fiction writer."

"That wasn't fiction." I said.

"I'll pay you two hundred bucks an article."

"What would I write about?"

"Whatever you want. Or I can give you assignments. Write one about packing for the run."

"Two hundred bucks?"

"Two hundred bucks."

"Deal."

This was a challenge that I was really into. I don't know why but I really liked the thought of getting published in the motorcycle magazine.

I tried writing a story. I was never a big book reader. I've read some books just not too many. Mostly when I was locked up. I knew any story I wrote had to have a beginning a middle and an end. That much I knew. I remember my dad telling me how 'A book was something that takes people where they have never been.' I thought about that. I stared using the Billy's computer after work to write my story on. I didn't even own a computer yet. It took me a couple of days and I wrote my first story. I thought the best thing to do was to write what I know, at least at first. So I wrote about me and my buddies, on out choppers, then breaking up the bar, just like we used to do.

'A Night at the Deuce' got published and everyone dug it. It was one of the times I think my father was proud of me. We weren't the best of friends, but getting published was a big one to him. He passed away shortly after that. I was always happy he got to see that before he left this plane of existence.

I started writing for the magazine every issue. I was definitely hooked. It was cool to see my words in print. Geno the publisher made a car magazine and offered me the space for my own article. I got the last page of every issue. I created a new character called Jimmy Carbone and my own column called 'Burnin' Rubber with Jimmy Carbone'

Jimmy Carbone was a drunken Hot Rodder, a completey screwed up motor head. Writing those articles was all fun. I always waited till the last day of the deadline or after Geno had called me two or three times to start writing. I learned I work best under pressure. I was getting addicted to accomplishing things.

After a year and a half the probation officer eased up a little. Like he didn't follow me into the bathroom anymore, but I still had to report, piss in a cup, show income and all that shit. Everything else was going smoothly with graduation approaching. My chopper was almost done and I was really looking forward to getting it on the cover of the magazine. That would be a huge accomplishment for me. That's what I wanted. By now Billy had many bikes on many covers. I just wanted one cover.

My life was motorcycles twenty four seven. Working at Choppers Inc. at the time I did was really cool. The whole Chopper thing was really taking off. Jesse James was big on the West Coast and Billy and Indian Larry were big on the East. It was very cool to be graduating from MMI and working at the Premiere Chopper shop at the same time.

Thirty six guys started in my class. Eight graduated, I was number three in that order. All my friends showed up and were yelling and screaming when I got my diploma. This was a great day. It had been about a decade since I had done dope. That feeling will never go away and I knew it. I had been exposed. But a decade had passed and I was on my way to achieve my real goals.

After school things got real slow in Melbourne. REAL SLOW. I started calling it 'Melbouring'. I got put on summary probation meaning I no longer had to report. I had paid my restitution which is usually what it's about anyway. I was no longer working at Choppers Inc. so I was assembling my

Chopper in my living room. I didn't have cable so every day I would put on Scarface and play it over and over while I assembled my chopper. I did all the body work on the frame it the drive way, then one of the local painters sprayed it in his shop.

I started seeing this really cute waitress from Hooters named Jenny and she moved into my place within a week of knowing her. Probably not the best decision but after the first ride she was both hooked. I still had some hookups that were paying off but my money was running out. Jenny always wanted to go out and spend money and party and I was saving to get the hell out of Melbourne.

Problem was I really liked Jenny alot. And it was screwing up my thought pattern. It was making me lazy. I wasn't working on the bike fast enough. I got complacent. I started stagnating. When my new bike was almost done I really needed money and I sold my old chopper to my friend Albie.

I was sitting in my front yard working on my new Chopper. I had just finished it and I was getting ready for the photo shoot which was in a week.

Albie walked up drinking a beer and smoking a joint. He was successful, relaxed and he loved to party. He wasn't really into bikes, he just had money and everyone had choppers so he bought one. He was maybe going to ride it twice a year.

"Nice bike."

"Thanks."

"Where you coming from?"

"Hooters."

"You saw Jenny?"

"Nope."

"She's working till closing. That's what she said."

"I didn't see her there."

"How long were you there? Ten minutes? It aint that big."

Albie squirmed with discomfort.

"We had three pitchers of beer and watched the game. If Jenny was there I would have seen her. Don't you think?"

"I'm gonna call." I went inside and dialed Hooters number. They picked up right away.

"Hooters Melbourne. Can I help you?" You could hear the crowd through the phone.
"Is Jenny available for a minute?"
"Jenny's not working today. Anything I can help you with?"
"No thanks." I hung up and walked back outside. My mind was reeling with jealousy and suspicion.
"I told you." Albie said.
"Shut up. I gotta go."
I jumped in my beat up Chevy truck and drove over to Hooters. I parked across the parking lot by the grocery store. I had a clear view of the parking lot. The sun was going down as I pulled up. Jenny had said she was working till closing so I didn't expect to se her before two a.m.
I sat in that truck real low and thought about what I wasn't doing. I had gotten caught up and was not chasing my dream. I wasn't chasing my dream because I got comfortable doing nothing. Nothing except wasting time and I couldn't figure out why. I had gotten too comfortable.
I had a bad feeling in my head that Jenny was lying to me and a good feeling in my head that if she was I was leaving. It was my way out. I couldn't say it was a good feeling, more of like a relief. I really liked Jenny a lot, but being from Miami, I never looked at a relationship all that seriously anyway. When you grow up in Miami you see new girls coming to model every year, year after year. So its safe to say the beach life party atmosphere was not conducive to relationships growing up. Girls would ask me, "Do you have a girlfriend?" and I would look around like I lost something.
"Why? Do I look like I am missing something?" I would answer. I always liked saying that. It's a good feeling. Like no one can have you. Only you can have you. It's a powerful feeling. Especially when you are young.
I wasn't feeling that feeling now. Sitting in the dark watching people coming and going from Hooters, drunk and having a good time. All I could think about is who the hell is Jenny with? Who is bending her over some car somewhere right now? Honestly I had no idea. We didn't have many friends in town. At least I didn't. Jenny was from Melbourne, she had lots of friends when in town.

I sat in that car for hours. Until no one was left in the parking lot except the waitresses and the clean up staff. All of a sudden I saw a shitty little motorcycle pull into the parking lot with what looked to be Jenny on the back. I opened the door of my truck and started jogging over toward them. As I got close I heard Jenny say,
"That's my boyfriend."
The guy looked up at me and his eyes got real big. He had the look of fear.
"Get off. GET OFF." He frantically said to Jenny who quickly jumped off the bike. She was a little too late. I hit that guy like a freight train. Him me and his bike hit the ground. The bike stayed running while me and the guy rolled on the ground punching it out.
"STOP. THAT'S MY BOSS." Jenny screamed. It didn't matter to me. I didn't believe her anyway. We stood up and punched eachother toe to toe till both of us was tired as hell. Some cooks and cleaning crew came out and broke it up. Jenny walked up to me.
"Why'd you lie to me? You weren'tworking today?"
"What are you stalking me? Is that what you are doing? We are through."
"You can believe that. Stay away for a day then you can come get your stuff. I'll be gone."
"Where you going? Amsterdam?"
"Don't matter. Not to you. Not no More."
"I'm coming to get my stuff tonight."
"I'll help you." The guy said. Turns out he was the general manager. And he was banging Jenny.
"Yeah. That's what you wanna do. Show up at my house with this guy. That'll end up good. Stay away for a day. Do yourself and everyone a favor. That way I don't get locked up and you and him get to keep on living."
I looked over at the Guy I just fought. "Hey dude."
 The guy was looking at himself in his rear view mirror. He looked over at me through his beat up face.
"You can have her."
I turned around and walked over to my Chevy, got in it and took off. I could see Jenny tending to his wounds. Sirens

started blaring in the distance. I don't know if it was for that or not. Either way I never saw any cops that night.
I woke up the next day, got a trailer for my bike, packed up my stuff and drove out of there by six p.m. Next stop, Miami.

58

It took about four hours to get down to Miami from Melbourne in my truck. I went to my friend Judd's warehouse, which is on the border between Overtown, which is the poorest part of town, and the design district, which is one of the richest parts of town. The warehouse was located right down the block from the Miami dopehole, where everyone could score dope. There was a crack dealer on every corner, some corners six or seven dealers deep.
I pulled into the lot and there seemed to be a commotion going on. I got out of my truck and Marko walked up to me and handed me a baseball bat.
"Let's go. This piece of shit outside named Bubba has been breaking into this place every night. We gonna set him straight." Marko is a serious customer. I grew up watching him bounce at every night club in town. I've seen him knockout countless people then toss them out of the club for misbehaving. That's what bouncers do.
I took the bat and about six of us walked over to the gate. There is this twenty foot tall gate surrounding the warehouse with razor wire at the top. Just like a compound. A compound covered in graffiti.
"You guys ready?" Marko asked.
I looked at everybody's face. They were way ready. People get tired of having their house broken into. Marko opened the gate and the six of us walked out on a mission straight towards Bubba and his crew who were standing on the corner, selling crack.
As soon as the gate opened and bunch of street people took off running. None of the street dealers did, but we weren't after them and they knew it. They were all strapped anyway.

Marko led the rest of us and we walked up. Bubba had four of his friends with him. They were all crackheads.
"Bubba."
"What you want MAAARRRRRKO? HUH?" Bubba got in Marko's face so I cracked him with my bat. He looked at me crossed eyed as he went down and everybody started swinging their bats. It was like a batting cage. I didn't like his attitude and I knew he didn't know me, so he wouldn't see me coming. He didn't. Bubba crumpled to the ground like a bag of chips. The crackheads all took off running. Marko stepped over Bubba and put a Glock nine millimeter in his mouth, but that's it he didn't fire that gun. Probably should have pulled the trigger. Bubba didn't stop breaking into our warehouse or any of the other warehouses in the area, until someone else finally stopped Bubba.
About six months after our run in with Bubba he was found with his head blown completely off at the jaw line. He was breaking into a warehouse that some locals were using to stash dope at. At this time there was no dope being stashed in the warehouse, just one lonely guard with a shotgun. He blew Bubba's head off with both barrels just as soon as he saw enough his head to blow off. I don't think there was much of an investigation. Just another dead crack head to the cops.
Judd had the warehouse as long as I can remember. He won it in a card game with a bunch of drunk Cubans he used to go fishing with. The guy owned the whole block and the warehouse when the neighborhood was even worse. When Judd got it when there was nothing but crackheads and Norwegian River rats that came in on the cruise ships. Big Rats. We cleaned up the whole place and the neighborhood more than once. He hung onto it through a lot of bad times when he could have sold it. Judd always gave me a place to crash whenever I came to town. Forever.
I got a job filling in at five different tattoo shops when artists had days off. My friend Ken owned five shops and I was the fill in guy. A couple of friends of mine lived in the warehouse also. My first motorhome was still in the warehouse yard with my old glass shop in it. That was cool to be able to work

glass n the side. Anything to make money. I had a plan. I needed to save some money, and get my stuff over seas.

Miami is an easy place to get nothing done and have a good time doing it, especially if you are from Miami. Being a local I knew all kinds of ways to make money, not all of them legal, but that didn't bother me. I never had a problem with smoking weed, or distributing it. If you were real good you just made the introductions and collected the dividends. Lets the grunts do the heavy work. Like my Jamaican friends would say, 'Its de healin' of da nation mon.'

I got my Chopper on the cover of the Horse Magazine shortly after I got to Miami. That was one of my lifetime achievements I've wanted that to happen since I was in high school. Junior high even. Just like everything else, it seemed so far away before it happened, then afterward I wondered why I took so long. I still wrote my monthly article for the Motorcycle mag, and now I was writing my own monthly column in the car magazine Ol' Skool Rodz.

Life was going just about as good as I could imagine it to be. Working in five tattoo shops all over Miami, riding my chopper everywhere, no helmet law. I was having fun. The only problem was I wasn't chasing my dream. I knew what I wanted to do, and where I wanted to do it, I just had to get there. I had an empty feeling that something was still missing.

I hung out every day with my pal Alex and we rode Choppers all over town. Five days a week I tattooed eight hours a day but the rest of the time was mine. It was good for me, a lot of structure.

Miami is like a live wire and we treated it like that. Every night of the week there was some club having a big party. Being a local we always got right in, even after people have been waiting in line for hours. You could always tell the out of towners. All made up in their silk clothing, all covered in hair grease or mascara, sweating like pigs on the way to slaughter. Locals never looked like that. We knew better, we grew up here. We know how hot and humid it is in Miami.

The Pre Scarface Miami was the cool one. The Miami where my grandparents would sit on the porch and look at the cars go by on Ocean blvd. There was a Dog Track and fishing pier and everything was quiet. Now it had become a back alley of glitter and house music over run with a whole lot of people that only come there a few months a year and think they own the place.

I was getting bored. Anxious. It didn't take long to get into all kinds of drama. It didn't matter how long I had been gone, soon as I was back I was right in the thick of it all. Home. One of my best friends was Jim Pep. Jimmy was from the beach. Most people thought we were real brothers. I ran around with a whole crew. Jimmy Russell Rey Red Alex Judd Marko Ken to name a few. I could keep on going. There was a special crew of people that grew up on the beach. It gave us a special bond. It's kind of special growing up in a vacation spot. The whole country was saving up their money to come to where I grew up for a week. And I couldn't wait to get out. Not like I hated it. On the contrary, I liked it too much.

Like I said I was getting bored and caught up in drama. Jimmy would get in fights all over the beach. All of us did growing up in Miami. Jimmy got in a fight with some guy from London named Bobby. Some muscle bound jerk who waited tables on Ocean drive in the day and bartended at night. I'm pretty sure it was over baby mama drama. It didn't matter anyway. If you were in the South Beach crew, like we were, we are ALWAYS right. Especially anything that happened on the beach. We ran that shit.

Jimmy walked into the tattoo shop. I was just about to get off work.

"You get it?"

Jimmy handed me a piece of paper with a number on it then sat down. I picked up the shop phone and dialed the number.

"Hello." Bobby said. He had a London accent. "Bobby?"

"Yes. Who is this?" "This s D.L. Do you know exactly who this is?" Bobby was silent for a moment."

"Yes I do."

"Good motherfucker. Where you wanna meet?"

"Why would I want to meet you anywhere?"

"So I can bash your fuckin' skull in you piece of shit. I saw what you did to my little brother. Now I'm gonna handle it. Where you wanna meet?"

"Why not let him fight his own battles?" I could tell Bobby was shaken. He didn't expect me to be calling him.

"WHERE YOU WANNA MEET MOTHERFUCKER?" Silence.

"Hello?" I said. No answer. He hung up the phone.

"He hung up." Me and Jimmy started laughing. Truth is he was probably waiting tables less than a few blocks away from the shop I was tattooing in when I made that call.

That was the beginning of a reign of terror I put on Bobby, calling him all the time, challenging him to fights, till one day I had enough. I was helping a friend paint a house and I took some acid to kind of help me get the job done faster. Instead of getting the job done faster, all I could do was think about Bobby walking around town talking about how he beat up Jimmy. I guess I got myself all worked up. I ended up leaving the job early. The house I was painting was in Kendall which is about an hour from the beach. I got in my paint van dressed in my painter whites and headed straight for the beach. I look back on this moment and these are the things that defined me, made me who I became. Standing up for what is right. This guy was in my town and misbehaving and I wasn't having it. As far as I was concerned I had let him know I was coming after him. He had gotten fair warning. He should have been on high alert after the first phone call.

I pulled over the causeway and onto the beach and looked for a parking space. The whole beach was slowly becoming one big parking lot. I wanted to be able to run to my truck after I beat this idiot down. That's about as far as I had thought this thing through.

I saw Bobby at least a block before he saw me. He was waiting tables on Ocean drive.

"HERE I COME BOBBY." I yelled as I was walking up. Bobby looked like he saw a ghost.

"I'm working."

"SO WHAT."

Bobby picked up a knife off the table and started swinging it at me. All the people eating and the other waiters all froze.

Everyone was frozen but me and Bobby. We were the only ones moving. Bobby was swinging that knife but as high as I was he looked like he was moving in slow motion. Every time he got close I smashed him in the face with a right or a left. His nose was bleeding and he looked frustrated. The other waiters were yelling at me to leave. In about a minute two squad cars pulled up, one from both directions and the cops jumped out with their guns drawn. Straight wild west shit.
"FREEZE." The cop said. They had stopped traffic with both of their cars in the middle of the street. Ocean drive is only two lanes. We both stopped moving. The cops approached us both and through us in handcuffs.
"What's the problem here?" The cop said.
"I'm the problem. I put extra gas in my tank, took the day off early cuz this piece of shit needs an ass beating and I'm the person who's going to give it to him." I took another swing at Bobby he ducked.
"He calls me all the time. He's terrorizing me. Make him stop." Bobby sounded like he was going to cry. The cops did everything they could to not laugh. I was as high as could be so I thought everything was pretty funny. These same two cops had arrested me at least once or twice growing up. Miami beach is a small town. They walked Bobby off to the side and talked to him for a few minutes, then they went in the restaurant for a few minutes, then they came and talked to me.
"They're not going to press charges."
"That's good."
"If you leave him alone." The first cop said.
"You are going to leave him alone, right?" The second cop asked.
"Yeah. I'll leave him alone." I thought the whole thing was amusing. The cops uncuffed me and I turned and took off in the other direction.
I knew it was time to split. I had waited long enough. I had gotten complacent, too comfortable. Once the cops have a lock on you, especially in a small town like Miami Beach, you know you are going to be harassed every where you go. And when your whole world is ten blocks wide and twenty one

blocks long, there is not a lot of places to go that you won't be seen. The cops didn't really bother me, not more than they bothered everyone else. It was just another reason to get on with my journey.

I knew my mom was not going to be too happy about me moving across an ocean so I went in my glass shop and made her a wine glass. It took three days to make that wine glass. I put everything I had into it. I wanted to give her something tangible before I left. Something she could put on the shelf next to all the glass art and perfume bottles I had made her over the years. I met my Mom on Lincoln road for dinner a few days before I left to break the news to her that I was leaving. We had a really nice dinner and she loved the wine glass. We took a walk up Lincoln road after we ate.

"That was a nice dinner." My mom said. We sat on a bench.
"I'm leaving."
"Again?"
"Yes."
"Where to this time?" I had left so many times in my life she wasn't surprised.
"Holland."
"Holland as in Amsterdam?"
"Yes."
"That's kind of far. Why?"
"It's just something I have to do."
"What do you have to?" I didn't know how to answer that one.
"I just want to go ride around Europe for a while."
"What with your motorcycle buddies?"
"Yes."
"Why can't you do that here?"
"It's just not the same." She thought about that for a moment.
"For how long."
"I don't know. Actually I do know. Forever."
"Forever is a long time." She started to cry and I hugged her. Some businessman saw us and started to come over. He looked at my mom.
"You ok lady? Is he bothering you?" Before I could answer my mom said through her tears,

"It's my son. He is leaving me." I looked at the businessman with a look that said back up or get knocked out and he left.
Me and my mom were always close. Still are. One thing for sure she knew if I had made my mind up this is what is going to happen. No matter what trouble I ever got in, she never let me go. She always supported me and encouraged me, no matter what.
I walked her to her car and we hugged like it might be the last time. As I watched her drive away I knew I was embarking on a whole new journey that I did not know the outcome. I just knew if I didn't go chase my dreams now they might get away from me and I would never have known if what I wanted is what was going to happen.
The next few days me, Alex, Judd and Marko built two crates. One for my chopper and one for all my tools and stuff. We took it down to the port and put them on a ship to Holland. To say I was excited is an understatement. There is no excitement like chasing your dreams. The worst day chasing your dreams is better than the best day doing anything else.
We had a quiet party at the warehouse, just a few friends to say goodbye. Within two days I was on a flight to Schipol airport in Amsterdam Holland.

59

Holland was cold when I first got there. Winter was coming. It was early September when I arrived. I was about to turn 37 years old in October. Over ten years had past since I had a bad dope habit and I was comfortable that part of my life was in my rear view mirror. I never spoke about it, thought about it. It was as if it had never even happened. Like I was never exposed, which is how I handled it. I have a great imagination.
I knew where I was going and why, which is a very cool feeling. Good to have direction. My friends lived in a small town called Ijmuiden, which is about 36 miles from

Amsterdam. Which if you have never been there, it is absolutely one of the coolest places in the world.

Ijmuiden is a small fishing village sitting on the edge of the North Sea. Big sea going ships would come and go through a series of locks, which let the water rise around the ship so they can make it in to the channel. My friends had a house across from one of the bars in the city and across the street from one of the two coffee shops in town and they all hung out there. Between folks drinking in the bar and people buying weed and hash from the coffee shop across the street it made for a pretty busy corner. I sat many a day on the bench in front of the picture window looking out at the North Sea at the ships coming in after months out on the open ocean.

I got to my friends house where I would stay until I got my own place. I landed with enough money to get started. I also brought all my motorcycle mechanic tools, my tattooing and glass blowing equipment, so I was confident I could make money. I had no plan 'B'. Only a plan 'A'. I was going to see my dream through.

I was unpacking my stuff and two of the brothers walked in.

"We have to talk to you about something." I looked at them and I knew it was serious. We all sat down at the table.

"You can not say 'Bro' to one of the brothers, not from any country." One of them said.

"We understand this is the slang from your country but you have to earn that here. And a foreign brother won't know you as well or as long as we do so he might not take that right." The other brother said.

"You have to change that to 'Dude' or something else. And we are going to give you the time to change it because we know it won't be easy."

I started saying 'Man' instead of 'Bro'. I absolutely understood where they were coming from. I did my best to change it quickly, which was no easy trick.

The Brothers have a love bigger than any I had ever seen. They greeted each other every day like they just picked their brother up from the airport, and they hadn't seen each other in a year. EVERY DAY. The love of this family is so overwhelming that it made me want to be a part of it. I cleaned the house and then fell asleep on the couch in front of the T.V.

I woke up early the next day and went down stairs to the bar for a cup of coffee. My friend joined me for a cup.

"So. How's it feel being so far from home?"

"Exciting."

"Give it time." He said with a smile.

"First things first you have to go check in with the foreign police."

"What? Why?"

"Because you are a foreigner. You plan on working and staying here. You need to check in and get registered. You have to pay taxes. This is a socialist government. You want to be part of it you have to check in. You also have to get a drivers license. That's very important."

He could see I was not too happy about checking with the foreign police.

"It's not as heavy as you think." He handed me a piece of paper with an address on it.

"Get your passport and I will drop you off at the boat that you will ride into town on."

"Boat?"

"Yes. There is a hydrofoil boat to the central station. It's like a bus on the water. Holds about forty people. It costs five guilders. Takes about 30 minutes. Come on. Get a move on. Be at my car in fifteen minutes." And with that he walked out.

I sat there realizing how big a trick this is going to be to turn, to make a complete life in this far away land. But I was determined to make it happen.

For five guilders it was a hell of a ride. The Euro hadn't been invented yet and the Dutch currency was guilders. We called them 'gliders'. The Hydrofoil boat was new to me but commonplace to everyone from town. This was the commute to the city for work for everyone. For me it was like a carnival ride.

I got out at the central station and walked for what seemed like an eternity until I found the foreign police office.

I walked into the office and every seat was taken it there was standing room only. The room was full of people from everywhere, all over Africa, Morocco, even all over Europe. I was the only American in the place. I took a number and sat down. I knew it was going to be a long wait. I always carried this little book that I wrote in with me. I was writing down every Dutch word that I knew and all the ones I learned. I also had that to write ideas for stories. I still wrote my monthly column for the magazine, so I always had a pen and a notebook with me.

After about three hours my number was called. I stepped up to the counter.

"Can I help you?" A real tall police officer asked me.

"Yes I would like to register, I just got here."

"Register to stay in Holland for how long?"

"Forever." I said with a smile.

"Everyone wants to stay in Holland as you can see. Have you a love interest here?"

"I got married to a Dutch girl about seventeen or eighteen years ago. It's been about that long since I have seen her."

The cop looked at me like I was insane.

"A love interest is about the easiest way to stay. Other than that it's very difficult. Can you bring her in with you?"

"I said I haven't seen her in about eighteen years."

"Then you are divorced?"

"No. I just haven't seen her. Even if I did I don't think she would come in here with me."

"In which country did you marry?"

"In the United States."

"You will have to produce that wedding certificate with your wife."

"But I just said I haven't seen her." I was getting g pissed off. It doesn't matter what country the cops are from they are still cops. I never did work well with authority.

"Or you must produce divorce papers from the country in which you were married in. You have an appointment in six months." He handed me some forms to fill out and a card with my appointment date. Six months away. I got back to Ijmuiden and my friend asked me about it.

"So how did it go with the foreign police? You get it handled?"
"I have an appointment in six months."
"Don't miss it." I got real busy after that and the appointment day came and went I didn't even notice. Neither did anyone else.

60

The life lessons started coming at me non stop. The lessons are actually always coming at you in some form or another it's up to you to get them. It also helps when you have some friends pointing them out to you along the way.
The first Saturday night there was a big party in the local bar called the Second Room. I learned later this raging party was every Saturday night. Also Thursday night. And sometimes on Wednesday night. Of course always on Sunday night. Come to think of it Monday was the only night there wasn't a big party in the local bar. The bar was closed on Mondays.
It was Saturday night and the bar was packed to capacity and raging. Like everyone is drunk and all singing together when a song comes on that they know. And everybody knows almost every song. The ones they don't know they fake. The brothers didn't sing in the bar, they just found it all amusing.
I had been there about a week. I was still waiting for my Chopper and all my stuff to arrive on the ship. I was just taking my time getting to know the Brothers that I didn't already know, and adjust to Dutch culture. Dutch people are relaxed. They work hard and party hard. I always loved it in Holland, probably why I moved there. There were fishing docks and canneries all over Ijmuiden and the people that lived and worked there worked hard. And partied harder.
I was standing in front of the bar and I looked over and saw a big guy pointing at me talking to one of the Brothers that I had just met. Both the guy and the Brother were big men. Six foot six and three hundred pounders. They both started walking over to me and the Brother stopped next to me. The big guy kept walking past me.

"He said you grabbed his girls ass. I told him you would never do that." The brother said. "He was talking about that guy."

I looked over and the big guy was beating the shit out of this very drunk guy from London. We stood there and watched the beating, which was especially brutal for about four minutes.

"All right, he's had enough. Come on that's enough." The brother said.

The big guy was out of breath and he walked back in the bar. The London guy was on the ground beaten and bleeding.

"You never know how it's going to go." He said to me.

"Guess not."

Just then the London guy jumped up.

"YOU BASTARD." He screamed as he tried to swing at the brother. He missed and I knocked him back out with a left hook. Before I could do anything else two young guys came running from out of the bar out and gave that Londoner one of the worst beatings I ever saw a man take at one time. These guys must have been around twenty. Probably played rugby or something. They beat the Londoner beyond recognition. His cheekbone was crushed. He was bleeding all over the place. One of the guys was kicking his head over and over when he was already unconscious.

"Enough." I said.

The brother had gone back in the bar so the only people on the street were me the two young guys and the Londoner who was on the ground bleeding and out cold. I grabbed a bucket and filled it up with water and poured it on the him. I wanted him to get up and leave. I knew enough to know we don't need some beaten bloody dude laying on the floor in front of the bar. I figured if he dies who's going to get blamed? Probably the guy no one knows. Probably me.

"We gotta get him out of here." I said.

Before I could say anything else the two guys from the bar dragged the guy about thirty feet to a small alley between two buildings. They were totally satisfied with their efforts, patting each other on the back as they walked back to the bar. I stood over the guy looking at him for a minute. It didn't look like he was breathing at all. I walked back to the bar and sat down next to one of the brothers. They were in mid conversation, which was all in Dutch so I didn't understand most of it. There was a break in the conversation and one of the brothers looked at me. He could see something was wrong.

"Tell me." He said to me. I leaned in close so I could say it quietly.

"We beat a guy real good out there. I think he might die."

"Show me." He said as he got up and walked out of the bar. I followed quickly behind him. We walked over to the alley where the guy was laying. The two guys were a few feet away having a smoke. The brother looked at the Londoner real close for a minute then at at me.

"Yes. If you leave him here he is going to die." He said and turned and walked back to the bar. He looked at the two guys.

"Cold out." He said with a wink. I stood there freezing with the two guys.

"We gotta get him out of here." I said.

"Gotta get him away from the bar." One of the guys said as they picked him up and carried him towards the main street. I ran ahead to look out for cars and when it was clear I signaled them to bring him along. They set him down on the other side of a cement wall that was there to stop cars from driving in the water.

By the time we got back to the bar everyone knew what happened. Another brother wanted me to show him the guy so we walked back down to where he was. We looked over the wall and the guy was still unconscious laying in a pool of his own blood.

"He looks like he was hit by a car." The brother said.

"Or a truck."

"I'm going to call an ambulance and tell them it was a hit and run." The brother said. That was the best idea I had heard all night. He made the call and they said help was on the way. Satisfied we walked back to the bar.

We walked in and the party was still raging, the whole bar singing together as drunk as can be. The brothers didn't sing, they found it all amusing.

I sat with the brother who told me if I leave the guy there he will die. Me and that began brother smoking joint after joint. We smoked solidly for over an hour. It must have been ten joints. We didn't say a word. Just smoked and laughed with all the rest of the folks. He passed the joint back to me and looked at me with a smile.
"Well you passed the first test."
"And what test was that."
"That you could sit here and just enjoy sitting here with a brother. That you didn't have too fill all the space with the sound of you talking. That you could just be here and that is enough."
It was a compliment and I knew it. I think he could appreciate the fact that I moved myself, and all my stuff across an ocean to this tiny little fishing village because that's where I wanted to be. The bar raged till six in the morning. As the sun was coming up I went outside for some air. You could cut the smoke in the bar with a knife. Everybody smokes weed or tobacco in Holland, and I mean EVERYBODY.
I stood on the red cobblestone street taking in the sea air. The seagulls were making a hell of a racket. I felt absolutely complete, confident, on top of the world.
I looked towards the Ocean to where the guy who got beaten earlier in the night was laying and I wondered if the ambulance found him. I started to walk over there and all of a sudden I saw a little red beach ball stick up by the wall. I rubbed my eyes and looked closer and I saw the guy climbing back up over the wall. He was having a hard time doing it. He looked like a red clown or something he had so much blood on him. He got to the top of the wall and fell onto this side. He got up and started walking towards the bar. I stood there and watched him limp closer and closer. He was wasted. I went back in side.
"HE'S COMING BACK." I said to whoever was left in the bar. Everybody got up and all squeezed into the doorway and watched the guy walk up. Nobody made a sound. The guy wobbled up to the bar and stopped right in front of it. He looked at the sign, then the bar, then all of us in the doorway. Nobody spoke while he tried to see what he was looking at. It

was another surreal moment. He then realized where he was and turned around and hobbled down the street. Everyone started laughing and went back in the bar. That party raged until two the next day. One of many, many parties that raged till the next day.

61

My chopper arrived about a week later. Me and one of the brothers went to the port and picked it up. I had made a really good crate to ship it over in. We uncrated it at the dock. The longshoremen who worked there really liked the crate and I left it there with them.
The bike was easier to transport on the truck without the crate anyway. Whether you knew bikes or not you could look at mine and know it was a serious machine. It looked like a frame wrapped around a tire with a big motor. I had an S&S 100 cubic inch, with an Avon 230 series tire. This at the time was the state of the art chopper. I had the second 230 series tire on the road. It used to be a Chevy rim. My old boss Billy chiseled it out, smoothed it, marked it had it dimpled, chromed then I laced and trued it and we brought it to the tire store to have the tire put on the rim. The tire guy had a hell of a time fitting that tire but he finally got it on..
People would lose their minds when they saw us coming up the block with our rigid frame, kick only, custom made choppers. Raked and stretched with big motors and fat tires in back. I had just gotten on the cover of the magazine with this bike a few months before I arrived in Holland. I built this bike from scratch and I loved it. I had to bend and weld the frame three times just to get the exact correct clearance for the rear tire. Everything was custom about this bike and you could tell just from looking at it.
We took it to the bike shop that one of he brothers owned and got it off the truck. At first the brothers tried to hold back the laughter, but then they couldn't and they broke out laughing real hard.

"What's so funny?"
"You are." Said one.
"That bike." Said another.
"Not every road here is straight."
Then to add insult to injury I kicked my bike about twenty times and it wouldn't kick over. Which only made the brothers laugh harder. It was kind of funny. After about a hundred kicks it kicked over and roared to life.
"We should go for a ride." One of the brothers said to me. It was sunny, not too sunny but clear and dry which was good. I was dying to ride my bike. It had been about two weeks since I had ridden any bike and I was jonesing.
We took off and rode slowly through town. We got to the highway and I wanted to hammer it, but I know better than to pass a brother like that. He could feel I wanted to take off and he waved me ahead, so I cut over a few lanes and I held that throttle wide open. It felt so great to take off in the crisp Dutch air. I could see him in the rear view mirror staying close to me so after I got my fix I slowed down and fell in behind him. He waved me up and we rode sided by side for a few miles. What a cool feeling. I waited my whole life to be right where I was and it felt good. And the fact that there was so much in front of me to get where I wanted to be felt even better. I love a challenge. You have to keep challenging yourself. Or life gets boring.
We rode like that for a while then we pulled off and the road quickly became a series of S turns. At every turn the brother was getting further away from me. I would stab the throttle on the straight away and try to catch up but it didn't matter. He kept getting further and further away. Then he started leaning into the turns and that was it and he really took off.
I started thinking about where the hell am I if he loses me completely. I had this cheap nylon jacket on that flapped so hard it fell apart. I didn't even have good foul weather gear yet.
Where he turned off was actually a back road to the bike shop. We pulled up and the brothers took one look at me, with my torn up jacket and they started laughing all over again.

"Bike like that might be nice over there, but here you need a different bike. You need an FXR."

The brothers all road Dyna's and FXR's with inverted forks made to ride across the continent. I always laughed at stock bikes but I knew he was right. I knew how important it was to be able to take advice from people who know better than you. That's a gift and a very deep lesson.

I rode my bike around town a little bit while I tried to sell it. A couple of Dutch guys looked at it but that's not the bikes they like. I called one of my friends in Washington state who could afford it and he bought the bike for twenty grand. He even flew over and brought me the money. He wanted to see the bike before I shipped it to him. Fortunately the shipping company kept the crate. They couldn't believe I was shipping the bike back within two weeks.

Like I said at that time the Euro wasn't invented yet so twenty grand converted into about thirty six thousand guilders. I was loaded. I rented a top floor apartment and built a complete grow room in one of the rooms. I broke the window in the attic and used it for the intake to take out and put in the fresh and old air.

I also started shopping for an FXR. In the crew I ran with at home we always laughed at stock bikes. If you didn't build it, then it wasn't the same for us. I hadn't ever really ridden a stock bike. Maybe once or twice but that was it. Every bike I had was a rigid frame chopper, even the first one. I shopped around for a few weeks and I found a 1994 Harley Davidson FXR with 5000 kilometers on it. It was almost new. Some dentist bought it and rode it a few times and left it in his garage. 1994 is the last year Harley made the FXR, except for an anniversary edition in 1999, but I didn't want that.

We drove over to the dentist's house to buy the bike. He didn't look like a biker he looked like a dentist, which I figured was good, he probably didn't beat up the bike.

We walked in the garage and I couldn't believe it. The bike looked brand spanking new. Like it had never been ridden before.

"I rode it a few times. I just don't have the time. My wife wants me to sell it."

I handed over the money.
"Nine grand." I handed him nine thousand Guilders. This equaled about five thousand dollars. There was no negotiating with him. The brothers did that on my behalf before we got there. He took the money and started counting it. We wheeled the bike out and put it on the truck. I wanted to ride it but the brothers wanted to go over it with a fine tooth comb first.
My first FXR. And I still had over ten grand. The grow room was working in my apartment. Quite a change from my previous life which was getting further and further behind me.

62

I still had a good bit of money left over so I bought a little caravan to build a glass shop in. It was a one room caravan with a sink and a shower that you towed behind your car or truck. We bought it from some Dutch gypsies about three hours away. It was in real good shape and I got to work on it right away. I had already made a few glass shops in motorhomes, mine or helping friends build their shops so I knew how to build it good. I had my own working glass shop with in two weeks. It was something to learn how to do this with different equipment than I was used to, they had different regulators and stuff like at the air and gas company, but I figured it out. The brothers let me put the glass shop behind the bike shop, which was a real good set up. I got to see the brothers alot, and they got to see one of the ways I make my money, and I was always near the action.
I had a travelling tattoo case also so in between tattooing folks in town and making glass pipes and selling them to the head shops I was doing ok. Having a harvest every nine weeks of a couple of pounds was just icing on top. But the weed had to be great. The competition was fierce. And bone dry. The guys at the coffee shop, which is where you sold

your weed, would grab a bud and break it in half. If it didn't 'CRACK' then it wasn't dry.

"Come back when it's finished." He would say with a smile.

The other thing that consumed my time was riding. The brothers rode. A LOT. It didn't matter what weather it was either rain or shine, they still rode. And I had just come from Miami. No helmet law and sunshine. I didn't even own decent rain gear. Rain gear for me was a plastic bag to put my cell phone in. These guys rode a lot to practice being the best. They rode in the tightest formation possible, inches apart, weaving in and out of traffic like a swarm of bees. We would be getting ready to leave, putting on all this rain gear and I would look out the window and the sleet, which is a combination of snow and hail and rain, would be so strong it was moving sideways.

"We're really leaving?" I would ask.

They would all laugh. These are the kind of storms in Florida that the cars would pull over to let go by, except way colder. We weren't going anywhere except on a ride. The starting point and finishing point are the same. It's just a ride. I was always in the back and I always stayed a bike length or two back. Riding the bike like it's synchronized swimming takes practice. You have to trust yourself and trust the guys you are riding with. And that takes practice.

I couldn't get the hang of the FXR. I was always a little too far in the back of the pack and it felt like the bike was slipping all over the place. I didn't feel confident enough on the bike to ride up in the tight formation. I was used to a rigid frame motorcycle, which is real tight in the turns. I got back to the bar and I was disappointed again with the ride.

"What's wrong?" One of the brothers asked me.

"Is that what these bikes are about? Slipping all over the place? Cause that's what they feel like."

The brother I was talking to looked at me like I was from Mars and walked out to look at my bike. He stuck his head back in the bar.

"Come out here." I got off my stool and went outside.

"Look at this." He pointed to my tires.

"These tires are dry rotted. That dentist had this bike sitting in his garage for so long the tires got dry rotted. They are cracking and too hard to grip."

He jumped in his car and I went back into the bar. In about twenty minutes he came back in with two new Dunlops.

"These are really sticky." He handed me the two new tires.

"Thank You."

"Go put them on."

I went down to the bike shop and one of the other brothers helped me change the tires.

I can easily say that after all the years of riding bikes a whole new world of riding opened up for me. I felt like I was finally having fun on my motorcycle. Now instead of me being way behind the pack I was in it. Right on the tail of the last guy only inches away. I have always been into Star Wars, since I am a little kid, so in my head was the voice of Darth Vader saying, 'Stay On The Leader'.

We rode all the time, rain or shine seven days a week. It seemed like the guys went faster in the rain. They would start splitting lanes and speed up.

"Why do you guys go faster when it starts raining?" I asked one of the brothers.

"Because we want to get home."

63

Days turned into weeks turned into months turned into over a year. I fell into a good schedule. I got a decent job at a place in the Red Light District at a marijuana museum called The Cannabis College.

I would make glass pipes at a big bench with three other glass artists. The tourists would walk by on a small tour about the history of cannabis, then end up at the glass bench and watch us work for a few minutes. They couldn't stand there too long, just long enough to make them want to buy a pipe.

The Cannabis College was connected to a head shop called The Flying Dutchman, which bought all the glass we made for top dollar. They had a really nice shop, real high end expensive glass. I was very proud to have my own glass in my own display case with my company logo, which was DL GLASS.

I started dating a girl that worked at the Cannabis College and fell into a very normal life. I was just letting time go by, which is what it takes. Many miles and a lot of time had to go by to get where I wanted to be. Nothing good happens over night.

By now I was in love with my FXR. I rode it everywhere. I used to look at the kids in the town riding their scooters all year long, no matter how cold it was. I figured if they could do it then so could I.

I rode with the brothers from Holland to Belgium to Germany to Switzerland to France. Through the French Alps on the way to 'Free Wheels,' which is a big motorcycle rally in the South of France. The brothers I rode with would pass everyone and everything on the road. They would stay in the left lane and stay so close on the bumper of the vehicle in front of us until they moved. That's European driving the left lane is for passing. We would pass whole packs of other brothers and just give a nod as we went flying by.

We left Holland and the weather was a combination of snow and rain. The further south we got the warmer it got. By the time we got to the French Alps everyone had gone from foul weather gear to just a T shirt and a vest. It took about a week to get where we were going. We would ride about seven hundred miles a day, which was from sun up to sun down, then the brothers would party till three or four in the morning. Then get up at the dawn and do it again.

After a week on the road I was comfortable, but I also did not have a clue where I really was, nor did I speak any language other than English. As we got further into the France we started riding into a series of winding roads that were moving through a forest. Some of the brothers started slowing down and kind of taking the scenic route. I was watching the front six guys getting further and further away from me. They were laying in to the turns hard and climbing up the highway. I started thinking about how I can't get lost out here, how I don't speak French and I would be screwed if I were to get lost here.

When I could hardly see the pack anymore I took off and passed the brothers that were taking the scenic route. I caught up with the pack and fell back in tight formation. I could see a few of the brothers see me in their rear view mirrors but the kept moving. They never stopped till they needed gas. Tank to tank that's how we did it.

We finally pulled over and I walked up to one of the brothers. He seemed surprised to see me.

"Is it cool if I stay with the pack?"

"CAN you stay with the pack?" he asked me with one eye brow raised.

"Yes I can." I said with a smile. He thought about that.

"Then I guess you can stay with the pack." We filled up our tanks with gas and smoked a joint and took off for another seven hundred kilometers.

I used to have real long hair. A real hippie. I never cut my hair or my beard. When I arrived in Holland I had long hair. Now it was almost two years later. When I got to Free Wheels I met many brothers young and old from countries all over the world. I met brothers from Denmark France and Germany and they all had a buzz cut.

"This is the fighting trim." One of the young Danish brothers told me.

"You can really control a guys head by his hair." Another said.

"Where the head goes the body follows." Another said and they all laughed.

One of the brothers from Denmark walked up to me.

"We're Always Ready." He said real serious.

"For what?"

"For whatever comes our way." I took that in. He meant it. His guys were on point. They had this air of competence around them. Like there was nothing they couldn't handle. They made a great impression upon me. I liked the way they all worked together, like they knew what the other one was thinking. They were all very focused.

After the run in the South of France we rode through the French Alps stopping at winery's and doing cool stuff like going white water rafting. After about a month on the road we headed back North to Holland. It got colder and colder as we got closer to home, but it didn't matter. It felt good to be getting back. We pulled into town and parked in front of the house next to the bar and the whole town came out. We had been gone over a month and they missed us. Everyone went into the bar for a drink and to unwind from the ride before they went home. I lived about two minutes from the house and I had one thing on my mind. I raced home and took out some scissors and cut all my hair off. I didn't do the best job, in fact it looked like I recently had chemotherapy or something. Like my hair had started to fall out. I cut it as close as I could and tried to even it up. It was quite a change. I put on a baseball cap and went back to the bar. When I walked in only a couple of brothers noticed. One yelled out.
"What did you do?"
"Tragedy." Another yelled. One of my favorite brothers walked up and took my hat off.
"Oh my gosh." He said. He was imitating me. "Why did you do this?"
"Those young Danish Brothers made such an impression on me that I just felt it was time." I said. He thought about that.
"I can understand that. But we are going to have to fix this mess." He went home and came back with a hair clipper and shaved the rest of my hair off.
"Now at least it doesn't look like you just had radiation.' He said. I kept looking at myself and my new haircut in the mirror. It was clean, sharpish. And it was hard to get used to.
I stuck to my routine. I would wake up and go straight to the gym. I made my own money so my time was my own. Then I would go for a ride through the sluizen. That's where the ships would come in from the sea and wait for the water to rise so they can pas in to the channel. The sluizen was a real narrow track that you could get to the other side of the channel with. It went back and forth in a criss cross pattern with these really sharp turns. It was great practice for riding my FXR.

I would do it as fast as I could make it across and back. I would time it and everything. It was definitely crazy because if you made a mistake you would go right in the water, or hit the crane, or the wall or something. It was just two lanes wide, two tight lanes of insanity at ninety miles an hour.

One time after I had just made another run across and back I was sitting on my bike rolling joint. I had been there awhile, almost two years and my riding had gotten a lot better. I had ridden across the continent with these guys twice. But I still knew I had lots to learn. A few of the brothers rode up and parked. One of them walked over to my bike and began looking it over. This guy was a real motor head. He knew the bike and he could really ride. He looked at my tires and pointed.

"That's good."

"What's that?" I asked

"The wear on your tires goes up the side wall. That means you have been laying low in the turns. That's good."

I was way proud.

"Let's go for a ride."

We all put on our gear and went for a ride. I had much better gear than when I first got here. Four hundred dollar all weather gloves. Bell full face helmet with a complete HD rain /snow suit. Good equipment makes a hell of a lot of a difference. Riding was very different also. It was now like synchronized swimming at one hundred miles an hour. Winding S turn roads on great pavement. The roads in Holland are very good pavement, like a racetrack.

Having a chopper all those years was cool. Choppers are cool. Cool in a death race two thousand type of way. Now I was now really having fun on my bike. I was having fun before this was different. It was now precision racing, not surviving to the bar.

We got back to the house and we all sat around for a smoke and a drink. One of the brothers looked at me with a smile.

"I have to build a bigger motor." He said to me.

"Why's that?"

"Because I can't lose you. You're always in my rear view." He gave me a slap on the back. It was a compliment. A big compliment.

64

I still took the boat to work five days a week. I only took my bike once in awhile, mostly when it was sunny, which wasn't that often. Parking was hell in Amsterdam and the boat was easy and quick and it dropped me right off at the central station. Then it was a quick five minute walk to my job making glass pipes at the Cannabis College.

Amsterdam is like New York City in the realm of that it is ALIVE all the time. The streets are always crowded. Girl's are in the windows and bars open till late and filled with everyone from dread locked hippies to English drunks singing the songs of their favorite football team to drunken teenagers having a girl for their first time to the way rich consulate general discreetly breaking all his rules, to legions of navy men from all over the world on shore leave banging everything in sight then getting drunk and tattooed to the poor Italian tourist who did too much dope and O.D.'s right on the street. That's Amsterdam.

The central station alone is like a huge shopping plaza with trains going through it to everywhere. As soon as you hit the street you can smell the aroma of hashish in the air. There were junkies everywhere, but much fewer than years before. They had now been regulated to one area called the nieuw market, and they stayed pretty much in that area. Anybody could still buy anything in that part of town, and not in a coffeeshop.

Life was better than good. I had a good job. I was dating a girl who worked at the shop, so I could come in whenever I wanted, or miss as many days as I needed. They always bought my glass for a good price. Then sold it for top dollar.

I was in the gym one day later than usual. Everyone was gone and I was the only one in the gym. I had the day off from work and the party the night before raged till the dawn, so I slept late.

I was on the bench press when the guys dad who owned the gym started banging on the window. I looked at him and he was waving at me frantically to walk towards him. I got off the machine and walked into the front of the gym. They had a little bar set up where you could get protein shakes and sandwiched and stuff. Above the counter was a television and it was on.

"Your country is under attack." He said to me. I looked at the screen and the World Trade Center was on fire.

"What happened?" I asked him.

"I don't know. I just turned the channel and there it was. Burning."

We both stood there and watched for a minute trying to make sense of it when a second plane came crashing into the other tower.

"Now for sure you are under attack." He said.

He started flipping the channels trying to find more news. I went and got my stuff and went home. I walked in my door and turned on the TV just in time to watch the towers fall. I took a shower and got cleaned up and went down to the bar. Everyone was watching the television. In every bar I passed, in every house that had the window open you could hear or see the broadcast. Later on in the evening on the news broadcast it showed some café's where the patrons all jumped up and cheered as the towers came down. I wouldn't know the difference from one religion to the next for most folks. I just never really paid attention before. I just always looked at everyone as people. But now it felt a little different to be an American abroad.

I took the boat to Amsterdam the next day and only two other people were on it. I thought that was kind of strange because it is usually full. I didn't think much of it until I got off the boat at the central station. The streets were empty. There were a few cops standing on various corners but no one else. Amsterdam looked like a ghost town.

I walked through the empty streets and almost all the stores were closed. Everyone had their hatches battened down. I got to the Cannabis College and it was closed. I called the owner and he told me that he was closed indefinitely. He said that I had to find another job. I called my girl and she had also got fired. He fired everyone and closed his doors for good.

A lot of people thought World War Three was going to happen. Everything slowed down after 9-11. Nobody was spending money on glass or tattoos. I started to think about getting a normal job. I was so close to where I wanted to be just not there yet. I had an indoor crop that was just about ready to harvest. I would have gotten money from that which I thought would hold me over until everyone calmed down and people start spending again and I could get my job back. Or get a different job in another shop.

I went on with my life like business as usual. Until the lights didn't come on in my house one day when I got home.

The electric meter reader must have come by and saw that I had tapped into the power by putting in a larger amp carrier fuse. He put a special lock on the electric box which I had to break into just to figure out he took my fuse. Fortunately for me I had an extra one so I turned the lights back on. But I had a bigger problem now. How long until the meter reader guy comes back to check it again? I had about ten to twenty days until harvest. Twenty would have been better. You always want to wait until the last possible minute.

I knew I had to figure out another way to make money. Everyone in town worked on the docks in one form or another. I started applying at all the fish canneries and on the docks and a dock worker. I applied everywhere I could and everywhere I applied they told me the same thing, that I needed a tax number.

I had no choice but to go back to the foreign police and try to get a tax number. In the end it's me who makes all the decisions, and me who will reap the benefits or pay the consequences for my actions or lack there of.

I wanted to stay in Holland no matter what so I made a decision to go back and try to get that tax number. I knew I should have followed through with it when I was supposed to, but I didn't. I had gotten comfortable. No one saw something like 9-11 coming, or knew how it would change things. But things got tighter everywhere.

I walked into the foreign police immigration office, it was the same one I had been in before, and it looked the same way. Every seat was full with every kind of person all trying to get their papers to stay. All a little more frantic about getting their paperwork in order than the last time I was here, about two years ago. I got a number and sat down. I knew I was going to be there for a while.

When my number finally got called I stepped up to the counter and it was the same immigration officer I had before. I don't think he remembered me but I remembered him. I stood there quiet while he looked over my paperwork. He kept going back and forth like he was confused.

"How long have you been in Holland?"

"About two years."

"Looks a bit more like three. Have you been working in Holland? Making money?"

"No Sir."

"Then how do you survive?"

"I have a rich girlfriend."

"Who is Dutch of course?"

"Of course."

He looked back at my paperwork again then he began stamping it with a stamper.

"You were supposed to have checked in with us when you arrived, which is over two years ago. It says you were married to a Dutch girl. Is this the same girl who is subsidizing you?"

"No Sir.' I could see this was going south fast. He handed me back my paperwork.

"You have seven days to produce the wife you are married to. If you can not produce her you will have to produce divorce papers from the country you got married in, and apply again for a tax number. In a year."

"In a year?"

"Yes in a year. You lived here illegally for over two years. You must now wait to apply again for three hundred sixty five days. Starting today. NEXT."

He was done with me.
I didn't think I was public enemy number one. I didn't think they would be coming to look for me when I didn't show up in a week. I knew I had to at least harvest the crop. I could use that money to get most of my stuff back to the states.
I explained to the brothers what happened at the foreign police and how I had to go back to get divorced from the Dutch wife that I hadn't seen in over eighteen years.
"If she saw you she would try to hit you with her car anyway." One of the brothers told me who knew her.
The day before I had to harvest the plants, the electric man came back and took the high voltage fuse out again and this time he left a note on the electric box. It was all in Dutch but I found out it was a summons to come before the electric board for stealing electricity. When it rains it pours. The house was in a phony name so I knew I just had to get out of there. I cut all the plants down and moved all my stuff over to my friends house and hung the plants to dry. I decided I could always buy more tools. I sold my bike, my tools and anything else I didn't need. While the plants dried. I kept my tattooing gear and shipped my glass tools and torch home. I sold all the weed within ten days and got everything ready to go. I didn't feel that my dream was shattered. I was disappointed for sure that I had such a set back, but I just looked at it as a set back and that's all it was. I never lost focus of my dream.
I had no real idea where I was going to go. That's when you always go home. I called my friend Red in Miami and he said his next door neighbor was moving out so I put a hold on that apartment. Always good to have a place to land, and you know what they say, there's no place like home. Miami Beach.

65

"What do you mean?" Red asked me.
"I mean I'm gonna put that shit back on the map."
"South Beach Underground? SBU? For real?"
"Yup. We run this shit. Gonna let em know it. Again."

"You are definitely back. Sign me up." Red went fishing and I was sitting in my new place. It was on third street and Washington avenue in Miami Beach. A little two story building with six apartments. Four apartments on the bottom with two on top. Me and Red had the top so we had a deck.

Below fifth street is the cooler part of town. Especially if you know a little of the history of Miami Beach like Joe's Stone Crabs, the dog track and the fishing pier. All long gone by now and replaced by night clubs and revamped art deco apartments, with huge parking structures to accommodate all the new people that are moving onto Miami Beach every day.

I had been back about a week and I was restless. I wanted to get something going. It didn't take long to get another chopper. In fact I got my old one back that I had sold Albie when I left Melbourne. He never even put it in his name. It was still registered to me. I just had to do one collection and he gave me the bike. I even got a quarter of the take. I usually get half. Albie never even rode the bike. It was cool to have a bike and a chopper at that, but now I wanted another FXR.

Some friends of mine had a bike shop that my pal Alex and me hung out at and they let me use the bench to do whatever work I wanted on my bike. Albie had this stretch tank put on the bike and had it painted flat black but other than that it was the same. The first thing I did was take the bike apart, put on a smaller tank and paint it royal blue with some candy in it. Bike looked sick with a 230 series tire. Nothing but motor, paint chrome and rubber.

It didn't take long to get my divorce papers in order but I still had to wait the year before I could apply again. So I started promoting parties. Everyone does parties in Miami Beach. Mine was called 'Local Party" which was the SBU party.

"Whenever you have a party every waitress in town tries to get the night off." One of the club owners told me. We had some wild parties with surf films, guys doing live graffiti, local and out of town bands and DJ's would come through. The SBU parties just got bigger and bigger. It became the biggest baddest party in town. I did it once a month. My pal Jim Pep always helped me put these together. Like I said

before everyone in town thought he was my real little brother, he wasn't, we just acted that way. Like real brothers. We would get girls to skate up and down Washington boulevard handing out flyers. Everybody in town came to the SBU 'Local Party'. One night before one of my bigger parties I had dinner with my mom. I had been back about a month.
'They made you a better man."
"What?"
"I didn't want you to go, but they made a man out of you. Your motorcycle buddies. Wherever you went it worked."
"What do you mean by that?"
"I mean you seem calmer. More focused. I can see the change in you. It's a good thing, not a bad thing."
It was really cool to hear my Mom say that. Especially since I knew she didn't want me to move so far away in the first place. She was happy I was back. She was proud. And that has a price tag on it money can't buy. I didn't know how long I was going to stay put in Miami, but for now it was fine. I had almost a year to waste until I could go back to Holland.

66

The Chopper was fun but I started saving and looking for another FXR. I had so much fun on that bike in Holland. I saved every dime I made and looked every day of the week for one. FXR's are the best bike Harley ever made in my opinion and for some reason they have the lowest resale value. At least in Miami you could pick one up cheap. I wanted a 1994, the last year they made them, so it had the least amount of wear. That was also the year of the bike I had in Holland.
All my friends hung out at the same motorcycle shop and worked on their bikes. The shop itself was huge and we covered every facet of motorcycle customization.
Me and Alex hung out there every day. They had this real big Pit Bull. Probably weighed ninety pounds. Me and that dog had a special bond. I would always show up with a bag of

cheeseburgers for him. I was the one who gave him a bath. Everyone used to say,
"Epstein is your dog D.L." and he was, even if he had a mind and a spirit all his own. He would roam the streets all around Overtown and the surrounding areas. The warehouse I lived in was a few blocks away. Epstein knew how to get there and back himself. He knew the route.

I finally found the FXR of my dreams. A ninety four with low miles. The guy only wanted six thousand three hundred for it. I had been seeing a girl for a few weeks and she give me a ride there. It was up by the Broward County line. That's where Florida changes, right on the Dade County and Broward County line. Once you cross that county line it becomes Redneck city. Below that line it's like living in Cuba. There are places in Miami, like little Havana where if you don't speak Spanish you're not getting served.

The guy met us on some side street. He had a big new Impala. Like the cops drive.

"Follow me." He said as he took off. He drove like a nut. Fast and reckless. We had a hard time keeping up.

"Hurry up." I said.

"I'm not getting a ticket." She said taking her damn sweet time.

"You're gonna lose him."

"No I'm not."

We were about five cars behind him. I think he saw that cause he slowed down a little.

He pulled up to a house and parked. In front of the house was a Broward County Sheriff vehicle. We sat in the car and he walked over to us. He was a very big man. At least six foot six and three hundred fifty pounds. He had a gun on his side and a police academy T shirt on.

"He's a cop." The girl said.

"A Sheriff." I said in amazement. He drove like a psycho.

"Let's have a look."

I got out of the car and walked over to his garage. A lady came out of the house in a cop uniform.

"This is my sister." He said. They were both cops.

"This is the bike." He pointed to one of two bikes in his garage. It was beautiful. I could see it was well maintained.
"We get our bike's serviced every five hundred miles so this is in great shape."
I walked around the bike and gave it the once over. It really was in great shape.
"Sixty three hundred?" I asked him.
"How about six grand."
"Deal." I took out sixty hundred dollar bills and handed them over. He counted them immediately.
"This is an FXRP. It's the Police special. You can't put on as many attachments but the frame is beefier, way stronger. And this is bike is fast, real fast. It's made for pursuit."
"Cool." I knew right away I was going to take this police special apart and rebuild it into an outlaw right away. I hit the button and it turned on and purred like a sewing machine. It was a little too quiet for me. Going to have to change that exhaust, among other things.
"You gotta be careful." The cop said to me.
"I know how to ride. I'm a five diploma Harley Mechanic."
"I got that. That's not what I mean. I'm big and fat, you're pretty skinny. That bike is REALLY fast. You got to be careful. That's all I'm saying."
We filled out the title, shook hands and I took off. He wasn't kidding. This bike was fast. When I stabbed the throttle one time it almost took off from underneath me.
I took it to the bike shop the next day and started taking it apart.
"Why are you going to take apart a perfectly good motorcycle. Why don't you ride it for a while first?" One of the mechanics asked me. "Cause I'm gonna make it my own."
I knew I wanted take that bike completely apart, put in a chrome bolt kit, tap every hole thread every bolt, polish the jugs, put on a chrome Thunderheader exhaust with chrome eighty spoke wheels. That's what it's like customizing your own bike. Not only was I going to get the bike I was exactly dreaming of but after you put it together, I would know every inch of it.

It took me about two months to get the bike completely done. I painted it black with Red flames and a white pin stripe on them. Only one overlap, old school style. All chrome with twelve inch risers. It wasn't every day you saw a completely custom FXR. Most guys kept those bikes stock.

The guy who owned the motorcycle shop was named Johnny and he had been on the run for six months. I'm not sure what he did but he knew he had to go inside for a while so he avoided the cops at all costs. It became this game of Cat and Mouse and somehow Johnny was always two steps in front of the cops. Everyone at the shop got used to the cops strolling in twice a week looking for him. They never looked too anxious. Like they knew he wasn't there and it was just a formality stopping by.

The day I finally got the bike finished I took it for a test ride around the neighborhood. The bike was clean and fast. One big thing out of the way, I got another FXR. All my friends rode choppers, I was the only one with an FXR. Until my buddy Al rode it. Then he got one too. Of my SBU crew in Miami Al was the only one with a motorcycle besides me. It was just our method of travel. We ride bikes.

Me and Al were in front of the shop after my test ride adjusting the clutch on my bike.

"FREEZE." Someone said behind us. We slowly turned and there was about twenty cops in face masks and full riot gear approaching us with their guns drawn.

"PUT THE WRENCH DOWN NOW. GET ON THE FLOOR." Everyone who was standing in the front of the shop got on the floor. Even the customers. The cops started making their way through the shop to the back. Johnny was standing in the back of the shop there smoking a joint when one of the mechanics opened the back door.

"They're here boss. For real this time."

Johnny started to run, then he just stopped.

"This was coming sooner than later. Might as well face the music." He hit the joint one more time just as the cops reached the back.

"ON THE GROUND. NOW."

Johnny was put in handcuffs and led out. The cops were gone just as fast as they got there. The customers got off the ground and all left. Me and Al went back to working on my bike but I couldn't stop thinking how my own clock was ticking. I had somewhere else to be. I got my bike and all my tools out of there and never went back. The shop closed about a month later. It's a car stereo place now.

67

You always have to be able to recognize the green lights and the red lights in life. You can't let any opportunity go by without extracting whatever you can out of it. And the only way you can do that is to have your eyes open.
Everything was moving along according to plan. I had already gotten divorced from the Dutch girl I had married and not seen in eighteen years. I hired an attorney, paid him and in about a month I was divorced. I still had about eight months to go until I could apply again at the Dutch immigration office, so I was just letting time go by. Miami is a cool place to let time go by. I got to see my Mom all the time which was great and hang out and go riding bikes with Al, just like we were kids. I had a chopper and an FXR so I alternated bikes all the time.
There was a bunch of thugs my buddy Red was getting a name building custom choppers, but he kept building them and selling them so he only had a bike once in a while.
South Beach Underground was really taking off. We were making T shirts and stickers and every one wanted them. I was putting the locals that I grew up with on the shirts. I had my own t shirt press and the shirts came out real nice. Everyone was wearing them. SBU stickers were all over town. On every car, every street sign and every door way on the beach.
The second time Hollywood got near my life I was a little more aware than the first time. A lot of water had passed under the bridge. Many lessons. Not only was I aware of

opportunities coming my way, I was looking for them at all times.

I was having lunch at Big Pink which is this jam packed restaurant one block from Teds Hideaway the local bar me and my friends hung out most nights. Both places are usually always packed to capacity and today was no exception. I had made some real good money at last nights SBU party, and I was taking Red to lunch. We had to wait about twenty minutes to get a table and when we got it, we were jammed in between two big tables each with parties of six. One table was Cuban and one was Haitian. It was kind of funny, everybody trying to talk louder than the guy next to him. It was July fourth weekend and the place had a line out the door. I was in an especially good mood because the party took in over ten grand the night before. Making money is always exciting.

Me and Red were in deep conversation about when to do the next party and where. I always moved it around town. Never the same club twice. A table of four sat across from us next to the Haitian table. It was an older guy with a younger couple and a real tall guy about thirty five years old. The old guy had a camera siting in front of him on the table. After a few minutes this guys slowly moved the camera so that it pointed at me and turned it on. I could see the little red light go on and I knew he was filming. And I didn't like it.

"What are you doing?" I asked him kind of aggressively.

"I would just like to film you for a minute if that's ok."

"What do you wanna do? Film a guy eating his lunch in this packed house?" I was being sarcastic. I didn't like that he put the camera on me I turned back to Red and we kept brainstorming the next party. After about six minutes I turned back to the guy with the camera.

"You got enough?"

"Yes. Thanks."

Right then the food came and we chowed down. When we finished I gave the waitress a huge tip.

"That's a pretty big top homie." Red said.

"You gotta throw the money around like that or it stops coming to you."

"Yeah. Ok." Red wasn't into throwing money around. He worked real hard for his dough. I was kind of superstitious. I walked up to the old guy with the camera. I had to squeeze past the customers siting at the table next to us.
"You can send my royalty check to Outcast Talent management." I said to the guy.
"Could I? Could I find you there?" he was excited. You could tell he was a somebody. He wasn't there vacationing.
"If you were looking. That's my friends agency." I bent down and bumped one of the diners next to me at the Haitian table.
"Watch it." The guy said to me. It was crowded and I almost knocked his plate over.
"What do you do?" The with the camera asked me.
"I tattoo in the oldest shop in town, Tattoos by Lou. It's here on the beach. I just read for the Bad Boys movie that they are going to film here but I don't think I'm gonna get the part. I don't read for parts too much. My buddy got me to go. A bunch of my friends are in it."
"You've got it. I've seen you on film and you've got it." He said. I stood up and hit the Haitian guys, girl's chair knocking over her water. She was not happy. The Haitian guy stood up fast.
"That's it." He said. I backed up like we were going to fight right in the restaurant.
"Excuse me." He said as he took an extra chair from the table next t us. He placed it in front of the guy with the camera.
"Sit down man. The man wants to talk to you. Sit down here and talk to the man man." He said in a thick Island accent. He had heard everything.
"Thank You."
I sat for a few minutes talking to the guy and his crew and when their food came I split. On the way out I paid the bill for the Haitian table. They must have freaked. It was over a hundred dollars.
I got on my bicycle and rode around the beach for a while. I had this beach cruiser with ape hanger handle bars. I went and found some weed and smoked a joint while I was riding along. Just a chill life.
I turned the corner and I saw the guy from the restaurant with the camera and his crew loading up a van with lighting

and camera equipment. I rode up to them. The big guy was loading the van and the older guy was adjusting his camera. The man and woman who I found out later were married were producers.

"Wanna smoke a joint?" I asked as I rolled up on my bicycle.

" We don't smoke joints." The guy with the camera said.

"I write." I said.

"Do you?"

"Yeah. I write pretty damn good."

"I bet you do."

"Yeah. I write so goddamn good that if we write a movie together it's gonna sell about a million tickets."

"I'm sure it would."

The big guy who was the camera operator looked down on me like I was insane.

"Do you now who he is?" he said to me with disgust. I looked up at him like he was insane. He was tall. Like six foot ten. I had to really look up.

"Do you know who I am? I am motherfuckin D.L.... Ask ANYONE around here." I looked back at the old guy with the camera. I could tell he was in charge.

"Wanna see something I wrote?"

"How long will it take?"

"Five minutes. I live two blocks away. You gonna wait?"

"Five minutes." He said and with that I took off in the other direction pedaling as fast as I could. I ran up my stairs and grabbed three magazines I had stories published in. I had been published at least twenty times at this point in the Motorcycle Magazine 'The Horse' at this point. I grabbed three articles I really liked. Then I rode back as fast as I could to where they were loading their van.

When I turned the corner they were standing in the middle of the street waiting for me. The old guy had a small Panasonic hand camera, probably state of the art for the day, and the big guy had a larger camera on his shoulder. I was riding up thinking to myself, 'You get a break in life right now. Cards are being dealt.' I knew opportunity was pulling me over again. Somehow I just knew I was being dealt great cards, RIGHT NOW.

I rode up and handed him the magazines and the lady producer walked up and grabbed the magazines. He started interviewing me, with both of them filming me. The big guy kept still and the old guy would move his camera in and out and take different angles.
"So what do you do?"
"I'm a tattoo artist. I ride a bike have fun live life. That's it."
"Are you from Miami?"
"Born and raised. I went to California when I was fifteen."
"What's next?" he asked me while he kept moving the camera around.
'What do you mean?"
"What's your next destination?"
"This is it."
"Miami?"
"No. The PATH is the destination."
He put the camera down for a second and thought about that. It was like a light bulb went off in his head. Then he smiled and picked the camera up again and pointed it at me.
"Can you explain that please."
"This is it so enjoy it. Wherever you are whatever you are doing is exactly what is supposed to be happening. So you are in your destination all the time. That's your path." They both put their camera's down. The producer lady, I think her name was Kim or Tina or something like that walked up with a release. I had seen a release before so I knew what it was. They had a real tricky one, and I thought they only had about five minutes of film so what would it matter, so I signed it. I gave him all my information but I didn't take theirs. When they drove away I still didn't know who he was. It wasn't until later that night at the bar did I find out he was some big time producer from Hollywood in Miami filming Wild on E with Brooke Burke. That night at Teds Hideaway all my friends were disappointed that I didn't get the guys contact info. Everybody was ostracizing me for letting an opportunity go by. It was crazy how disappointed they all were. Everybody was trying to be in the movies or on commercials. That's Miami. The bar is full of models and actors all trying to make it. I wasn't chasing that Hollywood dream so it didn't

mater to me. I had about eight months to go till I could go back to Holland. I had a different dream.
The next day my phone rang.
"David?"
"Yes sir."
I thought it was my dad. It sounded like my dad.
"This is the guy you met yesterday. With the camera, remember?"
"Absolutely."
"Are you busy?"
"No sir."
"Would you like to come down to the Mercury hotel. We can have lunch. I think it's right around the corner from you."
"It is. See you in five minutes." I hung up the phone and ran out of my house and across the deck to the stairs. Red was sitting on a lawn chair having a beer.
"Hey. Where you going?"
"Opportunity is calling?"
"The guy called back?"
"Yup. I'm on my way to meet him."
"Good luck." Red was always positive.
"Luck won't have nothing to do with it." I said as I ran down the stairs. I had no idea what was in store for me but I knew it was something good.
When I got to the hotel the guy was in front of the hotel with the man and woman producers. We went upstairs to his room and the camera guy was there with big camera set up on a tripod facing the bathtub. In the tub was a chair in front of a window which let the sunlight shine on it. I took one look at that camera and knew it was expensive, it had a small screen built right on the side of it. I had never seen a camera like that before. I started formulating a plan to come back later that night with my pals and steal it. What can I say? It's how my mind used to work. Old habits die hard.
We all sat down.
"Do you now who I am?" The old guy asked me.
"Nope."
"My name is Zalman King. I finish projects."

I immediately thought to myself what a cool line., 'I finish projects.'

"I have 36 episodes airing on HBO called Chromium Blue. Have you seen it?"

"No. I don't have HBO. I don't watch a lot of television."

They all took that statement in. Television was their business. Media was their business.

"I have also done a few films, maybe you heard of them. One was called, "Nine and a half weeks."

"I heard of that one. Mickey Rourke was in it right?"

"Yes. I also did a film called 'In Gods Hands'. It has surfing in it."

"You did that? I saw that."

"That's good. I'm doing a new project and I would like you to be the host of it. It's kind of like a video magazine."

"When do you want to do it?"

"Now. We have a camera all set up. If you could sit in that chair where the light is good I would like to interview you."

"That's it?"

"That's it. You will even get paid but that will be later."

"Have I got a time limit?"

"No."

"Can I smoke a joint while we talk?"

"Yes you can."

"Let's do this." I said. It was a no brainer for me. I knew I had nothing to lose. For the next two hours I had a conversation with Mr. Zalman King while I smoked a joint. When you grow up in Miami you learn all kinds of slangs and dialects, so some times I spoke like a Jamaican, sometimes like Tony Montana, sometimes like a cab driver from Brooklyn, and sometimes like me.

Zalman King was all class. He was a true gentleman. He had a calm excitement about him whatever he was working on. You could tell he oozed success from every pore. He was totally relaxed with a camera in his hand, having fun just making movies. I had no idea we would become the best of friends.

After the interview I signed a new release and we said our goodbyes and I didn't think about him or the filming again for awhile. It wasn't as if I thought anything was really going to happen from that interview. I stayed focused on my own dream. Until one day about a month later a package showed up for me from Los Angeles California. It was from The Z K Company and I knew it was from him.

I opened up the package and there was a DVD and a t shirt in it. I went over to Reds apartment because he had a DVD player and I put the DVD in the machine and sat back to watch it.

At first I thought it was pretty cool. The color was right, the sound. I could see that whoever made it knew what they were doing. That wasn't the problem. I looked like a stoner to me, and it just didn't sit right. I kept thinking about kids seeing it and that it wouldn't be the best thing. I'm not a role model but for some reason I just didn't want my mom or people to see me looking like some stoner. So I called Zalman King up on the phone.

"You got the package? How do you like it?"

"I don't."

"Why not."

"Because I look like I'm some stoner."

"You WERE smoking a joint."

"I know. It's just not what I expected."

"What did you expect?"

"I don't know. Not that. Maybe....more like a super hero or something."

"You are a super hero. You are STONER MAN."

"Not funny."

"Listen. Wait till you see what I do with it before you say no. I will take out the parts were you look really stoned. Ok?"

I thought about it for a minute. I trusted this guy. I don't think he is in business to fail. I didn't want to throw away a chance at something, even if I wasn't sure what it was.

"Ok." I hung up the phone. I was a little disappointed that the film was not what I expected. It was kind of like buying a lottery ticket. All week long you fantasize about how you are going to spend your winnings, then you are totally surprised that you didn't win when the odds were twenty million to one against you in the first place. That's how I felt. It was a good reality check. It just made me focus harder.

About a month later another package arrived from The Z K Company. This time I waited until Red got home and we watched it. Red picked it up.
"Sex Y and Z?"
"Yeah." Red rolled his eyes. "It's not porn. Right? Your mom wouldn't dig that."
"It's not porn."
We put the DVD in and it had me at all the breaks, and every now and then I would pop up. The editing was great. It had a whole bunch of other people in it, like Ice T and the Bishop Magic Don Juan, which was way cool to me. It also had extreme surfing, skiing, skating, and fine girls would be popping up all the time. Not naked or anything, just pretty girls would flash across then screen. It was like a video magazine and you were turning the pages about as fast as you could understand them. Just one clip after the next. It had these funny little skits in it also and a lot of extreme motorcycle jumping. It ended just as raw and abruptly as it started.
"That was cool." Red said.
"Different, that's for sure." I had never seen anything like it but I wasn't spending a lot of time in front of the T.V.
Zalman King called a few weeks later and offered me a job in Los Angeles. We were going to film a few episodes of his show and he said I could do camera work. I told him I was going to go buy a camera.
"Make sure it shoots 24 frames a second." Zalman told me.
"Why's that?"
"That's film speed. You are about to go to school. With the technology of today I can shoot something with a camera that I can hold in one hand, that can be sold to a network."
I ended up buying the same camera as Zalman had. It was a hand held Panasonic mini dv cam. It was the highest end consumer camera that I could find in my price range. It was almost five thousand dollars. This was a big investment for me, spending five thousand dollars on a camera. I figured I could always sell it if it didn't work out. I just thought it was important to come correct when I got to L.A. and show up with a camera. I was right because I was one of the guys with

his own camera so I always got to work. One of the other guys who was a real school trained camera man was always renting one. Or the company did when they needed an extra camera on set.

I still had six months until I could go back to Holland so I figured why not see what trouble I could get in on the West Coast. I could always jump ship anytime after six months goes by, so I figured the best thing would be to see how far I could take this deal in that amount of time.

Zalman bought me a ticket to L.A. and let me stay in his guesthouse, which was a few blocks from the beach in Santa Monica. His guesthouse was two story building in his back yard and it was bigger than my place in Miami. He let me stay in it until I got it together.

The day I walked in to Zalman's house he was having a dinner party with the heads of three major networks as well as a bunch of stars. His wife Pat is an incredible painter and sculptor as well as a gifted script writer. Both Zalman's daughters are artists. He definitely had a gifted clan. Extremely cool people.

"Tell them how we met." Zalman said as I walked in. I told the table the story about the restaurant. Zalman really liked that story. Then I went to bed.

I woke up the next day on East Coast time about three hours before anyone else. It must have been four a.m. I saw a Starbucks on the way into to town the day before so I walked over to it. I was used to Cuban coffee Miami style every morning so I ordered an eight shot espresso. I walked back to the house by five a.m. and I knew no one would be awake for a while so I started writing something. I didn't know the elements of a script yet, so I wrote a complete story only using the characters and the dialogue. This was a trick to get the story across with no description. But I didn't know any better. I wrote for about thre hours and it was about ten pages long.

Zalman had and office on Ventura blvd in Sherman Oaks. We rode in Zalman's Mercedes to work and I read him the dialogue. Zalman had a whole bunch of people working for him. He had a complete film company. They could do everything, write it, produce it, film it edit the film they shot, all of it, in one building. He had a bunch of interns and young people that were trying to come up in this business working on the cheap. It was a cool little pool of talent.

We got to the office the first day. We walked into the office of one of the interns. He was about twenty years old. Way younger than me.

"Teach him the script writing program." Zalman told him.

"Final draft?" The kid asked.

"That's the one." Zalman said as he went upstairs to his office. It took the guy a few hours to get me to understand the program and the elements of a script. I had been writing for years for the magazine, telling stories just not in script form.

"The script is like a blue print for whoever is going to help you film what you write. It's not just for the actors to learn lines. It's for guys to get cars, build sets, find locations." It all seemed so easy to him. I got the elements of the script fast enough and by the end of the day I had written my first script. It was a short story about sixteen pages long.

Zalman was impressed as he read it.

"Tell you what. You write funny skits and I will send you out with a film crew to film them."

"And pay me?"

"Yes and pay you."

"Once again you got a deal." We shook hands and I left his office. My friend Marko had an apartment off Western and Normandie on the other side of town that he let me live in free. I started writing scripts. The first script I wrote took a month and a half and was over three hundred pages long. I was so proud of it. I walked into Zalman's office and put it on his desk.

"What's this?" He asked me.

"My first script."

He picked it up and felt the weight of it then he dropped it back on the desk.

"No one is going to read this."

"Why not? You don't even know what it's about."

"Because it's too long. A page is a minute in film time. Ninety to one hundred and five pages, that's your limit. And you have to get them written within three months."
"Why's that?"
"You don't want to spend years writing a script. You want to be able to meet deadlines. " He picked up the script and handed it back to me.
"Go make two movies out of this." He said. I did. I turned it into a movie with a sequel.
I started seeing everything in three acts. I started writing three part trilogies. I would give my self all these different writing exercises. Writing the TV guide description, the back of the DVD description, the treatment, the script and stories. As long as I was writing something, completing projects, I was happy. Being a storyteller. I had been writing for the magazine for over a decade, so scripts were getting easier to write.. They were mostly dialogue and completing them became one of my favorite things to do. Soon I had a pile of them. I always finished within ninety days. Have to be aware of deadlines.
I started working for the ZK Company all the time. We even worked on weekends. Everybody there loved to work and make films. I was shooting different skits with Zalman and his crew. It was cool because I would be a camera man when I wasn't in front of the camera being an actor. Once in awhile he would send me out with the crew alone, but he would always show up. It was just like film school.
I worked hard and saved my money. I didn't know any one or go anywhere so I saved all my dough.
I bought a nineteen fifty two Chevy pick up. It was flat black and slammed to the ground and had a whole bunch of Mother Theresa's and crucifix's in it all over the inside. Like some Santeria voodoo priest owned it.
I bought it from an East Los Angeles Low Rider and this truck was dialed. His kids were screaming so bad because they didn't want their dad to sell it. When I got back to the office Zalman freaked on it. We shot a few skits in the truck but I figured it was time for me to keep moving. This was not my dream. We had made three episodes of the show and I had

learned a lot about camera work and script writing. I had gotten a lot out of being in L.A. but I knew it was time to go. I had somewhere else to be. I packed up my Chevy pick up truck, said goodbye to the friends I had made and drove back across the country. Again.

68

Driving across the country in the slammed 1952 Chevy pick up was a cool thing to do. At every stop some old timer would walk up and tell me about the first piece of ass he got in a truck just like that.
Everybody waved at me in the truck every where I went. The truck looked like a Rat Rod but it was dialed with a 327 motor, it went real fast. Three days and four nights of straight driving and I was back in Miami. It wasn't too comfortable sleeping in the truck but when there is somewhere else you want to be all you want do is get there. This wasn't a joy ride.
Miami was exactly as I left it. I wasn't focusing on the parties as much. I had been gone over four months and it was no secret I was planning on moving back to Holland. Jimmy and Red were taking care of the SBU parties for me. The parties kind of ran themselves. Once I picked a date and a bar to have it in they would just evolve into a party.
I still had a few months to wait till I could go back to Holland so I started writing like a man possessed every day. Red was welding every day. Either bike frames or big gates in front of rich people's houses. He would come home every day looking like he worked in a coal mine. I would be siting at my desk with a pile of crumbled paper behind me trying to write a script. Trying to write a coherent scene, trying to understand the elements of a script better. Writing a book was too far off to think about, so I stayed with scripts.
The first person to ever try and sell one of my scripts is my friend Vinnie. Skinny Vinny we called him growing up cause he is hella skinny. He is also one of those very efficient people. In a town full of decadence and a whole lot of people

trying things and failing, Vinnie was succeeding. We called him Mr. Efficiency as we got older. Vinnie owned a barber shop on Washington boulevard that was always busy. He called me up and asked me to bring him my latest scripts. I walked in and Vinnie was relaxing watching TV in the back. He saw me as soon as I got in.

"Hemingway. How's the writing going?"

"Good. Still at it."

"You should have never left L.A. That's where the action is. That's where I'm going."

"I got some where else to be."

"That's your problem and you don't see it. You got nowhere else to be except right here. That's why you walked in here. Did you bring the scripts like I asked you?"

"Yeah." I gave Vinnie my movie with a sequel.

"What's it about?"

"It's a love story."

"A love story? You wrote a love story?"

"Everything is a love story."

Just then a girl walked in and walked over to us and gave Vinnie a hug.

"D.L. this is Patty." We shook hands.

"Patty has a deal with a network and they are always looking for scripts. I want to give her yours. She's going to read them and see what she can do."

"If you trust her I trust her. When are you going to read them?"

"Right away. I will gat back to Vinnie by the end of the day." And with that she turned around and left. The entire barber shop stopped and watched her shake her ass the whole way out.

"At least she will give us the straight dope whether she thinks she can sell them or not."

It took about two weeks until I heard from Patty. She met me at Vinnie's barber shop again.

"I have news." She said.

"I sent the scripts to my friends at a big company in Los Angeles and they loved them. They gave me a list of things they want you to change."

"I thought you said they loved them."
"They do. Or else they wouldn't have sent the list of changes."
"I don't understand."
"Listen to her." Vinnie said.
"Let me explain how this works. Hollywood will take your scripts and throw them in the garbage and never even call you back. That's how Hollywood works. Nine doors out of ten slam in your face and one opens."
"I still don't get it."
"You got a call back. That's a big deal. Can you please fix the script according to their notes? PLEASE." I looked over at Vinnie.
"Just do it." Vinnie said. Like I said before trust is huge. I trusted Vinnie so I took the scripts back and left.
I went back to my place and looked at the notes. They were pretty precise notes. No drugs, no sex, no crime, no weed in every scene, they thought that my two films could be made into one film, which meant I had to take out almost one hundred pages. A bunch of notes.
I went over to the coffee counter near the warehouse. They were Venezuelan and I think they had a whorehouse upstairs. On Fridays the place would be packed with Venezuelan truck drivers and all the waitresses were all dolled up.
I got two cups of Cuban coffee and drank them both. I went back home and set up the scripts on my computer and attacked them. This went on all weekend until I had followed their notes and basically trimmed the fat off my two scripts and made a much tighter but I felt a less raw version of the films I had written. This was the first time I had to collaborate with another person on something I wrote. That is what's called development in Hollywood. EVERYTHING is 'in development' until it's on the screen and people are buying tickets to go see it.
I met Vinnie and Patty at the barber shop on Monday afternoon and handed her a new script.
"What's this?" she asked me.
"The script. I fixed it according to their notes." Patty looked at Vinnie in amazement. Vinnie just rolled his eyes.
"He doesn't suffer from writer's block." Vinnie said.

"Apparently not. I'll get right on this." Patty took the script and left. Once again the whole barber shop stopped to watch her shake her ass the whole way out the door. Then they went right back to cutting hair.

Vinnie sold the shop and moved out west like he said. I never saw Patty after that day. On the three hundred and sixty fifth day I decided to go back and visit Holland.

69

It was a big decision to move everything to Holland in the first place years earlier. It would be an even bigger decision to do it a second time. I had stayed in touch with the brothers that I knew over the year I was away. In fact we were in each others lives more than ever. I visited a couple of times and we talked often, so it was not surprising when I just showed up one day at the bar and said I was coming back.

I didn't get the reception I thought I was going to get. I didn't tell everyone at once. I just told one of the brothers I was close with. He was concerned.

"Are you sure you want to come back here again? Move all your stuff here again?"

"Yes. I am very sure."

"What about the paperwork. Getting divorced and all that stuff?"

"I took care of it from the states a few months ago, but now they are giving me a hard time. I thought I would just have to apply for a tax number at the foreign police."

"It's getting harder and harder to stay here. The immigration laws are out of control. They only want Dutch people getting Dutch jobs."

"I could work in the black market again. Or find some girl to marry for the papers"

He thought about that. The black market meant work under the table. Cash only. Basically the same problem I just had. He was one of those guys that really thought things through. He never rushed, always calm. I learned a lot from him.

"This is what I think. People leave us and we never hear from them again. Too scared to just be a friend. You stayed our best friend. What if for some reason things don't work out again for any number of reasons? I don't want to see you get thrown out of this country again after you invest a lot more time. Many things can happen. At least in the states they can't throw you out of your own country."

I thought about what he said. He could see I didn't like his solution.

"Talk to the brothers. It sounds like the consulate made the decision for you. Think about it. Maybe you could go ride with some brothers in your country."

"I don't really know any brothers from my country."

"We know them that means you know them. Think about it."

He left the bar and I looked around at everyone drinking and smoking and having fun. This is where I wanted to be, I just wasn't sure how I could work it out. I didn't think now was the time to start taking a poll so I just enjoyed the evening. In fact I got pretty loaded and passed out on the couch in my friends living room. I have no idea how I got there. That's when you know you had a good time. When you made it home safe and you don't know how you got there. It's a good feeling to know someone was watching out.

I had a splitting headache when I woke up.

"Take two of these." My friend put down two pills and a cup of coffee.

"What is it?"

"Paracetamol. It's for the hangover. You got very drunk last night. Looks like you needed it."

"I didn't need this hangover."

"I thought you didn't drink."

"I don't and you know it. I shouldn't have taken that first shot. It was downhill from there." I took the pills and chased it with the coffee.

"I have to work. Do you remember what we talked about last night before you got so wasted?"

"Yes."

"Good. Talk with the brothers. Figure out the tax situation. Make sure you can absolutely stay here before you move all

of your things back. I will see you later. Come by the bike shop." Then he left.
I sat there and waited for the pills to take effect, which wasn't very long at all. I got ready and went out not knowing how the day was going to turn out, at the same time knowing whatever outcome is going to change my future in a big way. If the answers were positive I was moving back to Holland, if not I wasn't.
It was as if I already knew the answer. I knew for me to come back it was going to be an even bigger mountain to climb.
I went to the foreign police the next day and showed them the divorce papers and asked for a work visa and a tax number. They wouldn't give me one and I could only get a tourist visa which said I had to leave in thirty days. It seemed like they knew who I was at this point. I'm sure they didn't, they see so many people in a day but it sure seemed that way.
I was depressed. I walked through the city back to the central station to take the boat back. To say I was depressed is an understatement. I was crushed. As soon as I walked into the bike shop my friend could see it.
"Didn't go so well at the foreign police?"
"No."
There wasn't a lot to say. We sat there and had a cup of coffee in silence.
"Listen. There is a big party here in about ten days. Can you stay that long? There will be some brothers from your country here."
"I can stay."
"Good. Then it's settled. Now cheer up. You can't be all doom and gloom around here." He was right. Being depressed wasn't going to help anything. I couldn't help it though. This is what I wanted and it seemed even further than ever.
I waited the ten days until the party. A lot of the brothers in Holland I know for decades were there and happy and surprised to see me so it was nice that I stayed.
I met a young brother from Oakland California and he invited me out for a visit when we got back to the states. I told him I was going to take him up on that offer.

I started to formulate a new plan. I knew a brother in Washington state that I was going to visit also, and now this young brother in California invited me for a visit. I decided to take him up on that invitation.

70

I got back to me Miami and went right back to work at the tattoo shop. I rented a new spot on the beach. Everyone moves around a lot on the beach. The rent is always going up or the apartment is getting torn down. Either way you got to move. I rented a studio apartment my friend Carlos owned on tenth street. It was about three blocks from the police station. Which is about four blocks from the action. It was going to take a few months to get it together to drive across the country. I had to do a lot of work on my motorhome to make it road worthy. It sat at the warehouse. The glass shop worked, which was great so I could get away from everyone and make some glass art, which was one of my escapes. I still had two bikes, the chopper and the FXR I just finished building. I had to make the motorhome ready to tow them and my belongings out west.

I was still writing for the Hot Rod magazine and the Motorcycle magazine, but mostly I was writing scripts. I had boxes of them. I would sit in the tattoo shop and write scripts while I waited for a customer.

I decided I would shoot my own short film. I wrote a short about a vigilante dad killing the drug dealers outside his house in revenge for killing his wife in a shoot out. I cast all my friends in it and shot it on my camera. My friend J A helped me with the permits and renting the cops, and we shot it right outside his office. My buddy Jim Pep's daughter played the daughter. Kids have a great imagination so they do everything with ease. She was awesome. She was like nine years old. She should have got an Oscar. Except it never went anywhere. I still have the footage around here somewhere.

Maybe one day I will dig it out. On the last day of the shoot one of the production assistants walked up to me.

"I know someone who would like your scripts."

"Who's that?"

"This movie Producer I used to work for named John. He's real cool. He's done some movies. He rides bikes. You'll like him. And he's getting it done." She handed me a piece of paper with his phone number and email on it.

"Give him a call. I told him you would." She turned around and walked through the set. Everyone watched her shake her ass. Then they went right back to work. It's a man thing. It never goes away.

I looked at the piece of paper and wondered to myself, is this opportunity calling or another obstacle to keep me from getting to where I want to be? One thing I knew for sure, a writer can write the best thing in the world but if no one reads it, who would know? No one. So I figured I better send him a script.

This guy was on the west coast and that was where I was going regardless so I emailed the guy and he was pretty cool. We both knew movies. We both knew bikes. I got his address and mailed him a package. I went in my glass shop and made a piece of glass and sent a script and some magazines I had articles in. It was a cool package. He is just a cool cat that I had something in common with. I was not chasing the Hollywood dream like a lot of people in that town. I had no hidden agenda. I just liked writing scripts. I was already on a steady course to get to the West Coast, so it would be cool to meet this movie producing guy. We talked on the phone a lot.

"David."

"John."

"I got nothing."

"Me neither." We became great friends.

I told him my plan about driving across the country and he invited me to stop at his ranch on the way out. Yes he said RANCH.

The SBU were still rolling the whole time I was getting ready to leave. Jimmy and Red kept running them. They had help from a few other people but as I got more focused on leaving and less focused on the parties they took over. Jimmy was also an ex junkie. Not as bad as I had been previously in my life, but bad enough. Like I said you can only become a junkie once, and once you become exposed that will never go away. An ex junkie can also always tell when someone is on dope near you. It's like you can smell it. Like your Spidey sense is tingling. That's why I'm surprised I didn't see that Jimmy was getting in too deep. I was going in and out of town so much I never noticed.

I came back from Holland and a few of our friends were going to have an intervention on Jimmy as soon as I got back. This is way before that was invented. We all grew up surfing together, which is a tight knit family. Jimmy used to come by my house every morning for coffee. He'd be whistling loud as hell, waking up the whole neighborhood just as the sun was coming up. We would get a Cuban coffee then swim out to the buoy and back. That's about as far as a football field and back. That's how we started our day. It always made you feel good hitting the shore again. Not only was it great exercise, you were just out there with the man eaters. The BIG SHARKS and you made it back alive. Hitting the shore was invigorating.

So five of Jimmy's surfing buddies and me got together and confronted Jimmy at his house. They picked me up from the airport and we went right to Jimmy's. They explained their plan on the way. Straight confrontation.

Confronting Jimmy didn't go over too well. In typical junkie fashion he let us know he had everything in control. SBU was taking off and he was fine. I had been out of town so I wasn't as aware of Jimmy's habit as everybody else was, but now that it was pointed out to me I could see clearly how strung out he was. We left the house and I got in his face to look at his eyes. The same way your parents did when you came home stoned. His pupils were tiny like pins.

"Are you slamming it?"

"What do you think? It's the only way to fly. Remember?"

I should have knocked him out right then. We had already been in plenty of fights in our life. I was standing in his way. It was kind of symbolic. He wanted me to move out of his

way. He wanted me to step aside to his behavior. I really had no room to talk in Jimmy's mind because I was an ex junkie.
"You mind?" Jimmy looked at me through stoned out eyes.
I shook my head and stepped out of his way. I watched him go down the block on his skateboard. One thing for sure I was convinced no one can save anyone that doesn't want saving. And Jimmy didn't want saving. Still, I should have knocked him out.
The next time I saw Jimmy was a few days later at the coffee counter. It was about seven a.m. and he was loaded. He looked like shit, been up all night, it was obvious he was strung out bad.
"Loan me a twenty till later." He looked like shit.
"How bout I knock you out instead."
"Don't be like that. Loan me twenty till later. Come on D."
"You're out of control."
"Look who's talking. You used to be the most out of control guy in town.
"Once upon a time. Yes. Them days are over."
"Don't be the village drunk. Loan me a twenty."
I looked at my buddy, my pal and my best friend. Someone who is like my little brother. Then I made another bad decision. I reached in my pocket and pulled some cash and gave him a few twenties. I remember being strung out and once in a while someone would hook me up. I remember how grateful I was.
"Thanks D."
"Listen. I don't wanna see you anymore like this. Just don't come around me till you clean up. It's hard enough with what's going on in my own head with out looking at my little brother stoned to the teeth."
"Come on man. You used to be way fucked up. Worse even."
"And I aint going back there. I mean it. I don't wanna see you till you clean up."
That was the last time I ever saw Jimmy.
Three days went by and I knew I had to start looking for him. I called Red.
"When was the last time you saw Jimmy?"

"He's right here. We're down by first street having a bar B Q. Russell got Thirtysix Mackeral. Can you believe it? Thirtysix. Tar Baby got some Snook. Come down."

"I'll be there in five minutes."

I ran out of the house and rode my skateboard down to first street. The party was in full swing when I got there. I looked all around and didn't see Jimmy anywhere. I found Red devouring a plate of Mackeral and a Corona.

"Where's Jimmy." Red looked up at me disappointed.

"He split soon as he heard you were coming. He was pretty wasted. He didn't want to deal with it. Everybody was saying something to him then he heard you were coming and he said 'I'm outta here.' He lit out the beach way cause he knew you were skating up Washington blvd. He didn't feel like running into you."

Jimmy O.D.'d in an abandoned building in Overtown later that night. Shooting dope with a bunch of low life scumbags he didn't even know. Instead of helping him they robbed him and left him there.

They found him around five a.m. and by six a.m. everybody had gathered in front of my house. Jimmy grew up on the beach. His passing rocked myself and a lot of people

Jimmy's paddle out was HUGE. I stood in the bar all night drinking till I dropped crying my eyes out.

"Go home D.L." The bartenders would say. I would hold up a shot and scream

"JIMMY." And the whole bar would scream his name. Losing Jimmy made me look at life harder. This was great loss for me. Like I lost my little brother. Like I failed him. It rocked me. I kept thinking I should have tried harder. But I didn't want to get too close that I fell back in that vein. I kept thinking you can't help a junkie. Not if he wants to keep getting high.

71

Gotta keep pushing my self at all times. Gotta keep moving forward. Gotta keep on keepin on.
Everything slowed down for me after Jimmy's death. It was a wake up call for a lot of people, myself included. Lesson one. I better never get too comfortable.
I was working a lot trying to save money to go back to Holland. Miami isn't the cheapest place in the world, but if you are from there it's pretty easy to have a few things going and not work a lot.
It took a few months to get back on my feet after Jimmy's death. It was really hard to shake the feeling of guilt. I would hang out at the bar depressed and my friends would see me there as they walked up and go to a different place because I was such a bummer.
Red was still doing the SBU parties and we hadn't had one in a long time so we decided to do one. I figured I had to get my mind into something so I could move forward. I started really working out the logisitic of driving across the country. Everything is an undertaking. Everything takes careful planning if you plan on succeeding.
When every day is the same they all seem to run into another and all of a sudden I was looking back at all the things I had not accomplished and the time I spent not getting it done. It was a vicious cycle, which I had to change. I was getting too comfortable in the sunshine riding my motorcycle every day with my friend Alex. I had become complacent. Sometimes that's hard to see while it is happening to you. Life was good, sun is shining, bike is running, but I wasn't getting anywhere. Not where I wanted to be anyway. I started working like a man possessed and saving every dollar. No more sushi every night, back to tuna out of the can. Got to get back to the dream.
I was still talking to the young brother on the West Coast alot and the Movie Producer once in a while so in my mind I had a place to go with a cool stop along the way. Time to get back to

chasing my dreams. As I got older the dream stayed the same, it just got a little more precise. I wanted to be in the family all my friends were in, and I wanted to make something out of my life. That's what I suffer from, it's called AMBITION.

Once my mind was made up to keep moving life got a little better. Everywhere I looked reminded me of Jimmy though and that was difficult. It made it hard to stay in Miami. It was time to go. But time to go and really getting out don't always fall in line. It takes work. Six weeks can turn into six months before you know it. Hopefully it doesn't turn into six years.

72

I was saving every dime I had and getting ready to split. I was about two weeks away from leaving. I had given up my apartment and I had to be out by the end of the month. The adventure was on again. I was out of my mind again with excitement. My new friends on the West Coast were expecting me and everything was going to plan. It felt right.

I had two bikes that I was bringing with me. My chopper which was immaculate, huge motor, fat tire, so clean you could eat off it. And my newly built Custom FXR all chrome with black paint Red flames with a white stripe. Both bikes were sick. I also had the motorhome running good with the glass shop operational in the back. I brought tanks of propane and Oxygen so I was self sufficient. I had been tattooing five days a week so I figured I could do that on the side. I was comfortable knowing I could make money when I arrived on the West Coast. Got to survive. The rent never stops coming. Ever.

I lived of tenth street about three blocks from Washington boulevard which is where all the action is. I kept the chopper at JA's warehouse and I rode the FXR everywhere. Everyone had choppers and now I was into FXR's. Me and Alex now had the only FXR's. Everyone else rode rigid frame choppers. I was planning to drive to Oakland with both bikes in an enclosed trailer. You never know how the wind can blow. I didn't want anything to damage my bikes.

I was laying in my bed around three a.m. I know it was three a.m. cause I had just gotten home around two a.m.. from working in the tattoo shop. I had gotten in a huge argument with the girl I was seeing at the shop and I ended up splitting to go home and she went to the bar to get drunk. I had to wake up early and cover a shift at the tattoo shop in Kendall and I wanted to get some sleep.

I heard a slight knock at the door. Da da da da da da da...you know that familiar knock. I thought it was my girl drunk trying to make up.......The door knocked again... da da da da da da.

I jumped out of my bed in mu underwear and ripped the door open. There were three men standing there. One was a decent dressed Cuban about thirty. One was a Haitian also about thirty tears old dressed in Miami Marlins gear and one looked like an over weight redneck about fifty five.

"What do you want?" I said as I ripped the door open. I think they were as surprised to see me as I was as seeing them. Everyone just froze for a moment.

"Is that you bike down there?" The redneck asked.

"It's gonna get towed." The Haitian guy said. I thought they were tow truck drivers. Three of them I should have figured they were cops.

I ran down stairs which was one flight and my bike was fine. I ran back up and only the Cuban and the Haitian guys were standing there. I reached for my door and it was locked from the inside.

"OPEN IT NOW." I said as I beat on the door. I was locked out of my own house.

The door opened and the redneck pulled a badge out from under his shirt that he was wearing on a chain.

"Miami P.D. You're under arrest."

"THAT'S BULLSHIT." I said as I tried to close the door and get back inside with them out. It wasn't happening. The redneck weighted about three hundred pounds. Everybody started swinging. I thought they were jackers. This became a fight with those three trying to subdue me. I blasted the Haitian with a right and the Cuban guy blasted me with a left. The neighbors who were sitting across the street drinking beer all night all started screaming with excitement. It looked like I was fighting three home invaders, which is what I thought they were. That big redneck could have bought that badge.

We were pretty quickly rolling on the floor. I lived on a second floor so it's lucky we didn't roll off. They had me in handcuffs and dragged me in my own apartment and ripped it apart with me watching them. And I'm in my underwear to boot. They were ripping my place apart in front of me.

"Can I put some pants on?"

The big redneck cop helped me put the pants on while I was handcuffed and I put my legs in the holes. Then he pushed me back on the couch. They continued to rip my place apart until they found a few ounces of weed I had in some jars.

"Jar weed. And it's all jarred up. That's possession with intent to distribute."

"Too bad you don't got a warrant or else that lie might work."

"What you say?" The Cuban cop said.

"I said I need a lawyer. I don't speak your language."

They collected all my weed and found a couple hits of and acid that I didn't even know was stashed in a book on the shelf. It was probably so old that if they bothered to test it nothing would have showed up anyway.

The whole neighborhood came out and was watching me get stuffed in the police car. Two squad cars pulled up to give back up.

"Call my friend to come get my bike." I said to the big Redneck cop as we passed my bike.

"Call him or else my shit will be stolen."

He thought about it and took out his flip phone.

"What's the number?" I told him the number. This is back when everyone remembered numbers. He spoke into the phone.

"Yeah you wanna come on down and pick up your friend's bike. He's being arrested. No, this is not a joke." The cop listened for a moment and the he held the phone up to my ear.

"Is this for real?" Red asked me.

"I am in handcuffs in the back of the police car. Hurry up."
"On my way."
Red came right down and took the bike.
The redneck cop opened the door of the back of the police car I was sitting in and looked at me. He leaned in.
"Ever been arrested before?"
"What do you think?"
"You can help yourself."
"I got nothing to say to you." He looked at me with a grin.
"I respect that." He slammed the door on me. Idiot.
It was a quick ride to the Miami Beach police station. About one minute. The three cops who were at my door walked me inside handcuffed with nothing on but my jeans. I had no belt so I was trying to hold up my past as I walked.
They brought me to a room full of people filling out papers and when we walked in they all covered their faces and screamed like they were in pain. They had brought me into a room full of undercover cops filling out their paperwork. IDIOTS. They slammed me up against the wall with my face to it so I couldn't see anything and all the undercover cops filed out real quick. When I finally sat down the only people in the room was the Redneck cop and two cops that used to stand outside a club called the Kitchen Club that I was a bouncer at many years earlier. They had watched me grow up and were sitting there with a grin.
The redneck cop sat down in front of his typewriter and put a piece of paper in it.
"What have you been arrested for?"
"Posession, assault, look it up you'll find it. I grew up on the beach."
They cop was having trouble typing with his two fingers. He looked up at me with disdain.
"Last chance to help yourself." He said.
"You don't know D.L.?" One of the cops said who was sitting behind me..
"He's not gonna tell you anything." The other cop said. I looked at them and they looked familiar. Then it hit me, these cops had arrested me years earlier. More than once. They were detective's now.

"Glad to see you're still at it D.L." One of them said as they got up.
"Yeah. Keeps us in business." The other one said and they walked out laughing.
The cop finished the paperwork and threw me in the holding tank. My friends got me out by morning. Getting out was the least of it. Now not only was I not leaving Miami when I thought I was, I now had to fight a case. I hadn't done that in a while.
For those of you that don't know, there is no fight like a fight for your freedom. Everything is different when you are fighting a case. And me with a few prior convictions things didn't look great from the start.
The court appointed attorney they had for at the arraignment was dump truck meaning he was into dumping me off a the first stop. The first meeting didn't go too well. He kept frowning and nodding his head 'no' while he looked over my rap sheet.
"So you recently completed probation a few years ago? Is that correct?"
"Yes sir."
He looked at the sheet some more and did some more shaking his head.
"You should take their offer. Possession with intent to distribute more than an ounce. You get three to five years. I'll have you out in two."
"You're insane. It was illegal search and seizure. I didn't invite them in. They went in without a warrant."
"That's not what they say."
"They are lying."
"Somebody in the neighborhood called on you. I don't know who and we wont know until discovery, and that's if we ever find out."
"Called on me for what?"
"For dealing."
"I wasn't dealing."
"They said you had a lot of traffic at that residence and they thought you were dealing out of it."
"Don't they still need a warrant?"

"Not if they smelled weed."

"I was sleeping."

"The are saying you attacked them." He looked at the paper and read, "The suspect opened the door and attacked the officers after they identified themselves."

"They went in my place and locked me out."

"Listen. You have quite a previous record. A few convictions. The judge is going to look at that. You get in trouble every three or four years. That sets a pattern. They have a ninety percent conviction rate in drug cases in this town."

He leaned in and whispered like he didn't want anyone else to hear him. He probably didn't. He was selling me up the river.

"Three to five. You do eighteen months. Think about it." he picked up his case load of folders and almost dropped them on the floor, but he caught them and left.

I sat there for a moment stunned. Then I got up and walked out. After I walked out of the swinging glass doors I turned back I read the letters painted on the glass, 'Public Defenders Office'.

I thought that's a laugh. Public Pretenders Office is what it should say cause that guy was pretending to help me. I had a clear cut case of illegal search and seizure as far as I could see it. And for what? Four ounces of weed? The acid never even showed up in the report. They must have kept it. It was probably twenty years old anyway. I never thought they would try to give me a few years for four ounces of weed. They have a zero tolerance policy in Miami.

I knew I had to figure out another avenue. I went and saw my mom and got the name and number of one of my father's friends who was still alive and still an attorney. It was on Brickell avenue in a high end building where really rich attorney's defend private clients with money. I rode my bike there and parked in a lot full of Mercedes and BMW's.

The attorney's name was Bill. The last time I had seen him I was about then years old. I knew he wouldn't remember me.

"You could be anyone." He said to me.

"Can I make a call?"

"Who are you going to call?"

"My Mom." He smiled and handed over the phone. She picked it up right away.

"Put him on." She said. I handed him the phone.

"My mom wants to talk to you." He took the hone with a big smile.

"Harriet? Yes. Good. Yes it has been quite a while." Then he listened. Then he laughed. Then I knew I was in. I knew he was going to help me.

He talked to my mom for about twenty minutes. They laughed for most of it. You could tell it was two old friends that hadn't spoken in a long, long time. He hung up the phone and turned to me.

"I am going to put one of the attorney's in my firm on your case. Don't worry about a thing. Me and your parents go way back. Since Beach High School. I am going to take care of your problem."

"Thank you Sir."

"It's going to cost three thousand five hundred dollars. If it was anyone else I would be charging thirty five thousand dollars. And getting the same result. Acquittal. That's what we do here. We win."

I stood up, shook his hand and left. I felt a lot better. I knew I just had to go through the motions of fighting the case and hopefully I will be acquitted. I knew first order of business is get the attorney most of his money. They don't work too well when you don't pay them.

I figured if the attorney has a private investigator they would talk to the witnesses who watched it and find out it was an illegal search and seizure and I could get back on my course. It's never that easy though.

It's almost impossible to think about anything else when you are fighting a case. It is the first thought in the morning and the last at night and most of the thought's all day. You might get you freedom taken away. Nobody can tell that's what's on your mind, but believe me, it is. I got a call from my new attorney, his name was Doug Haskell. He was the attorney Bill had appointed to my case. He had just started with the firm a few months ago. He was young and snotty and he was full of attitude.

"We don't even take cases this small. Who do you know?"
"Bill. He knows my mom. Bill is the lead partner of the firm. This is HIS firm, He is YOUR boss.
Doug went silent after that for a moment. I don't think people usually talk to him that way.
"Well, looking at your record it's going to be hard for me to get you just probation. You are going to have to do a little time. Six months maybe. Then a few years of probation. "
"Bill said you are going to get me acquitted. That's what you guys do. Win."
"Bill is not trying this case, I am. Don't call me I will call you when I have a date for the discovery and pre trial hearing. That will be the same day. I am going to try to expedite this process. I have big cases to try."
"This is a big case to me." He hung up the phone. I sat there not feeling too good. You have to be confident in your attorney. I wasn't. I started getting my head ready to go to jail for about six months. My attorney called me the day before the pre trial hearing. That's where they disclose the discovery, which is basically when they have to show their hand, witnesses, evidence, statements all of it. The first part is the arraignment which happens within three days. That's when you find out the charges and bail. This is the next part, which is when you see what you are up against. How good of a case they have against you. I didn't think the cops had much of a case at all. But that was just my opinion.
The Pre trial is usually a few months after the arrest. A good attorney will make a case drag out for years. People tend to care less when the incident is years previous.
I got arrested in mid August it was now almost Christmas. Backed up. That what they said. The courts are 'backed up.'
"Dress nice tomorrow. You have a suit, right?"
"Yes sir." Red took me to the thrift store and I picked out a suit from the rack.
"And be on time. You really are one lucky son of a gun aren't you?"
"What's that supposed to mean?"
"Don't worry about it. See you tomorrow. Third floor court room –C. Don't be late" and he hung up. He always hung up

the phone when he was done he never waited for a good bye or anything. Pompous bastard.

The night before court is always a sleepless one. Mostly because we stay up partying all night. Red picked me up the next day in his box van. I was waiting in front of my place wearing my suit from the thrift store. The same neighbors that watched the whole incident were siting on their stoop drinking just like always. They knew I was gong to court.

"GOOD LUCK." They started yelling from their stoop and waving at me and giving me the thumbs up sig. I gave then a thumbs up.

"Wow. You clean up good."

"Shut up. I feel like hell." The van did a slow unsteady take off from the curb.

"We gonna make it? I can't be late."

"Relax. I'm your lucky charm. Remember the trouble you got in with Jimmy years ago? The B and E's. You guys got off cause you brought me to court."

"We got off cause they didn't have anything."

"And cause you brought me. Relax. You'll see."

"There's nothing to see today. This is just the discovery. Can't this thing go any faster?"

"It takes a minute." We rolled down the highway to the courthouse in silence. Not a lot to say on the way to court. Just a foreboding feeling of what might happen.

"Try to think good thoughts." Red said.

"Shut up." Red was always positive. I was having trouble keeping a positive attitude. I had just completed probation less than three years ago. To the court that is like last week.

The court room was full of defendants. Most of them were crack heads or career criminals dressed like they were going to a tailgate party. My attorney and me were the only people in suits. As soon as he saw me he started walking to the hallway and waved to me to come meet him. The hallway was full of attorneys and clients all discussing their cases with great enthusiasm. Red found a seat in the court room and started watching cases. The cases were going by really quick. About a minute a case. Some crackhead defendant would stand in front of the judge in a football jersey.

"Ya Honor....I promise it was a personal crack rock." The defendant would say. Then his court appointed attorney would dump him off. Or they would get a fine. A lot of people that day would get fined three hundred sixty three dollars. It didn't matter what the charges were, that was the fine. It was like it was 363 dollar day. One defendant after the next would get the same fine.
My attorney and me found a corner to talk.
"How do you know Bill again?"
"He knows me my whole life. He went to Beach High with my dad."
"I just started with the firm. I'm on a probationary period to see my performance. It can last a year. This is an unwinnable case. It's your word against the cops word. But Bill told me if I don't get you off of this I will not have shown my worth to this firm."
"So I guess you have to win."
"I just disclosed to the prosecutor that my private investigator has eye witness accounts form your neighbors across the street stating they baited you out of your house then locked you out for over three minutes. I don't think she will proceed. These things cost money. They pick the cases they know they can win. With these eye witness accounts, they know there is more than a chance they will lose. They don't like losing."
He turned around and walked in the court room.
"Don't say a word." He said to me as we went in.
All the attorney's knew each other. You could see that my attorney was from the rich part of town. They called my name within a few a minutes. The big attorney's don't have to wait.
The case got dropped with me getting a fine for simple possession of four hundred eighty one dollars. The attorney was extremely happy and he ran out of the court to another case. Me and Red walked out of the court room feeling like Kings. I was totally relaxed. Like the weight of the world has been lifted off my shoulders.
"See I told you. I'm your lucky charm."
"Thanks for the ride."

You know that's a sign."
"What's that?"
"Every one all day long is getting fined three hundred sixty three dollars. Then you get fined four hundred eighty one dollars. The only one."
"The only one?"
"The only one. It's a sign I'm telling you. I hate to say it, cause I don't want you to leave, cause it's fun hanging out, but it's time for you to go."
Red was right.

73

Winning the case was a big deal. That put me back on track.
It was a few days until Christmas so I decided to wait for the holidays to pass until I got back on the road towards California. I didn't want to fight the holiday traffic. I wanted to take it easy, make my way across the country in a relaxed mode. No rushing, even though I felt like I was late. I had come to realize that is a general feeling I carry, that I'm always late. It makes you move faster. I still had to learn to slow and steady pace wins the race.
The bikes were dialed, I was getting the last few details on the motorhome with the hitch I had to install to tow the bikes, but everything was on track.
I went to the bar the night of the win t to celebrate with a few friends. My SBU crew showed up. It was a big deal. Everybody thought I was going back to jail for sure, so the fact that I wasn't was good news.
It was quiet, not too many people in the bar. We went outside to smoke a joint and when we came back in there was some guy siting in my seat. He was just a normal guy, same size as me dressed to go out for a night on the town in Miami Beach. I didn't know him, so he must not have known I was sitting there.
"You're in my seat."

He looked at me, then back at his drink. He had a pitcher of beer in between him and his friend.
"I said you are in my seat."
The guy stood up real quick. He towered over me. He was bigger than I thought.
"So do something about it." He said with more attitude than was necessary.
I smashed him with a straight upper cut. I saw where this was going, no time to waste. When in doubt knock 'em out is how I was taught. He didn't go down but he was dazed. Three of my friends got all around him quick. My buddy Al got right in his face. The guy realized he was out numbered pretty quickly.
"Oh yeah. Is that how it is? O.K." He said as he walked out of the bar real fast. Al looked at his friend.
"I'm just sitting enjoying my beer." The guys friend said. He didn't want any trouble.
"LOOK." Red said. He was looking out the front window. We all walked over and looked out the window. The guy walked over to his car, opened the door and looked around the back seat. He stuffed a gun in his belt. He covered it up with his shirt and started walking back to the bar. I looked at my crew.
"You guys strapped?"
Three of them nodded yes. We all went outside just as the guy was getting back to the bar.
"You ready?"
"The question is are you ready?" he asked me with confidence.
"Oh we're ready." Three of my buddy's lifted up their shirts showing they we had guns also. They smile on the guys face went away.
"Over a seat? You wanna have gunfight at the OK corral over a seat?"
The guy thought about it.
"No."
"Go back inside the bar and find another seat. No big deal." I said. The guy knew it was going to be all bad if he pulled his

gun out. He went back inside. Him and his friend found a table to sit at.

"Order them a pitcher from me." I told the bartender.

"You're such a sweetheart." She said as she shook her ass with a pitcher over to the guys table.

"Don't tell anyone."

I sat down at a table with Al. Nether of us drink but it was time for a victory shot.

"You got lucky today, winning that case."

"I know. The power of a private attorney."

"Private attorney or not you got lucky. You should be gone already. Months ago."

"I know."

He was right. He's usually right. I knew I got lucky today.

"Tell you what." I said as I lifted my shot glass. "Before the next incident happens I will be gone."

"How you gonna make a toast like that? How do you know when the next incident is going to happen? You don't. You gotta toast to something better than that."

"How about after the next incident."

"That's no good either. What if the next incident is the lock up? No that one aint no good either."

"Then you think of one."

We sat there in silence both trying to think about something good to toast to.

While we were sitting thinking three guys and a girl walked in. They looked like they had just turned eighteen. They were all dressed in white like they were in the navy. A short Mexican guy and a tall white guy and Fat Chinese guy and a white girl. One of the guys was about six four. They were coming through the entrance and the Mexican guy stopped in front of some customers.

"Permiso. Permiso." He said in this very drunken way. He was moving in slow motion like he was wasted or something.

"He's not drunk." I said to Al. We watched the four of them move through the bar like they were kind of casing it. It was getting late and the bar was starting to fill up with people.

One shot turned into two shots which turned into a few shots by the time later came me and Al were pretty drunk and still trying to think of the perfect thing to toast to. Sometimes things happen so fast that before you know it all decisions get made for you.

"There's a fight outside. DL Come on. THERE'S A FIGHT OUTSIDE." My friend Danny said as he came rushing into the bar. Everyone loves a fight so the whole bar started rushing outside to watch.

"Why not?" I said to Al as we got up to casually go watch whatever was happening. There was definitely some action outside. One of the locals from the bar was in the middle of the street slugging it out with the Chinese guy. The tall one was in the middle of the street challenging anyone who wanted to step up and fight.

"YOU'RE ALL GONNA DIE!!!" The girl who was with them started screaming, "YOU"RE GONNA DIE! YOU HEAR ME?" She screamed pretty loud I think everyone heard her.

I walked over to Red.

"What happened?" I asked him.

"I don't know. All of a sudden they said they were disrespected and they wanted to fight. They are from the Navy." Red said. Red has never been in a fight in his life.

The Mexican guy was now bouncing up and down and shadow boxing in front of my friend Frank. Frank is very mellow. He was holding his little dog in his arms. He had this little scraggly Benjy type of dog that he rescued. He took it everywhere with him.

"Mano y mano. Mano y mano." The Mexican guy kept saying to Frank while he bounced up and down shadow boxing. He kept swinging near Frank's face.

"I got a better idea. How about I just watch you get knocked out." Frank stepped up off the street on to the sidewalk and Danny started yelling at everyone.

"Get out of the street. DL is gonna handle it."

"What is wrong with you?" I asked Danny.

"Get 'em." Danny said. If you know Danny then you know he is nutso bat shit crazy, but in a good way.

"What seems to be the problem?" I said to the Mexican guy as I walked into the middle of the street. He kept bouncing up and down and shadow boxing like he was Sugar Ray.

"Mano y mano. Mano y mano." Was all he kept saying
"No problem. Here I am." I said. I kept advancing toward the guy and he kept backing up.
"I'm not gonna chase you dude. Let's hammer it out." I said. We were standing in the middle of the street with the whole bar outside watching.
"Mano y mano. Mano y mano."
The really tall guy was still standing in the middle of the street waiting for someone to fight with. This is all happening about two blocks from a police sub station and you can bet that not going back to jail was already on my mind. I kept advancing toward the Mexican guy slowly looking for that knockout punch. A car turned up the block and it was my friend Russell and his girl and they were in the middle of an argument. They were always in the middle of an argument which didn't always leave Russell in the best mood. One thing about Russell, he aint no joke. This is a real deal blue collar working man. He's a Captain on a fishing boat and he is salty. You can bet being out on the ocean day in and day out will make a man tough. And Russell was already tough. With a knock out punch that can't be beat.
As he pulled up he slowed down a little because there were a bunch of people in the street. I saw his face as he looked at the situation. As soon as he saw me he put his car in park right there in the middle of the street, got out and walked up to the big guy.
"What's happening?" and before the guy could answer Russell knocked him out cold. It sounded like a home run hit. The guy was knocked out cold on his feet, he fell down and rolled under a car, this big white a Cadillac that was parked in front. I should have known it was their car. Satisfied, Russell got in his car and parked walked over and watched the rest of the fight with the crowd from the bar. There must have been thirty people watching, the owner and all the bartenders. I thought for sure the cops were going to show up. The Mexican guy was still shadow boxing in front of me.
"Take a look around." I said to him.
"Your one friend is out cold, under the car." I pointed to the Cadillac where the guy was still laying on the ground. He

looed over. The girl was standing next to him but now she wasn't saying anything. She looked a little spooked.

"Your other buddy is getting mopped up." I pointed to his other friend who was now being beaten across the head with a full face helmet that Danny was swinging on him over and over.

As soon as he looked in that direction I slammed him with a right. He went down like a bag of chips. Out. Cold.

Russell looked at me from the crowd with one glance that said, 'That's enough. Get outta there.' I got off the street.

The big guy that Russell knocked out was awake, but dazed. He was now behind the wheel of the Cadillac. The girl was now screaming "WE"VE GOT TO GET OUT OF HERE." Her tune had changed. The other guy who was fighting Danny woke up the Mexican guy who jumped up and started shadow boxing again.

"Mano y mano. Mano y Mano."

"Lets go. You got knocked out." They told him as they stuffed him in their car.

"Who? Me?" he couldn't believe he got knocked out. I couldn't believe the cops didn't show up.

"Just like old times." Al said.

"Just like old times." I said.

I sat there and drank with my pals all night and went home wasted. And when I woke up I strapped my bikes in the trailer, packed up everything in my motorhome and took off for California.

74

Being someone who has driven across this country and a few others, a drive is a drive is a drive. I had a great stereo system installed in my motorhome and I don't think I turned it on even twice. I had too much to think about. The race is on. The dream was alive. Again.

I had a place to land in Oakland and I was going to stop along the way and visit the movie producer guy John in Santa

Barbara. We had become good friends by now so it was going to be a welcome stop. I had sent him a script I had written and he was going to tell me what he thought about it. After writing scripts for years I was excited about the possibilities of where one could go. Or at least hearing it straight from someone who really makes movies.

Everything happens when it is supposed to, if it is supposed to at all. I had learned to take my time and look around. To see what is around me, but on a higher level. I felt it was symbolic that I was passing the 'Welcome to California' sign at six a.m. as the sun was just starting to come up. The signs are out there if you can see them. And once in a while you get a gift. I still look at that sunrise that morning as a gift.

I drove straight through, no stops. That's the beauty of a motorhome. A quick cat nap at the rest stop and I was back on the road again. I made it to Santa Barbara in three days and three nights which is good time. Especially when you aren't speeding. That's just straight driving time.

I stopped at John's ranch for a day and rested from the drive. I wasn't going to spend a lot of time there. The next day after lunch he took out my script.

"I had a look at this."

"What do you think?"

"I think I can help you." He then took out his pen and started making big notes on each page.

"Don't need this. Nope. Not this either." He would cross off big sections of the script.

"What are you doing?" I said. I had never seen anyone do that to my work. It might happen, but I had never seen it.

"This is how it's done." And he continued to cross off what he didn't like and make notes along the way. He circled a scene.

"Here you go. Here's a good scene. This has to be moved closer to the front."

"Closer to the front?"

"Yes. Don't freak out. This is how it's done." I had no idea at the time but he really was helping me. Making movies aint easy. If it was everyone would be doing it. I reached into my bag and pulled out another script.

"What's that?'

"A motorcycle movie I'm writing called 'The MC'."
"Good title."
"Wanna see it?"
"Fix this one first." I took the scripts and put them away. I was a little discouraged, I thought it would be much easier.
When it got a little cooler I said goodbye and I got back on the road. I didn't want to get to Oakland too late.
Driving up the 101 as the sun set on the ocean felt like the perfect way to start this part of my journey. I had been preparing my mind and heart for what was coming at for my entire life.
Every time anything happened for the past few years I would ask myself, 'how does this apply?' How would this matter later? Well later was now. I got to Oakland and the young brother met me and showed me to my room. I laid on my bed that night, the roof was leaking on me, and in five other spots, and I was happier than I had ever been.

75

I moved into a big house that a few Brothers lived in. There were brothers living all around me in the neighborhood that I lived in in East Oakland. After doing so much growing up in the city I felt right at home in the Bay area. I used to always wear Raider gear in Miami growing up.
"Why you wearing that Raider gear?" My friends who are die hard Dolphin fans would ask me.
"Cause Oakland is a tough town." That was always my answer. I think that's why a lot of people still wear Raider gear worldwide. Oakland IS a tough town.
It was pretty cool to land with a custom chopper and a custom FXR.
I had my head on straight with my sight set on the prize. Even with all the money making skills I brought with me, I wanted a forty hour a week job.
I know what it's like to sit in the tattoo shop and wait for a customer to walk in and spend money, sometimes for weeks.

I had my glass shop set up but making sure I had my money for anything, any run I wanted to go on or if my bike broke or whatever came my way I wanted to be ready. So I got a job painting houses for a real cool guy who let me do my job and gave me enough space to achieve my personal goals. He had been in Oakland for years and had seen many people come and go and he knew how tough life can be. I painted houses the first year there forty hours a week.

I knew for sure I didn't want to get in any relationship. That would be way too complicated to deal with. This was my second time around the brothers. I didn't think I would get three so I had to make this work.

I went everywhere on my bike. I bought a flat bed 1952 Chevy pickup as soon as I got to Oakland and slammed it to the ground. It had a .327 engine in it and I used it to haul stuff in it on the side. If it wasn't raining I was on my bike and sometimes even if it was. I wanted the brothers to always see me on my bike.

When I got to Oakland the longest living brothers still alive in the world were there. And there was a whole bunch of young brothers popping wheelies on Harleys that wanted to be a brother just like me. It is in Oakland's culture.

There is a real lot of motorcycle riding going on in Northern California. Oakland is in Alameda County, which is the third largest county in the country. It's like the Wild Wild West in Oakland California.

They guys that I started riding with could really ride well. We would ride in the tightest formation possible, weaving in and out of traffic at ninety. All that riding in Holland was paying off. You have to be confident in the man you are riding next to when he is an inch off your wheel. I was confident.

It was exactly like summer camp. That's how I used to describe it. You are with all your buddies, you got a bunch of counselors and you are all doing fun activities. Sounds like summer camp to me.

One of the Brothers who had been around for decades lived down the block from me. He was as wild as any man I ever met. He had a son named Will and we became the best of friends. For as wild as the dad was the son was absolutely

chill. I can safely say he was the coolest person I ever met in my life.
Chilly Will. That's what we called him. Young Will. Little Will. He had a bunch of names. It depended on how you knew him. Once you knew him good enough you were family. He was always introducing everyone as his 'Uncle' or his 'Aunt" or Cousin. Some people have friends. Will had family everybody else was just an acquaintance.
When I first got to Oakland, Will ran everywhere with his next door neighbor named Korn. They were as thick as thieves. The best of friends. Will lived in a house with his dad and this big Rottweiller named James. Korn lived next door with his wife and three kids and his Aunt. I lived down the block. Not a day went by that I didn't see those two cruising around, laughing seeing what trouble the could get into. Will was always up for everything. Whatever was coming his way he was ready.
Will grew up motorcycling and could ride a wheelie for blocks. He was probably riding about the time he could walk. At the first party I was ever at he did a wheelie show up and down the boulevard with another brother for the crowd. The street was lined with folks on both sides like they were watching a parade.
I don't think anyone really knows what happened, but Will's friend Korn got a motorcycle and started riding around town. He must have been the victim of a hit and run within the first few weeks of owning his bike. Some guy in a big pink Cadillac hit him and killed him. We figured out it was the guy in the big Pink Cadillac because he was found a few exits further down the highway beaten to death laying in his car. Someone must have seen it and followed him. That's Oakland. That's Street Justice in its purest form. I definitely felt at home in Oakland.

76

I left my house with enough time to get gas. We were about to go on the road for over a month and ride to Wyoming for a big run and then to Sturgis South Dakota for a big motorcycle rally. It was going to be over a month on the road and I was excited.

I brought a hundred dollars for each day then an extra thousand just in case anything breaks on my bike. This was before I ever bought that extended warranty. I had never owned a brand new bike fresh off the showroom floor so I never bought the warranty. I didn't even know about it. I thought it was only for new bikes. Now I can't live without it.

I was already getting a name for just making it on time so I didn't want to be late. I got my gas and got back on the road. I got stuck at a light that just wouldn't change. I probably didn't weigh enough to trip the pad so I ran the light. Then I ran the next stop sign. Then the next one. Then I saw the red lights flashing in my mirror. There wasn't anywhere to go so I pulled over. Once in a while it's fun to let them chase you for a bit, but now was not one of those times.

I started to pull out my license and insurance. A real old cop walked up to me.

"You know why I pulled you over?"

"Yes sir."

"You ran a stop light and two stop signs. What's the rush son?"

"Going to meet my friends. Go for a ride."

"You all going to go to Sturgis?"

"Thinking about it."

"I remember when them boys just started out. I been here since the beginning."

He looked around and took a big breath.

"Get out of here. Don't run any more lights, ok?"

"Yes sir."

I jumped back on my bike and took off. That's what It's like in Oakland. The brothers are part of the mystery of the town. And that's cool.

I pulled up just as everyone was taking off and I fell into formation. We would ride like that from sun up to sun down gas tank to gas tank every day. Just like synchronized swimming, only faster on the pavement. It's cool when the best part of the trip is getting there. But you have to be a motorcycle enthusiast to feel that way. Not everyone is.

About three days into the trip we were riding somewhere near Omaha. It was about ten in the morning and we had already had our breakfast stop. It was sunny and dry and we were really moving fast on this two lane road. A real back country road with nothing but corn fields on either side. The road moved up and down and when you were in the ditch you couldn't see what was over the next hump in front of you. That didn't matter to me because I was the last guy in back. I was riding next to another guy who had recently decided he wanted to be in this family and was going to try and make it.

That's a very big decision. It's all about the time you put in. If you can relax and realize you are home, that these are your brothers, you are right where you are supposed to be, then everything will work out. As long as I remembered that this is forever then it didn't matter how long getting to forever would take.

We were clipping around ninety miles an hour on this two lane road when we came up out of a valley and the road straightened out. No more hills and Valleys. We really hit the throttle. We took a big wide turn and on the left of the road was what was left of a small town. A tornado had just passed through a few hours earlier and left nothing but splinters. There was nothing standing taller than your waist. The people were all picking through their belongings when we came flying past. We slowed down and we looked at them and they stopped picking up their stuff and watched us go by. It was a surreal moment. I was the last one in the pack so I saw the whole thing. As we passed they went right back to salvaging their stuff. It put a lot in perspective for me. These people just lost everything and I am racing down the highway chasing my dream. It made me realize again it could all be over at any minute.

We went to a big run where I met brothers from all over the United States. Some brothers I knew from Holland also showed up which was cool to see. I was one of the tattooers that was putting on the run tattoo, so I met and got to know even more brothers. It felt great to be the crew from California. It felt great to have stuck with it.

We left the run after three days and rode to Sturgis South Dakota. I had never been to a Sturgis Motorcycle rally before. I had been to a bunch of Daytona's and Biketoberfest but not Sturgis. If you have been to one then you know what it's all about. I had never been to one of these events with the brothers. Which was different because these guys are treated like the rock n roll stars from the street. Me and the young brothers were always waiting for anyone to get out of line. I used to get off my bike and look around and think, 'Who is my gift? Who has been sent here to get knocked out so I can show the brothers what I am made of. That was how I thought. No one told me to think that way. And it was never too long until someone stepped up to answer the call. It was almost as if they would tap me on the shoulder and say, 'Excuse me I know you are busy but can you knock me out?' I always obliged.

After thirty six days on the road and I was dreaming about sleeping in my own bed. We rode through a few states in a pack of about ten guys from Sturgis until the split, which is where anyone who is going North goes North and anyone who is going south goes South. Everyone except me and one of the brothers were going South. We were going back to the bay area alone. We said goodbye and went in the store to pay for our gas. When we e came out of the store. The sky was black.

"I hope you brought your rain gear." He said as he pointed down the highway we were just about to get on. The sky was as black as can be which would have been fine but it was only one in the afternoon. It was one of the worst rain storms I had ever seen.

"We can't wait it out?" I asked him. I once again had a really shitty set of rain gear.

"Nope. I gotta get back to work. Besides, it might rain for days." He said while he put on his rain suit. He found the whole thing funny. I had an old set of rain gear that I had brought from Holland. I almost never used it. It had duct tape on the leg where it had been burned from the exhaust pipe. I had a half shell helmet and a bandana so the rain felt like it was tearing my face off. The brother I was with had a full face helmet and a state of the art rain suit.

"Gotta be prepared." He said as we took off into the blackness of the rain storm. Lucky for us we only got the side of it. The highway we were on veered to the left out of the storm.

"Lucky you." He said at the next gas stop when we were putting the rain suits back.

Riding across the country on a motorcycle is something every man should do at least once. For some of us that's once a year.

When I got back t Oakland I got invited to a movie premiere from John my movie producer friend. It was down in Hollywood so I brought the young brother I was staying with and we went down to see John's new film.

This was pretty exciting for me, I had become great friends with John and this was the premiere of his newest film. He treated us like Kings. That was the first time I ever stood on the red carpet. It was at that famous Chinese theatre where they show all the new big films. Every seat in the place was taken it was standing room only. I would look around and see all kinds of stars but the thing I noticed was how everyone treated the brother I brought with me. Like he was the star. That made a big impression on me. Being at this movie premiere made me think that any dream is there for the taking, no matter how big. When I got home I took out the script John had put notes on and started a re write.

77

You never know what day is the day you will be called upon, but one thing for sure it's probably going to start out like any other day. When you are waiting to be called in and to be recognized and accepted into a family every day is pretty damn exciting. Being that day could be the day. Any day at all you just never know.

When you work at one thing for a few years of your life, no matter what it is, it's a rewarding feeling. It was for me. There is no greater feeling then the love you have in your heart when you are finally recognized and accepted into a family. I was now part of a world wide family, with brothers everywhere. Free airport pick up, free airport drop off, a place to stay, a bike to ride with other brothers when I get there. That's what it like in a Brotherhood. I had seen it for years, brothers getting picked up at airports being greeted by brothers they had never met, and acting like they grew up in the same house. Like REAL brothers do.

As soon as I became a brother, one of the older brothers loaned me twenty five grand and I stopped painting houses and starting building a tattoo shop. I was still tattooing on the side, another brother told me I could set up in his building so I built a five station shop. Will helped me build it.

Will had become my best friend. Breakfast lunch and dinner, we did it together. I was travelling all over and Will starting going with me. Everywhere. My day would start with the phone ringing about six a.m.

"I'm outside." Will would say. I would hurry up and get out there. As soon as I got in the car it would start.

"Let's get coffee."

"After we drop the kids off." That was Will. He picked up where Korn left off. A lot of people said it, but Will did it. He picked Korns kids up every day and dropped them off at school. Then we would go get coffee.

"What you wanna do today?"

"Make shit happen. We in the make it happen business. Today and every day"
"Well I'm going to Vegas today." I said.
"Correction. We are going to Vegas today. We can take my truck." We left right then, straight from the parking lot. Will was spontaneous.
There was some brothers on trial in Las Vegas so I went there to show support. I used to travel everywhere with my camera. I still had the film bug. I was still writing for the magazine every month, and writing scripts in my spare time. I wanted to go to the porn convention and make a film for one of the older brothers in the room. Not a porno movie. One of the brothers was a teamster and he got me and Will in the convention. I was walking around the convention floor with this big camera in my hand. I would walked up to any one of the porn stars.
"Excuse me. Can I pass my camera by you and when it passes you can you say, 'Hey Cisco. Wish you were here.'"
"That's it?"
"That's it."
"You don't want me to get naked."
"No. Just wave. Or blow him a kiss or something."
"No problem." I collected about thirty different 'Hello's' and I figured I had enough to make a short film for Cisco. I knew he would dig it. I was on the way out and I figured I better capture some 'B' roll. B roll is what I would cut in between the porn stars saying hello. Basically it was just going to be shots of the convention floor with the crowd and the lines of people waiting for autographs. The porn convention is like any other convention except they sell porn stuff. It's probably not what you think. There might be some wild parties at night but on the convention floor, it's all business.
Me and Will hung out until the convention closed then we got invited to a penthouse magazine party, in the penthouse of some big hotel. There were a few brothers there from all over and a bunch of cage fighters and porn stars. MMA was just starting to get big at this point. A real big guy walked in the door. He was huge, about six eight and four hundred pounds.

He was passing the bar and he looked at one of the brothers who was equally just as big.
"I bet I could kick your ass."
The brother put his drink down.
"Let's go. I'll give you a shot at the title right now." The brother said real serious.
"I'm only kidding." The big civilian said.
"I'm not. Let's go. Right now." The brother said who was now standing in a fighting stance ready to go. The big civilians lip started to quiver. He stood there frozen.
"I don't want any trouble." He said full of fear.
"That's what I thought." The big brother said. "Better watch what you say and who you say it to."
A few hours went by. Me and Will hung out in the back of the penthouse apartment with the brothers. The apartment was huge, a Las Vegas penthouse what did I expect? The living room itself was as big as a football field. Will spent the night talking to Ron Jeremy and two porn stars doing lines on a piano. In the middle of the rom was a whole bunch of couches with porn stars and cage fighters sitting watching old matches on the TV. I was standing next a few brothers when the big civilian guy walked past me and up to the big brother who was sitting in a chair relaxing."
"I still think I can kick your ass." He said and he took a swing at the big brother. I couldn't believe it. He must have been drunk or didn't like being put in his place earlier.
"That's it." The big brother said. But before he could get up I jumped on the guy from behind and put him in a backwards head lock and started dragging him out of the penthouse. The whole party froze. The guy was way bigger than me but I had him in a real good choke hold. He was on his heels and I made sure his head hit every post and table on the way out. As I got to the door the doorman opened it and I threw the guy in the hall. Before he could get the boots I got pulled back in the penthouse.
"That's enough." One of the other brothers said.
"Good job." Said another. I felt great. And I had only been in the family about a month.

We hung out there until the dawn then got back in the truck and drove back to Oakland. A few days later after I had edited the film I went by the house. I walked in and saw some brothers watching TV.
"I went to the porn convention and I made a film. Wanna see it?" They all piled in front of the TV and I put the film on. After about the twenty fifth porn star waving and saying, 'Hey Cisco wish you were here.' He looked up at me with a big smile.
"Can I get a copy of this?" Cisco asked me.
"I made it for you. That is your copy."
"I love you brother."
" I love you too my brother."
Life is an absolute roller coaster ride but it's safe to say at that moment I was on top of the ride. The best feeling in the world is to see your brothers smile. Have a good time. That's it.

78

The tattoo shop was working itself by now. I called it Evil Ink Tattoo, which was maybe not the best name, but I liked it. It was next to Oakland Custom Motor Cycle which was the local motorcycle shop in town. A lot of brothers always hung out there. In fact everyone in town riding a Harley hung out there. Probably scared away a lot of customers.

I have worked in so many tattoo shops in my life, all over the world, and always giving the owners half of my salary, fifty percent, of the take which is a basic shop percentage. I always dreamed about owning my own shop. So finally owning one was a big accomplishment for me. I really was living my dream.

I had my own station in my shop and there were four other stations. Business was slow and steady at first. We had only been open about a month. I had a few artists coming and going, maybe staying a few months before something flaky happened and they never showed up again.

I was boxing every day in the morning at Kings boxing gym then showing up at the shop around one in the afternoon. The guys who worked for me opened at noon so I always waited an hour or two before I showed up, unless I had an appointment.
I pulled up and walked in the shop one day and there was a big guy who was pretty wasted standing in the middle of the shop. One of the guys who worked for me named Tony was blocking the door.
"What's going on?"
"He doesn't want to pay." Tony said. I looked at the guy.
"Is that true? You don't want to pay?"
"He won't finish it." The guy said. He was wasted.
"Let me see." I said. The guy had a full shoulder piece, from his shoulder to his elbow, full color. It was finished.
"He just came in for a final touch up and to bring me the last of the money."
"How much does he owe?"
"Three hundred dollars." Tony wasn't having it, but the guy was way bigger than Tony. I turned around and closed the door and turned the deadbolt locking us all in the shop.
"You're gonna have to pay. The tattoo looks done to me." The other artist stopped tattooing and stood up. Now the guy was standing in the middle of the room with three guys around him.
"You guys are ganging up on me." The wasted guy said.
"Nobody is ganging up on anyone. Tony finished the work, now you have to pay."
The guy then did the stupidest thing I have ever seen he took out a pocket knife and flicked it open.
"Don't do that. You're gonna piss me off." I said.
"FUCK YOU." He said to me. I immediately knocked him out with a right. As soon as he dis respected me he got dropped. He was out cold. I didn't care so much that he had pulled a knife on me. Or didn't want to pay. Not as much as I cared that he had dis respected me.
I went next door and walked in the bike shop. There were a few brothers there and the owner of the shop who was in his sixties.

"I just knocked this guy out. He pulled a knife, he didn't wanna pay. Come have a look."
So the owner and one of the brothers walked back to my shop with me. I figured ut was better to have someone else there who has been around. Especially since technically my tattoo shop was on his property.
We walked in the shop and the guy was still out cold. Tony had grabbed the knife and his wallet, which had no money in it at all. I poured a cup of water on the guy and he woke up and sprung to his feet. He reached in his pocket for his knife.
"It's not there." I said. "Time to pay and since you have no money you are going to have to call someone to bring the money down." I handed him back his empty wallet.
He looked around at all of us and he seemed kind of dazed. He must have taken a handful of pills before he walked in to get tattooed. I would have never tattooed him if he walked in that wasted. Problem they aren't that wasted when they sit down, so Tony didn't know.
The guy looked at the door and I could see he was going to make a break for it.
"You gotta call someone. Who you gonna call?" I said again.
"Hey fella. This aint the place you wanna rip off." The owner of the motorcycle shop said to the guy.
"What do you know about it?"
"A lot. Time to pay." He said.
The guy pulled out his pockets showing he had nothing in them.
"Aint got no money." And with that he made a lunge for the door. He tried to push the owner of the motorcycle shop out of the way and I dropped him with a left. He walked right into it. His head cracked the tile we had just laid down a few months earlier.
"Shut the door. Get the plastic." The motorcycle shop owner said.
"Will you calm down?"
"Old habits die hard." He said with a smile. Just then the guys phone rang. The other brother looked at the screen.
"My Love. This must be his chick." He flipped it open.

"Hello. Yes he's almost done. He asks if you can bring down three hundred dollars to pay for the tattoo. Ten minutes? Great. Thanks." That brother talked to her just as smooth as silk and she showed up ten minutes later with the cash.
"What happened?" She asked as she handed over the money and looked at her bashed up boyfriend.
"I fell down." He said.
"Twice." I said. She looked at me like I was insane then helped him to the car. I'm pretty sure she dumped him a week later and started dating one of the brothers. That's how it goes sometimes.
I walked back in the shop and my phone rang. It was John my movie producer buddy. I didn't know it at the time but this was the third time Hollywood was calling.
"David."
"John."
"I got something."
"What's that?"
"I'm going to do a show. Sopranos west coast bikers style."
"Sounds cool."
"If I get it up and running I want you to be the technical advisor."
"For real?" He could tell I was excited.
"Relax. It's a long haul from the thought or the idea of a show until it gets to the screen. But if I get it you are in."
"Thank You."
He hung up the phone. Big guys in Hollywood do that a lot. Just hang up when the conversation is over.

79

Things started moving a little bit faster after that. Every day I would talk with John and he would tell me about the meetings for the show. It went to all the big networks but nobody was biting.
I didn't understand a lot about the business. It was still a far off dream that I wasn't really chasing anymore. I kept writing

scripts but I wasn't making any money doing it. I was just doing it cause I like it. I was in my own world already living more of a dream than I expected. I was a brother and I owned my own tattoo shop. There wasn't much more that I was looking for.

I started travelling all the time. There is always somewhere to go or something to do and someone to do it with when you are a brother.

Me and Will did everything together. He wasn't a brother but he grew up in the family and he knew the score. We went to Miami Beach, which is where I am born and raised. Soon as Will heard I was going to do a job in Miami Beach, he showed up at my door with his suitcase packed. He was always up for an adventure.

We got to Miami late at night and Al picked us up at the airport.

"Ready to work?"

"That's why I'm here."

'Wow." Will said as the heat of Miami hit him the minute we stepped out of the airport. It hit us like a wave.

"You aint seen nothing yet.." I knew Will was going to have a great time in Miami. That a whole new world was opening up for him. He also got to see where I am from which was cool.

We were always making big plans.

"Big things Big Things. That's what we're doing." Will used to say. "Gotta dream big."

We pulled up to Red's house and he was waiting outside.

"Red this is Will, Will this is Red. Red can Will stay with you for a few days?"

"Sure. He can crash on the couch."

I had a whole bunch of stuff to take care of in South Miami and that's where the job was and where Al lived and I wasn't going to go back and forth every day. That's about an hour drive each way and I had work to do. Got to make that dollar.

"Be good." I said to Will as I got in Al's truck.

"The best." Will said with a smile. There is a lot of trust on both sides when you can walk up to one of your friends and ask if another friend he never met can sleep on your couch for a few days. Especially when the apartment is a one room studio. Red had that trust. He knew I wouldn't bring over anyone who wasn't worth bringing.

Sometimes opportunities only comes along once in a while, maybe once a year and when it does you have to jump.

Al's friends would give a crazy low bid on a paint job. Under cutting everyone in time and money, then six of us with six airless sprayers would walk in and knock it out in three days. Three non stop twenty four hour days. Spraying a four story building, new construction inside and out is a big job. After the cost of materials each of us walked away with about eight grand. Not bad for a weekends work. Aint nothing wrong with good hard work. It builds character.

Al gave me a ride back to the beach when the job was over three days later and we found Will and Red outsides Ted's Hideaway, the local bar. I walked up and Will was outside with two strippers.

"Look at your boy." Al said as we walked up. Will was sunburned, with a brand new Hustler hat with a real loud button down Hawaiian shirt and some surfer shorts and flip flops, with a stripper on each arm and a mojito in each hand.

"Having fun?"

"My brother." He walked and gave me a big hug. He turned tight to the strippers.

"Have you girls met my brother D.L.?"

"No." They both said in unison. They turned around and walked back into the bar.

"I see you are right at home." Will smiled and opened his shirt.

"Ta da." He had a .38 snub nose tucked in the waist band of his shorts. Will was a gangster for real. He put his gun in his belt before he put his shoes on his feet. That's how it is growing up in Oakland for some people. Will was just for real on every level.

We stood there talking for a while in front of Ted's just standing on the side walk. It was a quiet night, I think it was a Tuesday. All of a sudden there was a big CLANG. Will's gun had slipped through the waist band of his shorts and hit the floor. Everyone froze. The bouncers looked at us and Will looked at them, the he kneeled down and picked his gun up, put it back in his waist band and acted as if nothing happened. Red freaked out.

"You guys gotta leave. Everybody saw that."

"Leave? The only place I'm going is back inside." Will said as he sauntered back inside.

"You need to relax." I said to Red. I walked over to the bouncers. I have known them for years.

"We good?" They looked inside and Will was back on the stage dancing with the two strippers.

"Yeah. We're good." The first bouncer said.

"Truthfully. Your friend is one of the coolest people we ever met."

"Yeah. I get that alot." I said.

"He was here with Red the other night, sat at the bar all night drinking Hennesey and talking stories. We had to carry them both home. It was hilarious. We laughed the whole way."

We all looked in a t Will having a blast. I looked at my phone and I had a missed call from my friend John.

"David."

"John."

"I got something. I think we might be in business."

"You are kidding."

"No. I'm not. I need you to meet this writer. He's going to write the show."

"I'm in Miami."

"Nice. What are you doing in Miami?"

"Visiting my mom. Did a big paint job with six guys. I'm here with Will."

"Time to come home. We have a job to do." He said before he hung up.

I looked in the bar and it was raging. I could have stayed in Miami another week or two but home is home. It's always going to be there. I was pretty excited about the possibilities. Will wasn't too happy about leaving he could have stayed another month. Then a new bug hit him.

"Hollywood Takeover in full effect." He started saying all the time. Will knew if I was going he was going. At least along for the ride. I started making arrangements and we left Miami two days later.

80

We got back to Oakland and life fell right back into line. Will always had ten things he was working on and he got right back to them. I went straight back to what I was already doing which was waiting for a customer to walk in my shop to buy a tattoo. I had to work. I had to make a dollar and I knew it. Or even better a stack of hundred dollar bills. STACKS of hundred dollar bills sounded good. Either way the hustle never stops. Ever. And I knew that.

John was going to bring the writer up to meet me so I started getting ready for that. I had no idea really what a technical advisor was for a television show. I knew I could discuss motorcycle life with him. What it is like to ride around with a bunch of brothers on bikes, but that is all. I knew I could not discuss my personal business or my brothers personal business and I let that be known at the beginning. I have been around guys on bikes my whole life, so that is what I discussed. They sent an art team also, and I had to go over the bikes we ride, the clothes we wear, all of it. Whatever had to do with motorcycle brotherhood life.

I had already been a cameraman for Zalman King so I knew what it was like to work with a film team but this was different. It was bigger it had a way more professional feel, like it was really going t happen. Everything about everyone I met was totally professional. They were very thorough. They asked questions I never even thought of, things I took for granted because I had been living this life so long it was all second nature to me. They had to understand this is a lifestyle, not a job.

John drove to Oakland and picked me up and we drove to The hotel the writer was staying at.

"There he is." John said as the writer walked over to our car. He got in and the first thing he did was give me a box set of the last show he worked on, some really successful cop show.
"I'm Kurt. This is for you." He handed me the set.
"I'm D.L. Thank you. Where do we begin?"

"I've got questions and you have answers so lets go somewhere so we can sit down and hash this out." He was one cool cat I could tell already. He knew what he was doing. And I was taking notes. I'm always taking notes. Mental notes.

John peeled out in his big bad BMW and we went to my house. We sat down and Kurt took out his legal pad and we sat and talked for hours. This went on like this for a few days. I learned a ton just by hearing the questions he would ask. I got to look into the mind of a creator. Someone who was already successfully writing and making a living in film, something I wanted to do.

After about a week of the question and answer bit, we went to my tattoo shop which was across the street from the house where a lot of my brothers hung out. Kurt met a bunch of my brothers, all shapes and sizes, ages and occupations. He got to see they were all regular people. Most just worked nine to five jobs and went home to their families. Just being motorcycle enthusiasts was our common bond.

We went over the bridge to the city with one of my brothers in his souped up Charger. Around us a bunch of my younger brothers did wheelies across the bridge next to our car. We went to the house where some of my city brothers hung out and there were some East Coast brothers where there. One of my brothers from the east can be considered pretty scary. He has a thick east coast accent. He knew I was hired to work on an upcoming TV show.

"Is that the TV guy?' He said real loud.

"Yeah." I said.

"Did you tell him I'm gonna cut his throat if he doesn't put me on the air." He started laughing at his own jokes. He knew he made people nervous. He liked that.

"No I didn't tell him."

"Give him my cod." He said in a thick North East accent. He held out his business card. I took it.

"Tell him I'll be expecting his call." My brother said as he chuckled at his own humor. Tough guy humor. All I could think was it's a good thing Kurt didn't hear that conversation. I wasn't sure if he was up on tough guy humor.

We jumped back in the Charger and high tailed it back to Oakland.

"I think I have almost everything I need. Lets sit down and go over these last few questions at your house and that should be enough for now."

"You got it Boss." I said. He was the Boss. I could see that already. We burned over the Bay Bridge back to Oakland weaving in and out of traffic at ninety miles an hour. After another high speed ride across the Bay Bridge we got dropped off at my house for the last round of questions. Hours later we were done.

"I think that just about does it." Kurt said as he started putting his notebooks away. I knew this was my opportunity. I held out three magazines I had articles published in. I had a pile of magazines under the table. I handed them to Kurt.

"I write. I have been writing for years. I have articles in all those magazines." I pointed to the stack of magazines. Kurt started to brows through the articles. I got up and put the DVD in the DVD player that I made with Zalman King. It started playing and right away I was on the screen. We watched it for a minute.

"Where do you see yourself on this project?" Kurt asked me.

"I want to be on it."

"You are the technical advisor."

"Exactly. Which means I will be around. When you are casting it I want a shot at a part just like anybody else."

"Do you act?"

"Every day's an act. I write. Which means I have an imagination. I have worked in film. I think I would help the show because of who I really am and what I look like."

Kurt thought about this for a moment then smiled.

"You just might be right at that. You can have a shot. Don't blow it. You only get one."

"You got it Boss."

He stood up and we shook hands and he left. We emailed a few times over the next few weeks. Not much, just fine tuning things he had questions on. Just by his questions I was starting to get an idea of what it would take to create a world and characters and back stories and what it takes to make a show. School was already in session and I knew it. The next time I saw Kurt was in the casting office. John was there with some producers. I was nervous. I didn't ace the casting and I knew it. I didn't get the part I read for. Didn't matter though. The forces to be made it happen for me.

81

It takes some time to create a television show and life went back to normal while that happened. I didn't hear about it much so I didn't think about it much either. I was already living my dream and more, riding bikes with my brothers and owning a tattoo shop. Even if there was no business it was still mine. And my tattoo shop was the hangout, which was cool. There was always some action going on around the shop.
"You love the drama." I used to tell Will.
"I do. I admit it. Better than no drama at all." Will loved the drama but he had a way of staying out of it. He just observed everyone else's drama with a smile on his face that said, 'better you than me.'
We sat in the barber chairs and watched the rain outside. It was pouring like Noah's Ark. There was a couple of guys getting tattooed in the stations and some kids checking out the flash.
"Check this out." Will held out a big purple bud.
"Nice. Twist it up."
"You got wraps?" I handed Will the papers and he grabbed a tattoo magazine and started rolling a few joints. This is what we did. Sat around and smoked weed and discussed the current affairs of the world. We always had some project going or some party to plan, go to, or recover from.
"It's really coming down." Will said as we looked out the front doors. Winter was coming and the rain was coming with it. There was a guy across the street trying to tie a load of cardboard boxes on his truck. Way too many at one time. He was having a hell of a time going from side to side trying to

keep them from falling. When he finally drove off they all fell and the next car ran them over. Then the next one then the next one. Until it was a big pile of paper mache'. Will passed back the joint.
"You ever wonder why?"
"Why what?"
"Why people that dont have clue get out of bed in the morning." I thought about that.
"They do it for the hustle. Same as us. The hustle is real."
"Yeah but they aint getting no where."
"Yeah but they don't know that. They're on auto pilot. Like most folks. Getting nowhere fast"
"But not us. We doing big things." Will said. "BIG THINGS."
Just then a big BMW pulled into the parking lot.
"Who's this?"
"It's John that movie guy I told you about. The one who is doing the show."
"I thought the other guy was doing the show."
"They both are. It's a long story. This guy thought of it and the other one you met creates it. Hollywood is something I haven't really figured out yet."
"We will." Will said with a smile and passed me back the joint.
John hopped out of the car with a young man about thirty and walked into the shop.
"Whoa." John said as he waved away the clouds of smoke.
"DL This is Charlie."
"Charlie this is DL."
"Wassup." We shook hands.
"Good to meet you. Charlie this is Will."
"Good to meet you Will." Charlie and Will shook hands. I passed John the joint.
"Check this out. OG Kush. LA Style." John handed me a bud. Me and Will examined it.
"Nice. May I?" Will asked.
"Absolutely." John said and handed over some king size papers. Will kept looking at Charlie and scratching his head. Charlie was looking around the shop just taking it all in. He had a totally relaxed calm vibration.

"I know you from some where." Will said. Charlie just smiled. He was as cool and as calm as any one man could be. Except for Will. He was just as cool. And game recognizes game.
We hung out in the shop for a few hours smoking and talking, just getting to know each other. There was always action in the shop and people were coming in and out all day long.
I usually waited till all the tattoos were done before I left. The shop wasn't in the best neighborhood, and I liked to make sure things got locked up tight. Will and Charlie talked for hours.
"I Got it." Will said all of a sudden and turned to Charlie. "You were in that soccer movie right?. It's about soccer fans right?"
"Football. Not soccer." Charlie said with a smile.
"I knew I knew you from somewhere. That movie was great."
"Thank you."
"So now you doing a TV show?"
"Time will tell." Charlie said. He was way relaxed. Just like Will. They were very alike and it was obvious.
"Gonna have to put me on it." Will said with a smile.
"I would have to vote yes on that." Charlie said.
We spent the next few days in and around Oakland. Will came over every day in the morning and the day was on just like usual. Charlie and Will bonded tight. It's no wonder they are two of the coolest people I ever met.
Every night my girl would cook us dinner. She is a straight up knockout. Gorgeous and a sweetheart at the same time. We had an understanding. I can be a little scattered and she put up with me. Or she was just my Angel. Charlie saw that. I would be getting ready and lose things and be screaming for her to help me find whatever it was lost.
"BABY BAAAAAABY! HAVE YOU SEEN MY KEYS? " Or whatever it was I had lost. And she would come in calm and quiet with whatever it was.
On Charlie's last night we decided to go out to eat instead of cooking at home. The rain was really coming down.
"You ready?"
"Ready." She said as she went outside. Charlie followed her.
"We're meeting John at the restaurant?" Charlie asked me.

"Yeah." I said. Then I remembered I wanted to bring John a script.
"I forgot something. I'll be right back." I said as I ran back inside. The rain was really coming down. I went into my office and dug through a pile of scripts until I found the one I wanted. I ran back outside and Charlie was still standing by the front door trying to keep out of the rain. My girl was waiting in the car.
"What are you doing out here? Why aint you in the car?" I asked him. He just looked at me with a smile, and I understood. It was out of respect. He wouldn't get in my car with my girl in it without me.
"Well then. We have established that you are kind of smart. Aren't you?" I said. Charlie just smiled.
"You ever worked a television show before?" Charlie asked.
"Nope."
"Well I did. And we are about to have a hell of a lot of fun. It's a lot of work. But It'll be a lot fun. Let's go."
We ran through the rain to the car and jumped inside and took off like we were supposed to. Like we owned the town.

EPILOGUE

The next seven years for me can only be described as some of the happiest times of my life. I made some of the greatest friends I ever had. I worked for one of the greatest and best companies in the world. I learned a ton about film production and about writing and about life. I launched a new career that I did not see coming. I lived an adventure of epic proportion.

Will got shot and killed on the way home from a funeral shortly after Charlie's visit to Oakland. Will's passing changed my life as it did so many other people,
Everyone you meet leaves something with you. Some people only leave a bad impression. Will always has something to offer, some insight, some valuable input, someway to look at things calmy and see the real in it.
I was sitting in my tattoo shop just about to tattoo a brother from Holland who was visiting me when my phone rang. It was one of my Oakland brothers.
"Will got shot." He said. "He's is San Rafael hospital." I hung up the phone and look at my Dutch brother.
"We gotta go."
We jumped in my car and raced to the hospital where Will lay. When we arrived a crowd of brothers had already gathered.
Will left this life before we arrived at the hospital. Wills passing was like being hit by a brick that I don't believe I will ever recover from. He took a little piece of my heart away. But knowing Will like I did, even for a short time, enriched my life and for that I am truly grateful.
I could go on and on but I have to keep some stories close to my heart. Will died too young. We were robbed. Will was good and just like they say 'Only the good die young'.

D.L. Late December 2015

Printed in Great
Britain
by Amazon